Teaching Interpersonal Communication: Resources and Readings

Teaching Interpersonal Communication: Resources and Readings

ELIZABETH J. NATALLE
THE UNIVERSITY OF NORTH CAROLINA
AT GREENSBORO

BEDFORD / ST. MARTIN'S
Boston ♦ New York

For Bedford/St. Martin's

Executive Editor for Communication: Erika Gutierrez
Development Editors: Noel Hohnstine and Lai T. Moy
Senior Production Editor: Irwin Zucker
Senior Production Supervisor: Joe Ford
Executive Marketing Manager: Rachel Falk
Art Director: Lucy Krikorian
Copy Editor: Sarah Zobel
Cover Design: Billy Boardman
Composition: Stratford/TexTech
Printing and Binding: R.R. Donnelley & Sons, Inc.

President: Joan E. Feinberg
Editorial Director: Denise B. Wydra
Director of Development: Erica T. Appel
Director of Marketing: Karen Melton Soeltz
Director of Editing, Design, and Production: Marcia Cohen
Managing Editor: Shuli Traub

Library of Congress Control Number: 2007921476

Manufactured in the United States of America.

2 1 0 9 8 7
f e d c b a

For information, write: Bedford/St. Martin's, 75 Arlington Street, Boston, MA 02116   (617-399-4000)

ISBN-10: 0-312-45542-9
ISBN-13: 978-0-312-45542-2

Acknowledgments
Acknowledgments and copyrights appear at the back of the book on page 209, which constitutes an extension of the copyright page.

Preface

In 1975, I took my first undergraduate interpersonal communication course with Dr. K. Phillip Taylor at the University of Central Florida. I benefited from Dr. Taylor's approach, which was a perfect blend of theory and practice, more than I was aware of at the time. Now, 30 years later, I realize that my own story as both an academic and a teacher parallels the development of the discipline. As interpersonal communication moved to the center of our field's research interests, we developed interpersonal communication courses as part of the core curricula (Wardrope, 1999). Studies show that the people who succeed in business, marriage, and other domains in life are those who can effectively communicate with others. Students need basic training in interpersonal communication, and now that they are utilizing computer-mediated forms of communication such as e-mail, instant messenger, and cell phones, they need a broader array of tools. Thus, further curriculum development is especially crucial. This leads us to consider: What are our roles as teachers of interpersonal communication? How can we help our students improve their basic communication skills in order to ensure that they engage in more productive, healthy, and worthwhile relationships?

I wrote *Teaching Interpersonal Communication* in order to help instructors develop more effective interpersonal communication courses. Over the years, I've noticed that too many new instructors get "handed-off" to teach the entry-level interpersonal communication course as if it were an easy thing to do. For those of us who are more seasoned in the field and in the classroom, we know that teaching the course is far from easy. Further taxing the new instructor is the fact that she or he may have taken fewer interpersonal courses than those of us who have "grown up" with the discipline. New instructors need an opportunity to develop a strong sense of the theory and discipline necessary to teach an interpersonal course with integrity, and they need guidance and support to overcome the problems and barriers to teaching the class effectively.

Teaching Interpersonal Communication: Resources and Readings serves as a reference for new instructors, adjuncts, and others with limited experience teaching interpersonal communication courses. You will find advice on constructing a syllabus, managing a classroom, selecting instructional strategies, constructing exams, and developing as a professional teacher. This book is about *teaching*, and it is designed to demonstrate how to integrate pedagogy and content to create a more effective course. It also provides avenues for developing and strengthening one's theoretical context. In this regard, even experienced teachers from all types of teaching institutions may benefit from this book.

Teaching Interpersonal Communication is divided into two sections: Part I, "Teaching Notes," consists of five chapters that mentor instructors in both personal development and course logistics. Chapter 1, "Teaching Approach and Philosophy," begins the mentoring process by asking the reader to consider himself or herself as a teacher in general and to set goals for becoming a better teacher. Chapter 2 is devoted to the syllabus as the basic tool of effective teaching. Chapter 3, "Student Challenges and Problematics," discusses common classroom issues, including using space, managing discussion, and setting up course policies and rules. It also discusses student challenges like disruptive students, nontraditionals, and co-cultural students. Chapter 4, "Structural Challenges and Problematics," examines five structural issues that affect the technical decisions an instructor makes to deliver an effective course: instructional strategies; balancing theory and practice; vocabulary; use of technology; and service learning. Chapter 5, "Evaluation and Assessment," studies the construction of assignments to support learning objectives, developing a grading system, and participating in assessment procedures. By the close of Part I, we will have taken a comprehensive look at a system for teaching interpersonal communication.

Part II, titled "Resources and Readings," consists of two chapters that show readers how teaching can be informed from the discipline's theory and literature. Chapter 6, "Theoretical Foundations and Readings," begins with a brief description of the history and range of theory that undergirds the field. To demonstrate how theory should support a course, I present five essential readings that theoretically support my own course: excerpts from Paul Watzlawick, Janet Beavin, and Don Jackson's *Pragmatics* (1967); an essay on relationship stages from Mark Knapp and Anita Vangelisti (1992); Martin Buber (1970) on self and other; John Wiemann's (1977) original work on the factors of communication competence; and Leslie Baxter and Barbara Montgomery's (2000) description of dialectics. Chapter 7, "Foundational Resources," offers a list of primary sources I judge important for one's professional development as a teacher of interpersonal communication. This chapter also provides an annotated bibliography of more than 70 sources that supports a basic course.

Teaching Interpersonal Communication is the first book in Bedford/St. Martin's new Professional Resource Series for Communication. This series was conceived specifically for instructors seeking best practices for instructing, managing, and developing a course. When asked to write this text, I accepted not only because I am passionate about the topic, but also because I was impressed with the editorial team's belief that a textbook publishing firm should attend to the needs of both students *and* professors. Thus, *Teaching Interpersonal Communication* not only offers sound advice and practical tips for good teaching; more specifically, it also approaches the introductory interpersonal course with a balanced integration of theory and practice.

It was my pleasure to work with all those involved in the writing, editing, and production of this book: Joan Feinberg, Denise Wydra, Erika Gutierrez, Noel Hohnstine, Lai Moy, and the production team headed by Irwin Zucker. In particular, I wish to thank former editor Vikram Mukhija for helping me to conceive the content and structure of the book and editor Noel Hohnstine for careful editing of the manuscript. I also appreciate the comments of the outside reviewers: Rex Butt, Bronx Community College, CUNY; Tim Cole, DePaul University; Alice Denise Danford, Delaware County Community College; and Loretta L. Pecchioni, Louisiana State University. Loretta L. Pecchioni was very helpful as the chapter-by-chapter reviewer, and I especially appreciate her enthusiasm for the content of the book.

I also wish to thank my colleagues around the country and at the University of North Carolina at Greensboro who shared their wisdom, techniques, experience, and course materials quoted in this book: Jen Baker, Marion Boyer, Michelle Burch, Lynn Weber Cannon, David Carlone, Elise Dallimore, Jessica Delk, Steve McCornack, Kelly Morrison, Mark Orbe, Robyn Parker, Chris Poulos, Bill Rawlins, Jen Day Shaw, and Julia Wood.

I wish to dedicate this book to all of the students in my interpersonal communication classes at UNCG over the last 22 years and to the teachers who influenced me to become the teacher that I am: Carol Wood, my second grade teacher at Pinewald Elementary who inspired me to become a teacher; Dr. K. Phillip Taylor, my undergraduate interpersonal communication professor at the University of Central Florida; and Dr. Gregg Phifer, my major professor in the master's program at Florida State University.

Jody Natalle

Contents

Preface   *v*

PART I   TEACHING NOTES   *1*

1   Teaching Approach and Philosophy   *3*

CONSIDERING YOURSELF AS A TEACHER   *3*
EFFECTIVE TEACHING   *5*
Start-up Difficulties in Effective Teaching   *5*
Coming to Effective Teaching through a Teaching Philosophy   *6*
What Effective Teachers Think   *8*
   From the Classroom: Affirmation and Community as Teaching
      Philosophy   10
A STATEMENT OF TEACHING PHILOSOPHY   *10*
PROFESSIONAL DEVELOPMENT   *16*
Teaching Portfolios   *16*
Professional Organizations   *17*
Training and Consulting   *18*
COMING TO CLOSURE ON EFFECTIVE
   TEACHING...FOR NOW   *19*
SETTING GOALS   *20*

2   The Basic Tool of Effective Teaching: The Syllabus   *23*

THE FUNCTION OF A SYLLABUS   *23*
THE ELEMENTS OF A SYLLABUS   *25*
Learning Outcomes   *34*
Organization of Course Content   *37*
THEORY-BASED, ON-LINE, AND SERVICE-LEARNING
   COURSES   *39*
A Theory-Based Syllabus   *40*
An Online Syllabus   *43*
A Service-Learning Syllabus   *48*
TEXTBOOK SELECTION AND SUPPORTING MATERIALS   *54*
LEGIBILITY AND DESIGN   *56*

3 Student Challenges and Problematics   57

CLASSROOM MANAGEMENT   *57*
   From the Classroom: The Challenge of a Large Classroom   59
DISCUSSION MANAGEMENT   *59*
The Influence of Classroom Climate and Teacher Ethos   *59*
   From the Classroom: Setting the Tone   62
Facilitating Discussion   *62*
Rules for Discussion   *64*
Tolerance and Diversity of Views   *66*
General Techniques for Classroom Management   *68*
Course Policies as General Classroom Rules   *69*
STUDENT CHALLENGES   *70*
Difficult or Disruptive Students   *70*
Ethical Considerations and Problem Students   *71*
   From the Classroom: The Most Common Interpersonal Communication
      Problem between Professor and Student   72
Nontraditional or Adult Students   *73*
Co-Cultural Student Populations   *75*
CONCLUSION   *76*

4 Structural Challenges and Problematics   77

INSTRUCTIONAL STRATEGIES   *77*
Locating Instructional Strategies   *78*
Getting Students to Read   *79*
Team Teaching   *80*
Instruction on the First Day of Class   *81*
BALANCING THEORY AND PRACTICE   *83*
VOCABULARY   *86*
TECHNOLOGY AND INSTRUCTION   *87*
SERVICE LEARNING   *89*
SUMMARY   *91*

5 Evaluation and Assessment   93

COURSE STRUCTURE AND LEARNING OBJECTIVES   *93*
GRADES AND GRADING SYSTEMS   *95*
Tips for Grading   *96*
EVALUATING CLASS AND HOMEWORK ASSIGNMENTS   *97*
EVALUATING MAJOR CLASS ASSIGNMENTS   *99*
EXAMINATIONS   *100*
Test Construction   *100*
Preparing Students   *102*
Test Administration   *103*
   From the Classroom: Cheating in the Large Enrollment Course   103
Grading Tests and Debriefing Students   *104*

ASSESSMENT   *106*
Program Assessment   *106*
Teacher Assessment   *109*
SUMMARY   *109*

PART II RESOURCES AND READINGS   *111*

6 Theoretical Foundations and Readings   *113*

A BRIEF HISTORY OF INTERPERSONAL COMMUNICATION
    THEORY   *113*
BASIC FOUNDATIONS IN INTERPERSONAL COMMUNICATION
    THEORY   *115*
Theory Is Organized Systematically   *115*
Teaching Needs a Range of Theory   *116*
Theory Informs Course Content and Structure   *116*
FIVE ESSENTIAL READINGS   *117*
    Paul Watzlawick, Janet Beavin Bavelas, and Don D. Jackson,
        Some Tentative Axioms of Communication   *119*
    Martin Buber, First Part from *I and Thou*   *128*
    John M. Wiemann, Explication and Test of a Model of
        Communicative Competence   *134*
    Mark L. Knapp and Anita L. Vangelisti, Stages of Coming
        Together and Coming Apart   *149*
    Leslie A. Baxter and Barbara M. Montgomery, Rethinking
        Communication in Personal Relationships from a Dialectical
        Perspective   *162*
WHAT ARE YOUR CHOICES?   *174*

7 Foundational Resources   *175*

PRIMARY AND SECONDARY RESOURCES   *175*
Types of Primary and Secondary Sources   *176*
READING RESOURCES EFFICIENTLY   *177*
BUILDING A PERSONAL LIBRARY   *178*
ANNOTATED BIBLIOGRAPHY   *179*

References   *203*

I

Teaching Notes

1

Teaching Approach and Philosophy

Teaching is an honor and earns the respect of others. As teachers of interpersonal communication, we bring honor both to the communication discipline and to the process that literally binds people together in society. Educating others is a serious responsibility that requires a teacher to know him- or herself before the imparting, negotiating, and interpreting of knowledge in the classroom can ever begin. How well do you know yourself as a teacher? As a person? Perhaps philosopher Martin Buber (1970) is correct that we are always *becoming* and never quite at a stage of *being*. Or, perhaps, as anthropologist Mary Catherine Bateson (1989) said, we compose our lives as improvisations in an ever-changing world. Life does not allow us to rest or become static. As professional educators, then, our goal is to become the best teachers we can be. Naturally, becoming our best will continue over the entire course of our careers.

I begin this book with an assumption: Although I am "author" and you are "reader," know that we are unified as college and university teachers who strive to be our best. Indeed, I hope this book will serve as a guide for teaching interpersonal communication. In this chapter I invite you to think about your approach to teaching. Based on your history and professional training, what would you identify as your strengths and weaknesses? What is your overall teaching philosophy? What are some of your professional goals?

CONSIDERING YOURSELF AS A TEACHER

You are a teacher, and you have what educator Parker Palmer describes as "the courage to teach" (Intrator, 2002). That's a good starting point, but have you ever thought about your history as a teacher? When did you know you wanted to become an educator? How has that knowledge shaped you to date? In my own case, I have wanted to be a teacher since I was in second grade. I made decisions all throughout my education that were relevant to my training. I majored in education as an undergraduate, volunteered in public schools, and taught courses for no fee as a graduate student in order to further my knowledge and experience. I call myself a *teacher/professor* when describing who I am to others because it is the single-most important aspect of my professional identity. What types of experiences have you had that likely prepared you for a career in teaching? If, for example, you have volunteered for Big Brothers/Big Sisters or were a Girl Scout or a Boy Scout, then you have gained experience that will help you teach. How have your experiences affected your basic ability to stand up in front of a group of learners and teach interpersonal communication as a college course? Beyond technical preparation in public speaking and organizing groups of people, how have those experiences shaped your basic approach to teaching?

In *The Joy of Teaching* (2005), Peter Filene, an awarding-winning teacher at the University of North Carolina at Chapel Hill, says that teaching is collaborative and personal. He likes to think about the student-teacher relationship as "heightened conversation." In other words, Filene sees teaching as an interpersonal relationship. He uses his strength of interpersonal style to focus on that learning relationship and be a "joyful," or successful, teacher. Professor Filene challenges his readers right away to consider themselves as teachers and ask, "Who am I?" I can't think of a better question. Once you consider your history and training, you will be able to identify your current strengths and challenges. Having a baseline allows you to teach with self-knowledge. Knowing that you will continue to evolve as both a person and a teacher, you can look forward to your own future with confidence. Think about some of your strengths and challenges as a teacher and record them below.

My strengths as a teacher

_____

_____

_____

_____

_____

My challenges as a teacher

_____

_____

_____

_____

_____

Until now, we have been reflecting on you as a teacher to try and frame your background and training. What I hope you have concluded at this point is that, although you undoubtedly have much to offer, you may still benefit from some additional professional development. We now turn to a more elusive topic—an ongoing goal you should try to achieve throughout your career: effective teaching.

EFFECTIVE TEACHING

What is effective teaching? Are all teachers effective? How can a teacher become more effective? Am *I* effective as a teacher? I have been thinking about these questions since my first experience teaching in the university classroom 30 years ago, and I am still working toward being the most effective teacher possible. These are not rhetorical questions, nor are they especially easy to answer. From a social science perspective, we have been testing teacher behavior for many years to pinpoint variables that contribute to teaching effectiveness (Frymier & Houser, 2000; Nussbaum, 1992); I will discuss some of that research in Chapter 3. In the section that follows we will explore the practical steps one can take on the journey toward professional success, as well as discuss how a solid teaching philosophy can serve as the central component, or foundation, to any course. We will also look at how we can continuously improve our teaching by taking advantage of professional development opportunities. These pragmatic goals serve as the theme for this book: to provide an organic look at what it takes to teach an effective class in interpersonal communication at the entry level.

Start-up Difficulties in Effective Teaching

There are a couple of ironies about effective teaching that we must face up front: first, although interpersonal communication is considered a core course in the field (Wardrope, 1999), we do not have enough qualified teachers to handle the demands of the class. It takes a highly experienced teacher with some degree of life experience to graft onto the theoretical knowledge delivered in the classroom. Like public speaking, there is often a need for interpersonal teachers, and we expect new MAs to pay their dues by starting their teaching careers with these two courses.

A similar situation occurs when temporary instructors or graduate students are given the responsibility of teaching the interpersonal communication course because just one more section of the course needs to be offered. For some inexplicable reason, there is a myth in our field that anyone can teach the interpersonal communication course. The faulty reasoning behind this myth is that we all participate in interpersonal relationships and, therefore, we should be able to teach interpersonal communication. Wrong! There is a significant difference between *being in relationships* and knowing how to teach the *interpersonal communication process.* This myth infiltrated my own department, as you'll see in the following constructive feedback given by a graduating senior in her capstone portfolio narrative:

> There should be more consistency in the department....I enrolled in relational communication three semesters before finally staying in the class. The second time I enrolled in the class I thought the class was more of a joke....One girl asked, "My boyfriend will not talk to me, what do I do?" The class members put their two cents worth in and we related nothing to the book or anything else relevant. I then dropped the class...it felt like a three day a week counseling session instead of a class. (Burke, 2005)

This type of feedback is not uncommon, and it testifies to the fact that we need to mentor instructors in these situations to grow and develop the skills appropriate to teaching the course. The question then becomes: What is effective teaching and what is it within the context of teaching interpersonal communication? What do you do as a new instructor who is under contract to teach this course as a new preparation? I recommend that you situate your technical skills (e.g., knowing how to create a syllabus, guiding discussions, grading assignments, and so on) within a larger teaching philosophy. We turn to that idea now.

Coming to Effective Teaching through a Teaching Philosophy

To be a competent teacher, one needs both technical expertise (knowledge of the subject matter; teaching skills) and a point of view or philosophy of teaching. Your own education provides you with the basic knowledge of interpersonal theory and concepts (see Graham & Shue, 2001, for a template on how to organize that knowledge); your life experience provides the working laboratory for application of knowledge; and time allows you to synthesize and evaluate knowledge and experience so that it becomes coherent and meaningful. Knowledge of pedagogy may or may not be a part of your educational training, and this book can help you with that. Although you can learn the technical expertise over a period of time, developing a philosophy of teaching to ensure effectiveness in teaching is, in my view, much more difficult to craft and apply.

A philosophy of teaching comprises a system of principles or a holistic viewpoint of how to impart your knowledge of interpersonal communication to students. This philosophy is grounded in cultural values, ethics, and morals. Developing a philosophy toward teaching interpersonal communication is somewhat difficult because cultural prescriptions for communicating, actual life experience, and the ideal prescriptions in textbooks may not always agree with each other. Because everyone has participated in relationships before entering the classroom, we all (teachers and students) come to the classroom with a mindset already in place that helps us approach relationships with a framework for seeing, doing, valuing, responding, and so forth in the social world. This comes from actual life experience as dyadic partners.

In the classroom, an interpersonal relationship develops between teacher and student. Again, learning relationships are deeply embedded in cultural conceptions of how learning should manifest and what the relationship between student and teacher should be. Onto these two layers we add the content of the interpersonal communication course, which is, indeed, a kind of metacommunication, or commentary, on the previous two layers. This is somewhat frightening to think about because, at any time, negative experiences from real-life relationships could jeopardize the content and/or the relationships involved in the teaching-learning process. Let's not dwell on the negative possibilities, but instead acknowledge that an interpersonal communication class is complicated because of the intersection of theory and real life. Developing a teaching philosophy toward communication is something that takes time and requires a balance in one's thinking about the ideal possibilities versus the messiness of the real world.

In trying to express a teaching philosophy, I like to think of cartography, or mindmapping. One of my greatest inspirations comes from novelist Cormac McCarthy. In *Cities of the Plain* (1998), the protagonist, Billy Parham, meets a fellow traveler on the road. In a long, lyrical discussion on life, the latter says:

> For now I can only say that I had hoped for a sort of calculus that would sum the convergence of map and life when life was done. For within their limitations there must be a common shape or shared domain between the telling and the told. And if that is so then the picture also in whatever partial form must have a direction to it and if it does then whatever is to come must lie in that path. (pp. 273–274)

I think about this passage a great deal because I am an advocate of mindmaps. I believe that each individual's cognitive mindset and life experience converge and carry that person forward on a path. *Philosophy, mind-map, calculus*—it doesn't matter what vocabulary you use, as long as there is a framework to guide you in your action as a teacher. You help shape students as they develop maps of interpersonal communication to guide themselves on the path of life. What tools help in this shaping process? New teachers are often influenced by their mentors, by peers, and by university workshops, as well as by the course textbook, which is actually a source of both knowledge and philosophy. For example, examine a text such as John Stewart's *Bridges Not Walls* (2002) and you see a humanistic philosophy in the tradition of Martin Buber, Carl Rogers, Jack Gibb, and Stewart himself; but a text such as Joseph DeVito's *The Interpersonal Communication Book* (2004) uses a social science approach that covers a broad range of research findings to help the learner approach a dyad with basic communication competence. Neither of these approaches is perfect, and a new teacher may not even be aware that the text itself is guiding his or her thinking and philosophical approach. A seasoned teacher, on the other hand, may supplement the text to fit his or her philosophy. Julia Wood and Lisa Lenze (1991) had to compensate for interpersonal communication texts that did not reflect their feminist philosophy to teach with gender inclusivity. Many texts are now more in tune with our gendered times, but the point is that unless you have a teaching philosophy, you do not have a complete approach to teaching. The text is only a starting point, so choose wisely and adjust as your philosophy develops over time.

Let's examine a statement of teaching philosophy made by David Worley, the recipient of the 2001 Central States Communication Association (CSCA) Outstanding New Teacher Award. In Worley's CSCA address, reprinted in *Communication Studies* (Worley, 2001), he demonstrates all that we have talked about here: he integrates his understanding of the nature of teaching (a lifelong impulse) with an orientation on teaching (student-centered) and places communication at the center of the process ("teaching *is* communication"). His basic principles include three things: teaching as a humanistic endeavor in which students and teachers come together authentically; relevance of course material to students; and engaging students in active learning in the classroom.

A slightly different statement, one based more on the framework of the classical philosophers Aristotle and Cicero, is evident in Paaige Turner's (2001) address. Professor Turner, the other CSCA teaching award winner for 2001, also supports the concept of an interactive classroom in which everyone is a teacher and a learner. Although her statement is more technical, relating structural (e.g., lesson plans) and operational procedures (e.g., class activities, exams) for effective teaching, it is a good example of how to think through the manifestation of philosophy in your actual teaching. Reading Worley's and Turner's statements can provide inspiration for your own teaching philosophy. Put your working statement in the teaching portfolio we will discuss later in this chapter, and try to rework it at least once a year.

Now let's turn to effective teaching across a range of disciplines to see what good teachers *think* as they approach the process of teaching.

What Effective Teachers Think

Ken Bain, Director of the Center for Teaching Excellence at New York University, came to the University of North Carolina at Greensboro and spoke to our faculty from his book entitled *What the Best College Teachers Do* (2004). When I arrived at the lecture hall, along with about 150 other faculty members, I noted and was impressed by who else was in the audience. There were a number of teaching excellence award winners, many new assistant professors—some with whom I have engaged in lengthy discussions about pedagogy, and a group of professors whose names I hear mentioned repeatedly by the students as "good" teachers. Over the next hour, Bain shared findings from his 15-year study with great teachers. As you might guess, the technical expertise demonstrated by effective teachers was learned, and such teachers have a formidable working knowledge of their disciplines. They learned classroom techniques along the way. But something bigger is at stake: Bain's study demonstrates that effective teachers approach teaching with a philosophy about human learning. After all the practices Bain (2004) describes in each chapter (preparation, expectations, conducting class, evaluation techniques), he boils it down to this eloquent statement:

> The magic does not, however, lie in any one of these practices. I cannot stress enough the simple yet powerful notion that the key to understanding the best teaching can be found not in particular practices or rules but in the *attitudes* of the teachers, in their *faith* in their students' abilities to achieve, in their *willingness* to take their students seriously and to let them assume control of their own education, and in their *commitment* to let all policies and practices flow from central learning objectives and from a mutual respect and agreement between students and teachers. (pp. 78-79)

Look at the four philosophical precepts that frame Bain's findings: attitudes, faith, willingness, and commitment. These are powerful concepts to consider as you think through your own philosophy, and I recommend Bain's book as part of that process.

In our field, Bill Rawlins of Ohio University is an exemplar of Bain's idea that good teachers have a philosophy of human learning. In his essay entitled "Teaching as a Mode of Friendship," Rawlins (2000) demonstrates that his research interests in dialectics and friendship converge with his teaching in interpersonal communication in the form of a mature teaching philosophy. The notion that we can learn together with all members of the class bringing knowledge to bear on life experience is inherent to Rawlins's philosophy. He sees teaching as the Aristotelian notion of friendship that embodies affection, equality, and mutuality so that classroom communication manifests goodwill as learners examine and create knowledge about relationships. Notice that Rawlins easily captures Bain's characteristics of attitudes, faith, willingness, and commitment. Once you read Rawlins's essay, you will fully appreciate his commitment to the teacher-student relationship.

However, the very idea that teaching is a mode of friendship is fraught with tension. Rawlins (2000) skillfully examines how common tensions in friendships manifest in the classroom. Through both his research (Rawlins, 1992) and his teaching experience, Rawlins observed that the four tensions of educational friendship comprise "the dialectics of the freedom to be independent and the freedom to be dependent, affection and instrumentality, judgment and acceptance, and expressiveness and protectiveness" (Rawlins, 2000, p. 8). Rawlins clarified his four tensions based on citations from passages written by his former students about those tensions. What fascinates me is the issue raised around *friendship* versus *being friendly*. Although Rawlins is personally committed to friendship, the student passages reveal a greater admiration and appreciation for a *friendly* classroom, where friendship had more of a potential than an actuality to develop. Rawlins certainly recognizes the problem inherent in negotiating what is comfortable for students and teachers, and he engages the reader in an excellent discussion of both the virtues and the limitations of educational friendship. What I like so much about this essay is the deep level of commitment to a philosophy that requires hard work and a payoff for all involved when the process works. Rawlins concludes:

> It [teaching as a mode of friendship] involves conscientious and disciplined practices, persistent orientations and sensitivities, and lived convictions. The rewards of these activities are their ongoing accomplishment, enriched relationships with fellow learners, and, it is hoped, enhanced humanity and education. (Rawlins, 2000, p. 25)

In the realm of interpersonal communication, what could be more fundamental than enhanced humanity and education?

Mark Orbe, a winner of six teaching and mentoring awards at Western Michigan University, is known for his core concept of *dumela*. I asked Professor Orbe to explain this after he visited our campus and I saw this concept in action. Read his response in the following box and then think about your own core concepts as a possible starting point for crafting a statement of teaching philosophy.

FROM THE CLASSROOM: Affirmation and Community as Teaching Philosophy

Dumela is a greeting used by the Basotho (Basutu) people, who live primarily in the northern parts of South Africa; it is Sesotho (Asutu) dialect. I was first introduced to the greeting by my pastor, who began to use it after a trip to South Africa. *Dumela* translates into "good day," but also connotatively communicates "I affirm you, I believe in you, and I see the great potential in you." I've been teaching the basic interpersonal communication class since 1991, and try to incorporate different things each time I teach the course. In 1994 I decided to start each class period by using "Dumela!"

Conceptually, the use of *dumela* fits perfectly with my teaching style. For many students, college is both an exciting and a daunting endeavor. By using this greeting affirmation, I communicate several important messages to my students—hopefully messages that are repeated/enhanced through other forms of communication. In many ways, it helps set the tone of the course—in which all individuals will be respected and affirmed as part of a diverse learning community. We may have contrasting ideas about different interpersonal topics (racism, sexism, language, sexual harassment, etc.), but when we become engaged with these subject matters true dialogue is possible because we begin with a sense of mutual respect, desire for understanding, and genuine affirmation. All this involves affirming where people come from, where they currently exist, as well as where their current learning will take them. In this regard, using the greeting *dumela* facilitates community in- and outside of the classroom.

Mark P. Orbe
Western Michigan University

SOURCE: Personal Correspondence with author, May 3, 2006.

A STATEMENT OF TEACHING PHILOSOPHY

Now I turn to a full statement of a teaching philosophy (Natalle, 2003). It is my own, and I share it with you so that you may dissect and consider it. I actually have two versions of this statement: one is a more objective statement that frames my teaching portfolio and the other is the story approach found here. In 2003, I was awarded the University of North Carolina at Greensboro College of Arts and Sciences Teaching Excellence Award. As part of the honor, the winner gives an open teaching lecture to the university. In composing my public speech (and there is a lot of pressure when the speaker is a communication professor), I decided to recraft my basic teaching philosophy statement into an appealing speech. I am presenting it here in its original speech form because it is actually more fun to read. As you read it, try to pick out the elements of the teaching philosophy that inspire you or confirm your perceptions of effective teaching. Note that the metaphor of children is quite different from Rawlins's idea of friendship, yet the qualities of friendship are here. I see friendship more as an outcome of the learning relationship, while the learning relationship itself is friendly. Note also that the notion of Confucian philosophy is embedded in a cultural context of benevolent authority. This is something to think about if you are a more democratic person. The speech text follows.

Teaching Excellence and the Confucian Ideal

I wanted to be a teacher since second grade, and I never deviated from that goal. So to stand before you as a Teaching Excellence Award winner is like winning the lottery in our profession. Today has technically got to be one of the best days of my professional career and, honestly, I wish my second grade teacher, Miss Wood, was in the audience. She was my original inspiration, and I still have her engagement announcement in my photo album from childhood. A personal note: Even though we are in the new science building and there is a real temptation to burst into a John Nash wielding of the chalk and put formulas all over the board (Howard, 2001), I'm going to refrain. Rather, I'm going to be a Girl Scout today and do my duty to "lecture" you on teaching excellence.

I have chosen the title "Teaching Excellence and the Confucian Ideal" for my talk, and there is a reason for the title. I am not a philosopher by training, but in my statement of teaching philosophy in my teaching portfolio I wrote the following: "In what might seem like an oxymoron, I have been able to take my childhood as a military dependent and my adulthood as a feminist scholar and mesh the two models to create an incredibly unusual ethical system that is a modern version of Quintilian's (1965) Good Man [Person] Theory. Ethics drive my life and what I take to my students. I believe in universal standards of right and wrong, of basic human dignity, fairness, cooperation, and justice. At the same time, I believe in the highest standards of achievement and that rewards come from honest hard work. I push my students to the limits that I know they can achieve, and then I push them one step further as a way to help them grow. One student once characterized my style as "tough love." I like that characterization. And, as many people know, I am not always the most popular teacher, and in fact, a lot of students don't care for me because I demand a level of commitment to the learning process that a lot of students cannot make. Without commitment on both our parts, there is no excellence in teaching or learning, and I can't accept that.

Note that I quoted Quintilian. When I developed my Case Studies in Intercultural Communication course, I selected T. R. Reid's (1999) fabulous book, *Confucius Lives Next Door,* as one of the texts. My students and I love this funny, insightful look at how living in Japan sheds light on what it means to be a Westerner, specifically an American. What I discovered, especially after going to *The Analects* (Confucius, 1979) is that Confucius and Quintilian actually have a lot in common. So to honor my students who are here today, I decided to go with the three Confucian lines that open *The Analects* that we learned in our class. I am using Reid's translation because it is so down-to-earth. So let us turn to Confucius and see what we can learn about teaching excellence.

I. Confucius said: Isn't it a pleasure when you can make practical use of the things you have studied? By training, I am a communication theorist, and it doesn't get any more esoteric than to theorize in the ivory tower all day. But when I was a graduate student studying group dynamics, my favorite professor, Gregg Phifer, quoted Kurt Lewin's famous saying, "There's nothing so practical as a good theory." For 27 years I have tried to use my teaching skills to make practical use of the theoretical knowledge I share with my students. The most recent example of that is my coauthored text, *The Woman's Public Speaking Handbook* (Natalle & Bodenheimer, 2004). My coauthor, Fritzi Bodenheimer, is one of my former graduate students, and we wrote this text as a practical application of feminist and rhetorical theories. It was pure joy to collaborate with a former student now turned colleague and to pool our knowledge for others' use.

One of the pedagogical techniques I work hard on is using real-life, practical examples to demonstrate how uncertainty reduction and dialectical theory, among many, many others, have practical application. When students return to me in class or even later to say that what we learned in class is happening in their lives, then I know we both receive pleasure in that knowledge and application of what we have studied together. Often, the students themselves find that practical use in their immediate lives, such as Andrew Strickland and Rich Jones using their relational skills in Sweden, or through the course activities such as the relationship analysis in Relational Communication, or the visit to the restaurant in Semiotics, or the ethnography on a gendered community in Communication and Gendered Communities, or the race and communication-style field observation in Cases in Intercultural Communication. There is one moment, however, that stands out above all others in practical realization.

In the spring of 2001, I taught our Persuasion and Western Culture course, CST 205. We were discussing Plato's Cave (Plato, 1985) in this class of 110 students. Jonathan Butler raised his hand and casually asked, "Well, don't you think *The Matrix* (Wachowski & Wachowski, 1999) is just a great example of Plato's Cave? I mean, Morpheus is the teacher-prophet who leads them out of the cave through Neo." Never missing a beat, I turned to my teaching assistant, Mike Toth, who was sitting at the A V console, and said, "Mike, you're the film man, what do you think?" Mike said, "Sounds good, I'll have to think about it." No one knew I was out of the loop and had not seen *The Matrix*! I went by the video store on the way home and watched *The Matrix* that night. Sure enough, the analogy worked, and I liked it even better than the usual one of Neo as prophet (Patridge, n.d.). Forty-eight hours later, I was congratulating Jonathan for his creative perception. But it got bigger than that because suddenly, the theoretical knowledge of Plato's Cave became a practical framework for how students in this class were analyzing their lives. Mike started calling me Morpheus, and I called him Neo. We decided to create the Cave in our auditorium. Using a host of volunteers, we positioned prisoners, the bridge was created, and using about a dozen Mini-Mag flashlights to project shadows on the cave wall, we were ready for the tableau.

Mike hit the light switch, the flashlights went on, and 110 people were in Plato's Cave. Through our study of rhetoric, we found our way out of the Cave that semester. It was awesome. The physical manner in which we moved from theory to practical application is a lesson my students and I will never forget. Confucius would be pleased with our creativity and the practical use that came from studying Plato's Cave.

II. Confucius said: Isn't it a pleasure to have an old friend visit from afar?   I have no children, as many of you know. My friendship circle, however, is wide and ranges in age from 20s to 70s. I like difference in my friendships because I learn new things from people who are not like me. I want to translate the word *friend* into *former student* because a number of my students are now my friends, and it is, indeed, a pleasure when they visit from afar. In today's world that visit is often by email or on the phone, but I am lucky this afternoon in that many of my former students are right here in this room.

When a student writes or calls it is often to say thank you. Here are some examples of what my "friends" say, and some of you in the audience know these former students.

David Redmond called me out of the blue one day to thank me for pushing everyone on APA style. What? This cracked me up, but David said, "Quit laughing. Look, I sell prosthetic devices to doctors. My job is difficult and there is little margin for error. I have to know exactly what's going on when I walk into a doctor's office and that means structure and format in my preparation. I got that skill from having to use APA style all the time in your classes." "I'll be darned, David," I said. "No one has ever said that to me before about the transferability of APA style. In a department where my nickname is The Queen of APA, I can't wait to tell my students in communication theory."

After a particularly dynamic semester in a graduate-level gender and communication class, DeAnna Chester wrote a formal thank-you letter to me in which she compared me to her eighth-grade teacher, Mrs. Moss. Apparently we both intimidated DeAnna by our sheer knowledge and demand on the student, but we are her favorites for caring and putting the responsibility on the student. DeAnna, who is now my colleague at a community college here in North Carolina, ended her letter with these lines: "If I ever work out all those role responsibilities in my life (most of which are socially constructed gender issues) and manage to get my doctorate, I like to think I will be a little like you in the classroom—structured, compassionate but not a push-over, and passionate about my teaching. I'm glad I had the opportunity to have a class with you. It has enriched my graduate experience." DeAnna and I talk by email about teaching as a regular topic.

One of my favorite emails is from Byron Beane, a public relations practitioner and aspiring actor in New York. His company handled the promotion for the stage version of *Tuesdays with Morrie,* and one evening he had the opportunity to meet author Mitch Albom backstage. What did Byron think of to talk to Mr. Albom about? He told Albom that we all read *Tuesdays with Morrie* (Albom, 1997) in the Senior Capstone course at UNCG and that we love the book. Byron was totally enthusiastic telling me this story, but there was a subtext. Morrie was Mitch's mentor and teacher, and Mitch honored his teacher with the book itself.

Byron honored me, his mentor and teacher, by telling me about this meeting with Mitch Albom. Even when I saw Byron the last time I was in New York, we mentioned this backstage scene. Byron smiled, and I glowed.

A physical visit I get every year is from faithful alumni who come back for homecoming. Jocelyn Fuller is one of those students who comes back every year for the tent party at our local corner pub. Along with another faculty member (we really are dinosaurs at this point), we show up at the pub to meet and greet the large number of communication alumni who attend the weekend activities. Jocelyn once told me that it just wouldn't be homecoming if I didn't show at the tent party. I am not even a beer drinker, but she knows I go to honor my former students and find out what their lives are all about. This is so much fun, but I am also consistently awed at the success of my students, most of whom live full and rewarding lives putting communication into practice everyday.

And how can I forget Love Crossling, truly one of my "children" who is now grown up? See for yourself—she is in our audience today. Love enrolled in my Gendered Relationships seminar her first semester in college. Although we come from very different standpoints, we clicked right away. Love double-majored in communication and psychology and took every class she could from me. She constantly excelled and pushed herself higher. She took a Masters in family counseling and then enrolled at UNCG for her PhD in higher education. One day, Love visited with a gift. She had made a statement for me, a thank you that she titled "Causatum" and mounted on beautiful paper with a glass frame. The statement she composed (Is it possible that I *caused* her to seek excellence? Perhaps I was an agent of change for her?) is hanging on my office wall and says the following:

CAUSATUM

Thank you for your diligence.	Now I seek diligence.
Thank you for your patience.	Now I seek patience.
Thank you for your passion.	Now I seek passion.
Thank you for your intuitiveness.	Now I seek intuitiveness.
Thank you for your warmth.	Now I seek warmth.
Thank you for the standard.	Now I seek the standard.
Thank you for your professionalism.	Now I seek professionalism.
Thank you for your nurturing.	Now I seek to nurture.
Thank you for your friendship.	Now I seek to befriend.
Thank you for your precision.	Now I seek precision.
Thank you for teaching me.	Thank you for teaching me

Why is all this visiting and thanking a pleasure? Because these students are, in part, a product of my teaching and their time at UNCG. They are my metaphoric children who have made good in the world. I can count on them to represent me, themselves, and their university well. My excellence as their teacher has transferred to them because we took the time to get to know each other. They are afar, but they are also always near in my heart and this is so much my pleasure.

In the Department of Communication there are many excellent teachers. We make jokes about each other's fan clubs because there is a little group of students near each of our office doors who are the fans. One day my doctoral student, Katie Ryan, witnessed a break between classes as we walked from my office outside the building. Along the way, we were interrupted numerous times—jokes in the hall, students calling out to me, a young woman coming up and hugging me, more laughter. Katie remarked, "Gee, that's not what the hallway is like in my building." Well, poor Katie spent most of her life in McIver Building, so what can I say? But you know what she saw. It is my pleasure that Katie sent me a note just this past Saturday in which she outlined her third year of teaching at West Virginia. If you are a professor without a fan club, start recruiting. They are your pleasure and they are a measure of your teaching excellence. Today in my audience is Lynn Fick-Cooper, one of my original "fans" from 1986. She honors me with her outstanding work at the Center for Creative Leadership, and she speaks often to my students in the Senior Capstone course. We have been friends all these years, and she now has children of her own. [Lynn called out from the audience that day, "Hey, Jody, that makes you a grandmother now, metaphorically speaking." The audience laughed heartily.]

P.S. Take your camera to school and capture your students on film. You will enjoy their images long after they graduate, and it is fun to show former students their photos as they do return to visit. Now, with digital cameras, it is even more fun when students send me pictures over the Internet.

III. Confucius said: Isn't it a sure sign of a gentleman that he does not take offense when others fail to recognize his ability?   First, let's take that notion of the Confucian "gentleman" and translate it into "good person." Here's where Quintilian (1965) and Confucius (1979) merge, so I don't mind whether you go Roman or Chinese—either philosophy will get you where we need to go. I am pleased that I have been recognized for teaching excellence in the College of Arts and Sciences. The College is at the heart of the making of good citizens, or good people, or gentlemen and women. Through the work of art, history, science, communication, math, psychology, theatre, and all the disciplines that make the arts and sciences, our students become people with moral character that fits them for adulthood. Confucius believed that a good person was born, but needed refinement or cultivation. We are the tools of our students' cultivation. That is an awesome responsibility and one that professors know is at the core of their professional life.

What are the virtues possessed of a good person? Confucius believed those virtues included benevolence, translated as love and obligation between family members; the ability to follow rules; wisdom or intelligence; courage; a reliability for keeping promises and speaking from fact; a reverence for responsibility including sacrifice for others. How do these qualities come to fruition? Through excellent teaching, of course, but also through service to community once those students graduate. In my audience today are a number of my students: Chelsey, Richard, Kristi, Katie, Rhiannon, Brandon, Lynn, Melissa Jane, Love. They are all good people because they possess the qualities of moral character I have just described. I have worked hard in conjunction with their parents and ministers and other role models to get them to do things like follow rules, be smart, have courage to do the right thing, sacrifice for the people you love most, and be honest above all else. My students do not need to be recognized for their ability; they already know what they possess. That is the mark of an educated person. They only have to honor themselves and all their teachers so that each night they can sleep with a clear conscience and a loving heart. Excellence speaks for itself, so there is no need to tell anyone about your abilities. Just do it!

Conclusion.   I hope that Confucian philosophy makes you think anew about the meaning of excellence in both teaching and learning, for surely those two processes merge when education is functioning in its ideal state. It is my commitment as a teacher to see that teaching and learning happen every day inside and outside the classroom, for without moral character to cultivate, what would we be but uncivilized animals in chaos? S. I. Hayakawa said, "Cooperation through the use of language is the fundamental mechanism of human survival.... Human fitness to survive requires the ability to talk, write, listen, and read in ways that increase the chances for you and fellow members of the species to survive together" (1992, p. 12). An ethic of cooperation through communication literacy is my aim in teaching excellence. Without moral character, our communication efforts lead nowhere. To my students: Thank you. To my colleagues: May you have the pleasure of teaching students similar to those I have had over the years at UNCG. To learn practical applications of theory, to take pleasure in visiting with one another each day in a quest for knowledge and character development, and to do so without pointing out our abilities is a life of the "good person."

PROFESSIONAL DEVELOPMENT

Having an approach to teaching means considering yourself a professional in the classroom and establishing a philosophy that guides your instructional methods. From the point of view of technical expertise, professional development—keeping your skills up and staying current with the trends in the field—is the primary tool for furthering the growth process. In this section I will discuss three recommended avenues for professional development:

- creating and maintaining a teaching portfolio;
- participating in training conducted by the National Communication Association or similar professional organizations; and
- using your own consulting and training opportunities as a mechanism for bringing real-world feedback into the classroom.

Teaching Portfolios

A teaching portfolio is a record of your teaching accomplishments. A portfolio can serve as both a professional development tool and evidence for your own advancement or promotion and tenure. Virtually all instructors in the field of education now maintain teaching portfolios, but it is only recently that instructors of communication have begun to assemble portfolios. In general, a portfolio will:

- reflect you as a professional teacher—your philosophy and training as a teacher and some of the experiences you have had over the course of your career;
- serve as a demonstration of your effectiveness as a teacher because evaluations are contained within the portfolio;
- provide an historical picture of you as a teacher because there is a chronological record of responsibilities—you can reflect on your past achievements, present activities, and future plans.

Portfolios are ultimately a tool to improve teaching.

There are many books (e.g., Campbell, 2004) and articles (e.g., Quinlin, 2002; Syre & Pesa, 2001) available through your school library that can show you basic standards for setting up a portfolio and thinking about how it will be reviewed by colleagues. My own portfolio is based on the criteria of my university's teaching excellence award. I update it every summer. The contents include:

1. statement of teaching philosophy
2. methods used to achieve educational goals (including sample syllabi, student papers, honors thesis, etc.)
3. teaching goals for the next five years
4. current vita, including list of courses taught and developed at UNCG
5. interdepartmental and/or interdisciplinary activities related to teaching
6. information documenting advising activities, guided student projects, supervision of honors projects, graduate theses/dissertations
7. letters of teaching effectiveness (peer reviews, letters from students)
8. numerical and/or descriptive data by students from course evaluations

Other items might be useful in a portfolio: copies of books or articles to accompany the teaching philosophy (item 1 above); coauthored publications with students to support item 6 above; awards received if portfolio is used for promotion and tenure or a job application; photographs of student activities to enhance items 5 and 6 above; course proposals to support item 4 above; copies of conference or workshop presentations given to demonstrate teaching expertise. You should carefully review your university's expectations as you compile your portfolio. You can find this information in promotion and tenure guidelines and in calls for nominations for teaching awards. Don't wait! Assemble a basic portfolio now and use it to develop professionally throughout your career.

Professional Organizations

The primary professional organization for communication educators in the United States is the National Communication Association (NCA), founded in 1914. On its Web site homepage (www.natcom.org) the association describes its purpose, in part, by stating: "NCA works with its members to strengthen the profession and contribute to the greater good of the educational enterprise and society." I recommend membership in the NCA as a wise investment in the discipline of communication. When you register, be sure to affiliate with the Interpersonal Communication Division so you receive the newsletter and other information of specific interest to you. The NCA Web site itself is a marvelous resource to help you think about ways to develop professionally. For example, the pull-down menu on the homepage that is labeled Instruction has 11 links on topics such as online communication courses, assessment resources, preparing future faculty, service-learning, and the scholarship of teaching and learning. As I investigated the online communication courses link, I found an online interpersonal communication course offered at Clark State Community College that is described by its instructor, Michelle Burch. Not only can you see a sample syllabus for such a class, you can gain deeper knowledge of the requirements for both teaching and taking an online course.

The NCA is also the publisher of many journals that offer articles to improve your teaching. For example, *Communication Education* and *Communication Teacher* offer a range of theoretical, research-oriented, and practical pedagogy that can enhance both your knowledge and your skill as a teacher of interpersonal communication. As a communication educator, you can enjoy current knowledge of the field by reading such publications. Select a journal that will enhance your teaching, and make a commitment to yourself to read through four times a year. At a faculty meeting in my first year of teaching, one of my senior colleagues suggested that we all receive our journals at our home addresses. He argued that a person would be more likely to read at home, whereas at the office we might just shelve the journal without taking a significant look. For 26 years I have received all my journals at home. He was right.

Professional organizations offer training in the form of workshops and panels at their annual conventions. I use my state organization to attend Great Ideas for Teaching Speech (G.I.F.T.S.) panels. Usually these panels consist of a series of short presentations by members in the Carolinas Communication Association who teach public speaking, interpersonal communication, or hybrid courses. These practical "gifts" offer creative strategies to make the classroom a better learning site. At NCA you can sign up for short courses on topics relevant to interpersonal communication. Short courses usually run for three hours and often include copies of texts, sample syllabi, and course activities.

Make it a priority to join a state, regional, or national organization as part of your professional development agenda. Go to the annual conferences and subscribe to journals that will broaden your scope and depth of interpersonal communication knowledge. Attend at least one workshop or panel every year and take the suggested activity back into your classroom to try it out.

Training and Consulting

Depending on where you are in the course of your teaching career, you will receive calls to train or consult with agencies and organizations that need help with interpersonal communication problem solving or employee training. About five years into my career I started training managers and employees out in the community. For many years I worked with managers in state government and taught a regular interpersonal skills course that constituted about 20 hours of training. For the last five years I have taught a diversity course in a management development program that targets managers in my region of North Carolina. In between I have worked with corporate managers, hospital social workers, city employees, student officers in university organizations, attorneys, university faculty and staff, speech and hearing clinicians, and employees of the federal judiciary. Because I take interpersonal concepts, skills, and theories out into the community, I have a strong knowledge of how interpersonal communication process works in the real world. It's like a testing ground to see if what we are teaching our students has applicability beyond the classroom. At the same time, I bring the concerns and issues of my students' future employers back into the classroom. The back and forth between my students and my clients is an excellent way to teach information that is up-to-date and practical. My own professional development is enhanced through these training and consulting opportunities, and I am ultimately a better teacher. I encourage you to take advantage of such opportunities when they come your way. Think through your expertise and how you will respond when you receive your first call from a community agency. What can you do and, just as importantly, what can you *not* do? If you are a senior professor, invite younger colleagues to go with you as a co-trainer so they can see firsthand how beneficial such opportunities are.

COMING TO CLOSURE ON EFFECTIVE TEACHING . . . FOR NOW

Some people think good teaching is a knack—that we come to it naturally if we are good at it. Maybe there is a "teacher personality," and those of us with such a personality gravitate toward the profession. I agree with Bill Rawlins (2000) and Peter Filene (2005) that teaching is inherently relational and that effective teachers bring a philosophical orientation on relationships and teaching when they enter the interpersonal communication classroom. This chapter highlighted some of these philosophical characteristics by looking at the thoughts of professors in both education and communication. If you are a new teacher, make a list now of key phrases and concepts that you perceive to be core components in your teaching philosophy.

_____	_____
_____	_____
_____	_____

Over the next several months, craft a written statement that will guide you more effectively and that you can have as part of your teaching portfolio. If you are a seasoned teacher, take out your statement of teaching philosophy now and review it. Make amendments as appropriate. No matter where you are in your career, you have to love students and the learning process for this career to mean something to everyone involved.

SETTING GOALS

Now is the time to set goals for your own development as a teacher of interpersonal communication. To assist, I will outline possible areas of goal consideration. Depending on where you are in your career, your goals should reflect a logical point for improving your teaching. For example, do you have knowledge-based goals? ("My goal is to develop a deeper knowledge of the conflict literature to close a gap in my teaching on that interpersonal topic.") Do you have philosophical goals? ("My goal is to commit a philosophy of teaching to paper so I can use that philosophy to be a better teacher of interpersonal communication.") Perhaps you have technical goals. ("My goal is to take a professional development workshop on interpersonal communication to help me manage my classroom more effectively.") Knowing that you cannot set and reach multiple goals overnight, prioritize your goals as short-term or long-term. Decide for yourself what *short* and *long* mean. Try to be as specific as possible so that you can be realistic in goal setting.

Short-term Goals

Goal #1: _____

_____

Strategy to reach goal # 1: _____

_____

Goal #2: _____

_____

Strategy to reach goal # 2: _____

_____

Long-term Goals

Goal #1: _____

_____

Strategy to reach goal # 1: _____

_____

Goal #2: _____

_____

Strategy to reach goal # 2: _____

_____

Review these goals and strategies at the beginning and end of each semester. Make changes as appropriate. Discuss your progress with colleagues or a mentor. On a separate page, develop a unified plan for professional development by outlining what you've read about in this chapter: strengths, challenges, teaching philosophy, goals, and strategies. This plan will help you stay on the path of professionalism and effectiveness. To help you gain more insight into what really works in the interpersonal classroom, the next four chapters reveal helpful information on constructing a syllabus, managing the classroom, dealing with student problems, developing instructional strategies, and implementing a system for evaluating student work.

CHAPTER

2

The Basic Tool of Effective Teaching: The Syllabus

The syllabus is the backbone of the interpersonal communication course. Without this fundamental skeletal component, the course would not work. A syllabus links teacher and student so they can effectively manage and accomplish the course objectives. In this chapter we will look at the function of a syllabus. We will then dissect the syllabus I use for my course, reviewing the scope of the course, the learning objectives, the organization of course content, and how supporting materials enhance a syllabus. Finally, we will look at variations on a syllabus, including one emphasizing theory, one focused on service-learning, and another created specifically for an online course. After reading this chapter you should be able to construct a syllabus that will serve as a strong foundation for your introductory course and help you be a more effective teacher.

THE FUNCTION OF A SYLLABUS

A syllabus serves several purposes, all of which are interconnected. For me, the primary function of a syllabus is to organize the course so that learning can be successful. The syllabus delivers essential information to help the student navigate the course. The organization outlined serves as a study guide when students prepare for examinations. The syllabus also functions as a policy document because it typically contains important protocol about attendance, the implementation of exams, grading, and other departmental and university policies. Finally, the syllabus is a legal document that binds professor and student in contractual agreement. All of these functions are interconnected because technical, legal, and pedagogical details are needed in the learning environment. Even so, I like L. B. Curzon's advice that "above all, the teacher's own interpretation of the learner's needs at his or her current stage of development" (2004, p. 189) is what should underlie the syllabus. This is good advice and keeps you on track in your job as the instructor. In her compact and useful book titled *The Course Syllabus: A Learning Centered Approach,* Judith Grunert (1997) lists 16 functions of a syllabus that include everything from setting the tone of the course to communicating the role of technology—all of which aid the educational development of the student. Look at Table 2.1 and see if these functions sound reasonable to you.

TABLE 2.1. Judith Grunert's 16 Functions of a Learning-Centered Syllabus

1. Establishes an early point of contact and connection between student and instructor.
2. Helps set the tone for your course.
3. Describes your beliefs about educational purposes.
4. Acquaints students with the logistics of the course.
5. Contains collected handouts.
6. Defines student responsibilities for successful course work.
7. Describes active learning.
8. Helps students to assess their readiness for your course.
9. Sets the course in a broader context for learning.
10. Provides a conceptual framework.
11. Describes available learning resources.
12. Communicates the role of technology in the course.
13. Can expand to provide difficult-to-obtain reading materials.
14. Can improve the effectiveness of student note taking.
15. Can include material that supports learning outside the classroom.
16. Can serve as a learning contract.

From Judith Grunert (1997). *The Course Syllabus: A Learning Centered Approach* (pp. 14–19). Bolton, MA: Anker Publishing.

Because students tend not to read a syllabus thoroughly or understand how much it can contribute to student success (in fact, first-year students in college may be seeing a syllabus for the first time), I go over the syllabus on the first day of class. I then usually begin the second day of the semester with this invitation: "Now that you've had time to review the syllabus and think about what's ahead this semester, do you have any questions about the syllabus or the course?" There is usually at least one question.

To counteract casual student attitudes about the role of the syllabus, I emphasize our use of the document throughout the semester. A tightly structured syllabus helps me implement the various functions of information delivery, policy archive, semester organization, and study guide for exams. After all, as educator Ruby Higgins argues, the syllabus is "an aspect of the instructor's role of communicator" (1994, p. 408). And now that technology (course home pages, email lists, and so forth) makes it easy for students to reprint syllabi, the most common complaint—"I lost my syllabus"—no longer stands as a valid reason for a student's falling behind.

Overall, a syllabus should align with your teaching approach. For example, if you have a skills-based course, the syllabus should make that clear. Also, check that it organizes the semester accordingly. The same criteria apply to all types of courses, such as service learning-based courses or distance learning-based courses. A student or a peer instructor reviewing your syllabus should be able to locate in the document the purpose of the course, stated learning objectives, class schedule, and any description of activities related to the course.

Why is this important? A straightforward statement of approach tells everyone in the learning community where they are going and what they are striving to achieve. For example, if you are teaching a skills-based course, a student should be able to see that certain skills need to be learned and that those skills will support enhanced interpersonal communication in the real world. In fact, a skills-based approach is the most common scope of an entry-level interpersonal communication course.

Generally, most courses are tied to textbooks that teach skills based in research and theory. If, however, the course serves a research function or a service-learning function as part of the departmental curriculum, then it is a good idea to make that clear on the syllabus so that your students have some context for the course. In my own department, our introductory interpersonal course is also a required core course that supports the department's mission statement: "We teach the strategic and ethical uses of communication to build relationships and communities." On my syllabus I make it clear to the students that the course fulfills a role in delivering the relationships component of the mission statement.

THE ELEMENTS OF A SYLLABUS

While doing research for this chapter, I examined many different syllabi from introductory interpersonal communication courses, and I will share portions of some of those syllabi later in the chapter. Although I found many similarities among the syllabi that I studied, each still reflected the unique teaching style of its respective instructor; this testifies to the fact that there is no one correct way to structure a syllabus. Most instructors tend to order a syllabus with access information first, followed by learning objectives, policies, assignments, and a daily schedule. This organization may reflect more custom than pedagogical logic, but the end result should be clear information that guides the student through the course. Communication pedagogy expert Jean Civikly-Powell (1999) advocates that a syllabus has two good payoffs: to reduce "student uncertainty and anxiety about the course and expectations for successful performance" (p. 70) and to serve as "the all-in-one-place reference manual" (p. 70) to reduce class time spent on procedural issues. Such payoffs are well worth the time you will invest in constructing a syllabus.

I now share with you the syllabus I created for my own introductory interpersonal communication course. Let's examine it carefully and dissect the basic elements. If you are an experienced instructor, you may want to compare yours with this one to see if it sparks any new ideas; remember, however, that it is just one example of how a syllabus might be structured. Note that this class also serves as a writing-intensive course and would be called a "marker course." Many institutions are now using marker courses, so named because they are marked with letters to indicate what the course promotes, such as writing (W) and speaking (S) across the curriculum or service-learning (SVL). We will talk about this later and again in Chapter 4.

SAMPLE SYLLABUS FOR AN ENTRY-LEVEL INTERPERSONAL COMMUNICATION COURSE

CST 207W-01

T-TH 12:30-1:45 p.m. Room TBA

Relational Communication Writing Intensive

Syllabus

Fall 2005

Instructor

Dr. Jody Natalle

Office: 112 Ferguson

Phone: 334-3841 Email: ej_natalle@uncg.edu

Office Hours: T & TH 3:30-5 p.m.; or by appointment

Purpose of Course

CST 207 introduces the student to the study of the strategic and ethical uses of communication to build relationships. The emphasis of the course is on the practical application of concepts and strategies. In addition to gaining knowledge through lecture and reading, students will increase awareness of relational messages through skill-based activity, discussion, and a relationship analysis. As a writing-intensive course, there are also the purposes of (1) improving basic writing skills and (2) learning to think through writing. This course treats writing both as a means of learning and as a skill to be learned. This core course supports the departmental mission statement that "we teach the strategic and ethical uses of communication to build relationships and communities."

General Objectives

Upon completion of this course, the student should be able to:

1. define and use a vocabulary of relational communication terms.
2. apply major theoretical concepts in the field of relational communication to real world relationships.
3. analyze his or her own role in interpersonal relationships in a family, professional, friendship, interracial/intercultural, or intimate context.

4. apply both practical and theoretical knowledge to increase his or her own competency in relational communication skills.
5. evaluate the effectiveness of an interpersonal relationship.
6. write more effectively and correctly than when the semester began.
7. use writing to express ideas about interpersonal communication.

Text and Supplies

Text: DeVito, J.A. (2004). *The interpersonal communication book* (10th ed.). Boston: Pearson Education. (required text)

Hacker, D. (2000). *A pocket style manual* (3rd ed.). Boston: Bedford/ St. Martin's. (optional text/available UNCG Bookstore)

There are also readings on e-reserve, including a course packet, at the library. See attached reserve list.

Each student should also purchase a pocket dictionary and some kind of a writing guide. Dictionaries and Strunk's book are available in the reference section of the bookstore. On reserve for you at the library are the following sources:

The elements of style (4th Ed.) by William Strunk, Jr. & E. B. White.

The elements of grammar by Margaret D. Shertzer.

You will also need two (2) Scantron sheets, Form #882-ES (available at the bookstore) and about a dozen 5×8 plain index cards.

Bring cards and course packet to class at all times!

Attendance

You should attend every class session. The course is designed for participation by students and includes many in-class exercises. You should expect to be called upon during the semester. **There are no free cuts.** For each day you are late to class or that you depart early, one point will be deducted from your final point total. For the first three unexcused absences, five (5) points will be deducted from your point total. Upon the fourth unexcused absence, your final grade will be lowered by one letter. Five absences will result in being dropped from the course with a WF. An excused absence includes illness, accident, family emergency or funeral (call or email the professor to let her know what is happening), attendance at an approved UNCG event such as athletic team competition or academic conference (bring the notice from the appropriate sponsor), or unavoidable company travel for full-time employees. Job interviews and roommate problems are not excused absences! Pay attention to this policy. There are no exceptions. Make coming to class a top priority and be on time.

In-Class Behavior

Everyone deserves the respect of others. Turn off your cell phone. Eating and drinking in class are not appropriate. If you are suffering from illness that requires a water bottle or cough drops, do bring those with you. Getting up in the middle of class to go to the bathroom or get a drink is not acceptable—take care of these needs before you arrive. You are adults and are expected to demonstrate adult behavior. You should be able to sit through a class period by staying involved and showing consideration for others. Your class participation points reflect not only your thoughtful and constructive contributions to class discussion, but also your ability to conduct yourself in a positive, mature manner.

Exams

Two quizzes and two exams will be administered during the semester. A quiz will follow Unit I. At the end of Unit II, a comprehensive exam will cover the material in both Units I and II. A quiz will follow Unit III on only the content in that unit. At the end of Unit IV, a comprehensive exam will cover the material in both Units III and IV. Dates for quizzes and exams are in the daily assignment sheet. No quiz or exam may be made up without a doctor's note or university excuse. **If you go to the UNCG Health Center, make sure you get a written note from the doctor, or proof that you were attended to by a health care provider.** If you miss an exam and do not bring a valid excuse, you will receive a zero for that quiz or exam.

Homework

A number of assignments will be given as homework, including a major assignment that involves a relationship analysis. All homework must be turned in on the due date at the beginning of class in order to receive credit. **Late assignments will**

be substantially penalized. Since this is a writing-intensive course, students will be allowed to draft and revise both major assignments once. Original and revised copies of the assignment must be turned in when submitting a revision. Note that the revised grade is what stands in the final point total. If you receive a lower grade on a revision, that will be the final grade for that assignment.

Honor Code

It is the responsibility of everyone at UNCG to obey and to support the Academic Honor Policy. Students should become familiar with the Honor Policy by reading in the 2005–2006 Undergraduate Bulletin. You will be asked to sign an honor pledge for all major work submitted in CST 207. Violation of Honor Policy will result in full and appropriate penalty by the instructor.

Grading

Final grades will be based on the following breakdown:

Possible Points		Final Grade
Quizzes 25 pts. @	50 pts.	392–400=A+
Exams 100 pts. @	200 pts.	372–391=A
Homework	70 pts.	360–371=A−
Class Participation &		352–359=B+
Exercises	50 pts.	329–351=B
Writing Improvement	30 pts.	320–328=B−
		312–319=C+
Total	400 pts.	289–311=C
		280–288=C−
		272–279=D+
		249–271=D
		240–248=D−
		239–Below=F

Units of Instruction and Daily Assignments

Units I and II emphasize the **transactional philosophy** and **relationship development.**

Unit I Overview of Relational Communication

T Aug. 16   Orientation/Introduction

Homework: Buy text & supplies

TH Aug. 18   Definition and Perspective

Preparation: Read Chp. 1

T Aug. 23   Writing: A Skill and a Way to Think

Preparation: Review Hacker, Strunk & White, Shertzer

TH Aug. 25   Context and Transaction

Preparation: Review Chp. 1, pp. 10–20; Packet Item #2

T Aug. 30   Models of Effectiveness

Homework: Conduct Interview & Complete Model Exercise;
Packet Item #3

TH Sept. 1   Share Models/Perception

Model Exercise Due (15 pts.)

Preparation: Read Chp. 4

T Sept. 6   Perception (cont.)/Attribution

TH Sept. 8   Attribution/Uncertainty Reduction

Homework: Complete Revision of Model Exercise

T Sept. 13   The Self and Self-Disclosure

Model Exercise Revision Due

Preparation: Read Chp. 3

Homework: Study for Quiz

TH Sept. 15   **Quiz #1 (25 pts.)**/Introduction to Relationship Development

Homework: Select Relationship for Analysis; Packet Item #4

Unit II The Relationship Cycle

T Sept. 20   Interpersonal Process/Attraction/Conversation

Preparation: Read Chps. 9 & 10

TH Sept. 22   Social Exchange/Equity Theory

Preparation: Read Chp. 11, pp. 252–263; Read Wood, E-Reserve

T Sept. 27   Rules and Power
                    Homework: Read Chp. 14; Packet Item #5

TH Sept. 29   Negotiating Selves/Confirmation-Disconfirmation
                    Preparation: Read Chp. 7, pp. 170–177; Packet Item #6

T Oct. 4   Deception and Ethics/Deterioration
                    Preparation: Read Chp. 11, pp. 264–277; Packet Item #7 & #8

TH Oct. 6   Relational Deterioration
                    Units I and II Review
                    Homework: Study for Exam

T Oct. 11   Fall Break. No Class.

TH Oct. 13   **Exam #1 (100 pts.)**
                    Bring Scantron Form 882-ES and a No. 2 pencil

Units III and IV emphasize **competence**.

Unit III Relational Communication Skills

T Oct. 18   Competence: Skills Assessment
                    Return Exam
                    Preparation: Review Chp. 1, p. 12; Packet Item #9

TH Oct. 20   Dialectics
                    Preparation: Read Baxter, E-reserve; Packet Item #10

T Oct. 25   Assertiveness and Social Manners
                    Preparation: Read Chp. 6, pp. 142–152; Packet Item #15
                    Homework: Finalize relationship analysis

TH Oct. 27   Listening
                    Relationship Analysis Due (50 pts.)
                    Preparation: Read Chp. 5; Packet Item #11
                    Homework: Complete Listening Exercise

Preregistration for Spring 2006 runs October 26-November 11. Don't forget!

T Nov. 1   Language

Listening Exercise Due

Preparation: Review Chp. 6; Read Chp. 7

TH Nov. 3   Nonverbal

Preparation: Read Chp. 8

T Nov. 8   Conflict Management

Preparation: Read Chp. 13; Packet Item # 12, 13, 14

Competence Diary Due (5 pts.)

Homework: Study for Quiz

TH Nov. 10   **Quiz #2 (25 pts.)**/Introduction to Friendship

Unit IV Communication Competence in Relationship Contexts

T Nov. 15   Friendship/Intimate Relationships

Preparation: Read Chp. 12, pp. 280–293

Relationship Analysis Revision Due

TH Nov. 17   No Class. Dr. Natalle at NCA.

T Nov. 22   Gender, Race, and Culture Perspectives on Friendship

Preparation: Read West et al., E-reserve;

Read Chp. 2; Packet Item #16 & 17

TH Nov. 24   Thanksgiving Holiday. No Class.

T Nov. 29   Family Communication

Preparation: Read Chp. 12, pp. 294–303

TH Dec. 1   Final Summary and Activity

Units III and IV Review

Last Day of Class

Homework: Study for Exam #2

TH Dec. 8   **Exam #2 (100 pts.)**

Noon–3:00 p.m.

Don't forget your Scantron Form 882-ES!

Final Grades

You may check your grades via the Internet by going to the UNCG Homepage
(www.uncg.edu). Click on *Campus Pipeline* or *uncGenie*. Log in with your user
name or Student ID and PIN numbers. Follow the instructions. See also p. 20 in
the UNCG Fall 2005 *Schedule of Courses* bulletin for more information. No grades
will be posted or given out over the department telephone.

First note the basic elements of the syllabus: course title, professor access, course purpose and learning objectives, textbook and supply information, course policies (attendance, behavior, exams, homework, honor code, and grading), and the daily schedule. Try to be succinct and complete. On this syllabus I did not initially include a classroom location because at the time it wasn't available to me. However, try to make it a general practice to include it as a courtesy to students or other guests who may attend your class during the semester. If you can update your syllabus electronically, and thus avoid having to photocopy a document that doesn't include all the essential information, then do so. (Stating a room number is no small issue. I once received a critical comment on a peer teaching evaluation because this information was lacking.)

Some syllabi may include university policies concerning students with disabilities, class rules for participation or behavior, a statement of prerequisites, or written instructions for specific assignments throughout the course. The "reference manual" approach advocated by Civikly-Powell (1999) means that a syllabus could be ten pages or more by the time it is finished. However, others, such as Ruby Higgins (1994), administrator and former dean at Grambling State University, suggest that a syllabus be no more than three pages long so that students do not suffer from information overload. It is your decision how to honor university, departmental, and personal policies and preferences, but rarely do I see three-page syllabi these days. One can supplement a syllabus with a course packet, as I do. My 29-page packet contains assignment instructions, handouts, class exercises, and an extra copy of the syllabus that I post on Blackboard so students can have access to these course materials at all times. (The dog can't chew up the instructions for an assignment and leave a student high and dry!) Although a course packet can take the dramatic suspense out of class discussions because some students have looked ahead, the fact that such a resource is available makes it worth having.

Although I do not include a teaching philosophy per se on the syllabus, I attempt to enact my philosophy every day in class. I have seen syllabi on which a teaching philosophy is stated briefly, but I am more likely to see statements that invite students to participate in class discussions and/or activities, or that indicate something about the positive communication climate created by the instructor. I have also read syllabi that presented a potentially negative learning environment by using "dos and don'ts" as the approach for rules and policies.

Granted, the tone in my own syllabus is much firmer than when I first started teaching 30 years ago. One reason for that is because I feel the need to respond to a student population that, over the years, has actually become less respectful of both classroom and peers. My policy on in-class behavior, for example, may at first seem quite negative. However, if you examine it carefully you'll see that there is some humanity implicit in the policy. For example, I encourage water bottles if a student is suffering from a cold. Yet I discourage bringing a burger bag and a large drink into the classroom just because a student feels like eating lunch in my class. Student feedback to these instituted policies typically consisted of "Thank you! I wish other teachers would have these policies because I don't want to be distracted by people jumping up to run to the bathroom or people unwrapping food and eating instead of participating." This positive feedback encourages me to retain my policies of "tough love." Such policies help me maintain control over the environment for pedagogical success.

Learning Outcomes

Learning outcomes are the skeletal structure of the syllabus; they comprise the actual foundation for the course in interpersonal communication. A professor sets the learning outcomes and then provides a learning environment in which those outcomes can be achieved. All course activities and materials support the expected outcomes, and the syllabus must reflect the choices made to match activities and materials with outcomes. There is no magic number when it comes to how many objectives should be on a syllabus. I've seen no outcomes stated when a course purpose seems to indicate what is expected from student learning, and I've seen as many as a dozen learning outcomes. Be sure there is a logical connection between the learning outcomes specified and all that follows. When you think about students taking five classes per semester, it starts to become unrealistic to think that a student could achieve as many as ten learning outcomes per course and retain what is learned. Be reasonable in your expectations. Just like a parsimonious theory, craft the smallest number of learning outcomes to achieve the most effective results for the body of knowledge under study.

I first learned about learning outcomes in an undergraduate education course I was taking on how to construct behavioral objectives, examinations, and other assignments. We used a great book called *Behavioral Objectives and Instruction* (Kibler, Barker, & Miles, 1970) that taught us how to write behavioral objectives based on the work of Benjamin Bloom. Originally offered in 1956, Bloom's famous taxonomy of educational objectives and his six categories of cognition have been the mainstay for teaching aspiring professors how to write statements of expected learning outcomes. (Note that the original term was *behavioral objective*. We now say *learning outcome* to better reflect that what we are trying to teach can have cognitive as well as emotional results. You will hear both phrases used interchangeably.) Bloom outlined an ascending order of six cognitive domains: *knowledge, comprehension, application, analysis, synthesis,* and *evaluation.* These domains are intended to propel a student forward on his or her mastery of a discipline. The absolute beauty of this taxonomy is that it provides a way for the professor to write learning outcomes, as well as to set up course activities and exams appropriate to the cognitive level of the expected outcomes. For example, take a look again at the basic student objectives for my course:

1. Define and use a vocabulary of relational communication terms.
2. Apply major theoretical concepts in the field of relational communication to real-world relationships.
3. Analyze his or her own role in interpersonal relationships in a family, professional, friendship, interracial/intercultural, or intimate context.
4. Apply both practical and theoretical knowledge to increase his or her own competency in relational communication skills.
5. Evaluate the effectiveness of an interpersonal relationship.

I have used the verb forms of Bloom's taxonomy in writing the objectives in items 2, 3, 4, and 5. Knowledge is the first domain in Bloom's taxonomy; therefore, I made defining terms the first and lowest level of expected cognitive mastery. I use the vocabulary of interpersonal communication everyday in class so that students become familiar with terms such as *dyad, self-disclosure, social exchange,* and *dialectics;* I engage students in vocabulary activities (e.g., let's construct a Johari Window to see what are the implications for your self-disclosure with your mom); and I test vocabulary on an exam by using something as simple as a matching exercise of terms and definitions.

Untrained instructors who teach entry-level classes often set the expected outcomes at the level of application or below. But once you know Bloom's taxonomy, you can stretch yourself and write learning outcomes that push the student toward higher levels of cognition. In real life, for example, we need to *apply* communication skills in dyads, but we will also need to know how to *evaluate* the effectiveness of the relationships in which we participate if those relationships are to grow and remain healthy. An introductory course can achieve both expected outcomes with the right learning outcomes, such as I did in learning outcomes 4 and 5 on my syllabus.

David Krathwohl, a collaborator of Bloom's from the beginning, recently described a revised version of Bloom's Taxonomy that he developed with some new colleagues (Anderson & Krathwohl, 2001; Krathwohl, 2002). The taxonomy still contains six cognitive dimensions, but there are changes as noted in Table 2.2. The *synthesis* category has been dropped and a *creative* category added. In addition, verbs replace nouns as the names of the categories.

I can see the creative category of knowledge at work in one of my colleague's interpersonal courses. He requires students to create a working relationship with someone in the class whom they do not know in order to practice interpersonal skills and to generate activities for themselves and other classmates. Toward the end of the semester the dyads evaluate how well they achieved their assignments together. Using the Bloom and the revised Krathwohl taxonomies will improve both your effectiveness as an instructor and your ability to create the *appropriate* learning outcomes to serve your course and your students' needs.

TABLE 2.2 A Comparison of Bloom's Taxonomy and Krathwohl's Revised Taxonomy

Bloom's Taxonomy	Krathwohl's Revised Taxonomy
Knowledge	Remember
Comprehension	Understand
Application	Apply
Analysis	Analyze
Synthesis	Evaluate
Evaluation	Create

In planning your learning outcomes, you may need to conform to a departmental syllabus or to the expectations of "marker" courses such as speaking or writing intensives. My syllabus demonstrates two outcomes related to writing, and they follow the objectives of our university-wide program to improve writing. A departmental syllabus may already have learning outcomes specified. Using your own professional judgment and range of academic freedom, be sure that those outcomes honor the learning situation as you see it and can teach within its boundaries.

In addition to designing learning outcomes that satisfy course, student, and departmental needs, there is now the pressing responsibility to conform to assessment expectations. Although the assessment movement has swept the nation since the 1970s (Banta, 2002), many institutions are just now conforming to the demand for assessment. State legislatures have put much pressure on community colleges and universities to measure learning outcomes on both the level of general education (e.g., writing, reading, critical thinking) and within the disciplines that comprise degree programs (e.g., communication, sociology, etc.). Accrediting agencies, such as the Southern Association of Colleges and Schools (SACS), which serves an 11-state region, have responded by incorporating evaluation criteria into their accrediting procedures that look at assessment. Institutions that do not demonstrate a systematic approach to an assessment process risk losing accreditation.

Assessment itself is simply the technical process of systematically measuring how well students achieve learning outcomes and then making adjustments to improve the learning environment based on the results of the assessment process. For more than a decade, the National Communication Association has assisted communication professionals in creating learning outcomes and developing assessment procedures (Morreale & Backlund, 1999). If you log on to the NCA Web site at www.natcom.org, click the Education button, and then go to Assessment resources, you will find eight different items to help you set up an assessment plan. You can also attend workshops on the assessment process at NCA, regional, or state professional conferences. Another good source is Linda Suskie's *Assessing Student Learning: A Common Sense Guide* (2004).

I have been the chair of assessment in my department since 1997. My colleagues and I have struggled hard with assessment, and we have resisted it on both psychological and practical grounds. Many educators in higher learning believe that we are following a high school model that doesn't apply to college education. Some believe that the real payoff from a college education doesn't show up until college graduates are out in the so-called real world; hence, assessment isn't a valid way to measure what students learn. Our resistance is to no avail because the university has mandated compliance with assessment. We are just now putting our departmental learning objectives in place for 2006 and figuring out how to embed departmental outcomes in course objectives so that the actual assessment of student learning can proceed with some degree of ease. My department has probably now entered the mainstream, but there are many communication departments well ahead of us—including, for example, Delaware Technical and Community College (DTCC). On DTCC's interpersonal communication syllabus, the 11 learning outcomes are stated as "college-wide core course performance objectives" followed by *measurable* performance objectives for all 11 learning objectives. For example, the first core objective and its corresponding measurable objectives are:

1. Describe the communication process, including major elements of a communication model.
   1.1 Name the components of a typical communication model.
   1.2 Explain each component of a communication model.
   1.3 Compare and contrast major communication models.

The evaluation standard for proficiency on the measurable performance objectives (items 1.1, 1.2, and 1.3, above) is set at 75 percent. The student would then have to achieve a 75 percent or better on whatever the measurement tool is for all three of the performance objectives in order to pass the overall learning objective. Note that the measurable performance objectives reflect Bloom's cognitive domains of knowledge, comprehension, and analysis/synthesis.

Whether or not you agree with assessment, be sure to construct your syllabus so that it reflects the demands of your university. The idea behind assessment is to make the learning process better reflect the knowledge and practice of the discipline so that students are better prepared for life. Knowing about learning outcomes, how they link to Bloom's taxonomy, and the state of assessment from a nationwide perspective will help you meet this important challenge effectively and professionally.

Organization of Course Content

Let's now consider the day-to-day content of the course and how that content is posted on the syllabus. In examining syllabi from other instructors, I noticed two commonalities in about 95 percent of them. First, the course content was generally arranged in the same order as the chapters of the textbook in use, and second, the syllabus was structured topically. For instance, the syllabus would start with chapter one of the text and then work its way through the book during the semester. Daily topics followed a progression paralleling the text such as models first, then perception, then language codes, then nonverbal communication, then conflict, and so forth. If you are a novice teacher, it's fine to trust the textbook; after all, textbooks are written by colleagues who have taken on the responsibility of synthesizing the current state of the interpersonal communication scholarship. Popular textbooks in the field tend to systematize the content of what most people teach across the country in entry-level courses.

But it isn't only content that is standardized across the field. The most popular structure for an entry-level course is a theory-practice combination in which the instructor introduces theories and concepts from the interpersonal communication scholarship and then has students practice skills that are derived from those theories and concepts. This is why virtually every course covers topics such as self-disclosure and conflict management. Again, this is not a bad thing. However, I'd like to offer you an alternative way of thinking about organizing your course to help your students learn more about the complexities of interpersonal communication.

Return to the last section of my syllabus and examine the units of instruction and daily assignments. You will see that the course is divided into four total units, with two units comprising each half of the course. The course progression is based on a theory-practice model, but the course reflects a larger philosophy about the nature and function of communication and relationships. Further, the learning outcomes for the course are reflected in the units and assignments as well. Philosophically, I believe that effective interpersonal relationships are a combination of personal philosophy and the execution of strategies (skills) to achieve a competent dyad. So look at the headings that group units (and note that in my department we say *relational communication* rather than *interpersonal communication*):

Units I and II emphasize the **transactional philosophy** and **relationship development**.

Unit I Overview of Relational Communication
Unit II The Relationship Cycle

Units III and IV emphasize **competence**.

Unit III Relational Communication Skills
Unit IV Communication Competence in Relationship Contexts

In the first half of the course, I am setting students up to see that relationships just don't drop out of the sky and *voila!* we have satisfying romance, for example. Relationships result from communication behavior that helps us construct social bonds, and thus function in the world and realize our humanity. I teach that before a dyad even comes into existence, before we even approach other people, we need to develop a philosophy toward relationships in general. My philosophy is based on an interpretation of the transactional philosophy that comes out of my study of, among others, Martin Buber (1970) and the axioms of Paul Watzlawick, Janet Beavin Bavelas, and Donald Jackson (1967). (Chapter 6 in this book provides readings by these scholars and the inspiration behind the content of my course.) I also believe that dyads are really a three-part entity that constantly negotiates the perspectives of those three entities:

one partner, the other partner, and the dyad itself. Hence, the first unit of the course orients the student to the communication process itself, the self, and the transactional philosophy. The second unit then works the student through the stages of the relationship cycle so we can see how communication works in the everyday dynamics of relating. Mark Knapp and Linda Vangelisti (2005) provide a good framework. Within the stages we explore a wide range of theoretical and practical ideas about communication that help students see the complexities of interpersonal process and the way a relationship philosophy keeps a partner on an even keel as the dyad progresses over time. Units I and II are building blocks that work together, and as we move through the first half of the semester, the students work on a relationship analysis, where they evaluate a relationship in which they are a partner. Note how learning outcomes 1, 2, 3, and 5 are addressed in the first two units.

The second half of the course changes tone and style slightly. With communication competence as the overarching theme, we shift to the mechanics of skills. My approach here is that in order to have a completely competent relationship one needs to combine philosophy with skills. After all, what good is a transactional philosophy if a person can't manage a basic conversation? Note again a progression from Unit III to Unit IV. Although we learn about a range of general skills that help us be effective communicators in relationships, I take time in the last unit of the course to talk about how effectiveness is related to the type of dyad in which one might be a partner (see the readings in Chapter 6 from Baxter & Montgomery, 2000; Wiemann, 1977). We talk about the oddities and ironies of how some people can be great in their roles as friends, but may be less competent as sons or daughters. We talk about choice making and relationship goals and how different types of dyads really do need different types of competencies for a relationship to be effective. For example, competent friends have joking skills because cutting up and having fun is such a central part of communication in friendship, but an intimate relationship would require the ability to express love in both verbal and nonverbal ways. In the second half of the course I address learning outcomes 1, 2, 4, and 5. We conduct daily assessments and activities to build skills and increase competency. Each half of the semester constitutes flip sides of the same coin. Together the course considers the complexity of the process of interpersonal communication. Note that the structure of a syllabus can easily go beyond topics (which I think is a fragmented way to teach) and put together a meaningful study of relationships. If you haven't already, I urge you to try restructuring your syllabus as soon as you feel confident about doing so. (Note: It took me about ten years to figure out that there is a more meaningful way to structure a course than a simple presentation of topics.)

THEORY-BASED, ONLINE, AND SERVICE-LEARNING COURSES

Up to this point, we have talked about the most common syllabus in the field: a combination approach of theory and practice that is delivered through lecture-discussion-activity as class meets two or three times a week. There are other types of introductory interpersonal communication courses, and each requires a slightly different set-up that should be reflected in the syllabus. Visually, a syllabus for a theory-based, online, or service-learning course might look similar to the sample presented in this chapter, but the information will be additional or different to reflect the course approach. In particular, the course descriptions and learning objectives will tip you off as to the specific approach. In this section of the chapter, I will share with you syllabi from colleagues who teach with these different methods. If you are asked to teach an introductory course with such approaches, these syllabi will provide you with good models to adapt.

A Theory-Based Syllabus

Theory-based interpersonal communication courses emphasize the theory and research behind the concepts under study and usually aim to teach students basic research procedures. The syllabus that follows was developed by Robyn Parker of Kent State University in Kent, Ohio. Note that research is combined with experiential activities so the entry-level student is not overwhelmed by theory. As with all of the sample syllabi used here, I have edited out contact information and course policies since that was covered in my syllabus. The daily course schedule is also abridged and simply gives you an idea of how a topical approach is structured.

SAMPLE SYLLABUS FOR A THEORY-BASED INTERPERSONAL COMMUNICATION COURSE

Course Syllabus

Interpersonal Communication (Comm 2001/002)

Fall 2001

Dr. Robyn E. Parker

Kent State University

Required Texts

DeVito, J. (1998). *The interpersonal communication book* (9th ed.). New York: Addison Wesley Longman.

Rubin, R. B., & Nevino, R. J. (1988). *The road trip*. Prospect Heights, IL: Waveland.

Course Description

This course is designed to increase your understanding of the interpersonal communication process by acquainting you with existing theory and research. Additionally the course is designed to facilitate improvement through experience.

Course Objectives

1. Facilitate both increased knowledge of "self" and understanding of how self affects and is affected by interpersonal communication.
2. Explore the influence of culture in interpersonal encounters.
3. Experiment with nonverbal communication and research how it functions in a variety of interpersonal communication contexts.
4. Acquaint you with relationship development stages and explore the role of power and conflict within interpersonal relationships.
5. Introduce you to the research process as it relates to interpersonal communication.

Course Requirements

1. <u>In-class Learning Activities</u>. The experiential design of this course requires regular attendance, out-of-class preparation and in-class active participation. Our classroom learning environment is co-created by all of us, together. There is no way to "make-up" for missed in-class activities. The learning opportunity is lost. Therefore, attendance will be taken at each session, and in-class work will be collected and evaluated.
2. <u>Out-of-class Assignments</u>. You will receive "homework" assignments at least once per week. Assignments range from mini-content exploration papers to conducting field and Web-based research. One virtue of this course is the immediate applicability of its content to your daily life. Assignments will be designed to help you make those connections.
3. <u>Interpersonal Communication Theory Mini-Paper</u>. You will be asked to research an interpersonal communication theory of your choice, subject to instructor approval. In this paper you will be asked to explicate the theory and apply it. The paper is limited to five high-quality pages. You will receive separate instructions for this challenging assignment.
4. <u>Exams</u>. There will be two tests and a cumulative final examination. All course material (text readings, in-class discussions, weekly assignments) is "testable."

Evaluation

3 EXAMS	1=100, 2=100, 3=200 PTS.	40% OF COURSE GRADE
WEEKLY ASSIGNMENTS	300 POINTS	30% OF COURSE GRADE
THEORY MINI-PAPER	150 POINTS	15% OF COURSE GRADE
IN-CLASS LEARNING ACTIVITIES	150 POINTS	15% OF COURSE GRADE

Proposed Course Outline

DATE	TOPIC	READING
8/27	COURSE INTRODUCTION	
8/29	INTERPERSONAL COMMUNICATION PROCESS	UNIT 1, DEVITO
8/31	AXIOMS OF INTERPERSONAL COMMUNICATION	UNIT 2, DEVITO
9/3	NO CLASS (LABOR DAY)	
9/5	INTERPERSONAL RELATIONSHIPS/ COMMUNICATION ETHICS	
9/7	CULTURE	UNIT 3, DEVITO
9/10	THEORIES OF CULTURE AND COMMUNICATION	
9/12	PRACTICE	
9/14	SELF-CONCEPT	UNIT 4, DEVITO
...		
10/10	THEORY APPLICATION	
10/12	REVISITING INTERPERSONAL PROCESS, SELF-CONCEPT, AND PERCEPTION	CHAPTERS 1–5, ROAD TRIP
10/15	EXAM REVIEW	
10/17	EXAM 1	
...		
11/28	FAIR AND UNFAIR USE OF POWER	
11/30	CONFLICT IN RELATIONSHIPS	UNIT 19, DEVITO
	MINI-PAPER DUE	
12/3	WORKING THROUGH CONFLICT	
12/5	REVISITING NONVERBAL COMMUNICATION, POWER, AND CONFLICT	CHAPTERS 11–15, ROAD TRIP
12/7	EXAM REVIEW (LAST DAY OF CLASS)	
	FINAL EXAM PER UNIVERSITY SCHEDULE	

SOURCE: Personal correspondence with Robyn Parker, July 25, 2006. Used with permission.

An Online Syllabus

Online or distance-learning courses are now offered by many colleges and universities. What distinguishes this type of course is the method of delivery—that is, use of email and the Internet rather than face-to-face classroom interaction. Although the objectives for the course may be the same as a typical theory-practice approach, the assignments are more likely to include online discussions of concepts, e-journals, and exams completed at home and emailed to the instructor. A syllabus might look quite similar to that of a face-to-face class, but the syllabus and all supporting information would be distributed through a software program, such as Blackboard, or a course Web page.

Below you will find portions of an online syllabus created by Michelle Burch at Clark State Community College in Springfield, Ohio. Professor Burch's syllabus is an excellent online syllabus because it demonstrates a complete synthesis of philosophy and structure to achieve the objectives of an online interpersonal communication course. In fact, this syllabus is featured on the NCA Web site at www.natcom.org as an exemplary syllabus. You may find the complete syllabus and supporting documents by clicking on Education and then Online communication courses. It is easy to see that this approach to teaching has been well thought out, and Professor Burch even includes important information about the types of skills needed to succeed in an online course. The sample syllabus you see is abridged; it does not include all of the course policies and weekly assignments. I simply want to give you a general idea of what an online syllabus looks like and what needs to be considered if you are asked to create an online course.

SAMPLE SYLLABUS FOR AN ONLINE INTERPERSONAL COMMUNICATION COURSE

Course Syllabus

COM 111: Interpersonal Communication

Clark State Community College

Instructor: Michelle Burch

Credits: 3

Prerequisite: CPE 061 & 071

Enrollment Limit: 25

Offered: Year-Round

Course Description

This is a full online course in Interpersonal Communication, which focuses on techniques, understanding and skills required for effective communication, focusing on linguistic, psychological, and cultural factors affecting the communication process.

General Requirements

1. Able to use word processing programs
2. Able to submit papers via email, as instructed, by the due dates provided
3. Able to use email, discussion boards, and chat rooms
4. Able to take tests online, with a reliable Internet connection
5. Able to read Adobe files with an Adobe Reader (free installation)
6. Ability to read and work independently, and complete work by prescribed due dates

Online courses are not for everyone. Interpersonal Communication is offered in the traditional setting; see the course schedule for more information or call the instructor. If you are not sure if you are a good candidate for an online course, you can check out the *WBE 001, WebCT Student Learner's Guide* prior to getting started in the class.

Textbook/Workbook

Burch, Michelle. *Interpersonal Communication: Building Your Foundations for Success*. Dubuque, IA: Kendall/Hunt, 2005.

Course Goals

- Learners will be able to judge effective communication behavior.
- Learners will be able to explain inappropriate communication behaviors and link communication theory to reality.
- Learners will be able to assess problems in relationships and generate solutions for maintaining and improving relationships.
- Learners will be able to analyze communication situations and accurately apply communication concepts.
- Learners will be able to exercise interpersonal competency through an increased sensitivity to multiculturalism (showing respect for various cultures), while decreasing their ethnocentrism.
- Learners will be able to employ effective listening skills in interpersonal relations.
- Learners will be able to generate facilitative emotions and minimize the effect of debilitative emotions.
- Learners will be able to evaluate the influences of self-disclosure.

Teaching Philosophy

Today's teacher must be an example, a leader, and a virtual communicator. I teach through student-oriented discussions, group activities, and real-life experiences. Using these tools, my students gain their own presentation styles, communication skills, negotiating abilities, and diagnostic skills.

Course Grades		Course Grading Scale	
Discussion Points	125	**A:** 90–100%	**473–525**
(25 points x 5 discussions)		**B:** 80–89	**420–572**
Individual Portfolio Project	100	**C:** 70–79	**368–419**
Team Intercultural Project	100	**D:** 60–69	**315–367**
Midterm Exam	100	**F:** 50–59	**0–315**
Final Exam	100		
Total Points	**525**		

Assignment Descriptions

Discussion Points:

You earn these points by participating in the weekly discussions. Typically, you must post your first message by *Wednesday* of any given week (see schedule and discussion board for specifics), all discussions wrap up on *Saturday* evenings. You must log in to the class, and check the topic for discussion, at the beginning of the week (i.e., Monday) so you know exactly what is expected of you in a given week. The discussion may be large group, small group, or an individual assignment. If you do not participate in a given week, you will not earn the possible points. *Discussions are not extended and cannot be made up.*

Individual Portfolio Project:

The purpose of this assignment is to provide you with an opportunity to explore who you are, what your place is in the world, and what you want out of your life. Interpersonal communication can only be successful if you begin *intrapersonally* communicating. The portfolio project is explained in your textbook, in Appendix B, with supplemental information listed in the web course. You must read the project in the textbook in order to successfully complete the project.

Everything in this portfolio is developed for the purpose of allowing you to intrapersonally communicate. The portfolio will be reviewed and graded to make sure that you are following the objectives and completing the sections. However, everything in this portfolio is completely confidential. Nothing will be discussed outside of the comments between you, the author of the portfolio, and the instructor.

Intercultural Team Project:

The purpose of this project is to learn how communication works and is practiced in another culture. You will examine the various aspects of intercultural communication, apply the intercultural concepts to one culture, develop examples and/or scenarios for a paper, and finally, you will post a team paper to the class for discussion.

Midterm Exam:

This will be a multiple-choice test covering the first six chapters in your book.

Final Exam:

This is a comprehensive final covering all of the chapters discussed in the course.

Sample Schedule

Week 1: Assignments/Activities

1. Send instructor email, following the directions on the homepage.
2. Participate in the discussion topic, "Introductions." Follow my instructions in the "Start Here First" posting.
3. Read the syllabus, where you can review a summary of assignments.
4. Print out this schedule, so you can reference it as needed.
5. Read chapter 1, in your textbook, for next week's discussion.
6. Read the section on Communication Foundations, which can be found under Unit I on the navigation bar.
7. Begin sections 1–3 of the Intrapersonal Portfolio project, which is explained in both the textbook (Appendix B and in this classroom). Sections 1–3 of the portfolio are *not due* until week 4.

Due Dates

Discussion. To be completed by Saturday at midnight, with your first posting by *Wednesday* at midnight

Week 2: Assignments/Activities

1. Participate in the discussion topic, "The Communication Process." Follow my instructions in the "Start Here First" posting.
2. Read Chapter 2 in your textbook for next week's discussion.
3. Read the section on Listening Works, which can be found under Unit I on the navigation bar.

Due Dates

Discussion. To be completed by Saturday at midnight, with your first posting by *Wednesday* at midnight

Week 3: Assignments/Activities

1. Participate in the discussion topic, "Listening Works." Follow my instructions in the "Start Here First" posting.
2. Read Chapter 3 in your textbook for next week's discussion.
3. Read the section on Your Perception is Your Reality, which can be found under Unit I on the navigation bar.
4. Continue working on sections 1–3 of the Intrapersonal Portfolio; it is due *next week*.

Due Dates

Discussion. To be completed by Saturday at midnight, with your first posting by *Wednesday* at midnight

Week 4: Assignments/Activities

1. Participate in the discussion topic, "Elements of Perception." Follow my instructions in the "Start Here First" posting.
2. Read Chapter 4 in your textbook for next week's discussion.
3. Read the section on Verbal vs. Nonverbal Communication, which can be found under Unit II on the navigation bar.
4. **Sections 1–3 from the Intrapersonal Portfolio are due.** You must (1) Email the three sections to me as one attached document. (2) The name of the file must be your name, and it must be submitted in rich text format (file name example, "Burch, Michelle.rft"). See the portfolio project for more specific directions.

Due Dates

<u>Portfolio</u>. Due Friday by midnight

<u>Discussion</u>. To be completed by Saturday at midnight, with your first posting by *Wednesday* at midnight

---

SOURCE: http://webct.clarkstate.edu/public/COM111E1/index.html. Used with permission.

A Service-Learning Syllabus

Service-learning courses are becoming more popular across the country and include community service as part of the pedagogy of the course. For an interpersonal communication course, a theme of building effective relationships might be focused on a particular type of relationship, given the community sites available. For example, a nursing home as a community site will focus on college-age students building relationships with senior citizens. Other types of interpersonal relationships that could be the focus of service learning include children, the homeless, immigrants, and HIV-positive patients. Appropriate readings and service activities would support the traditional texts and activities found in an interpersonal communication course. The syllabus will need to reflect all of this by adding appropriate information to the descriptions of course purpose, objectives, readings, grading, activities, policies, and the calendar. Service-learning courses usually require 10 to 20 hours of on-site participation in addition to regular classroom meetings. If your university has a service learning office, consult them for policies and procedures that affect the information needed on a syllabus because there are sometimes legal requirements that need to be incorporated.

The sample syllabus that follows was created by Elise Dallimore of Northeastern University in Boston. Professor Dallimore has served as both a consultant and an assistant director in two teaching and learning centers. Her tightly constructed syllabus is an excellent example of how a service-learning approach frames an entire semester of study in interpersonal communication. Dallimore's students complete approximately 30 hours of service on site, with at least two hours of service over the course of 13 weeks.

SAMPLE SYLLABUS FOR A SERVICE-LEARNING INTERPERSONAL COMMUNICATION COURSE.

Communication (CMN) 230

Interpersonal Communication

Spring Semester 2006

Instructor: Dr. Elise J. Dallimore

Required Course Materials

1. Text for Purchase:

Stewart, J., Zediker, K. E., & Witteborn, S. (2005). *Together: Communicating interpersonally: A social construction approach* (6th ed.). Los Angeles: Roxbury Publishing.

2. Reserve Case Text: This text is available on reserve in Snell Library (1st floor—Reserve Desk).

Braithwaite, D. O., & Wood, J. T. (2000). *Case studies in interpersonal communication: Processes and problems.* Belmont, CA: Wadsworth/Thomson Learning.

Course Description

Communication (CMN) 230 is a four-credit course in interpersonal communication. This course is designed to enhance your awareness, knowledge, and skill level in interpersonal communication in order to assist you in making more active, thoughtful choices in your communicative life. The course focuses on the communication you experience daily with friends, significant others, family, peers, coworkers, and others. We will explore interpersonal communication through a social constructionist lens and will explore how our identities are negotiated through communication. Further, this course has a service-learning component designed to provide you with an educational opportunity that meets identified community needs and encourages reflection upon the service activity in such a way as to gain further understanding of the course content and an enhanced sense of civic responsibility.

Course Objectives

This course is designed to help you meet the following general objectives:

1. to understand various ways to view communication and the benefits and drawbacks associated with each.

2. to demonstrate a self-reflexive awareness of the communication in your life.
3. to apply theories of interpersonal communication to practical interpersonal situations (including service-learning opportunities).
4. to develop a commitment to service activities as a means of enriching your life as well as the lives of others.

More specifically, the course is designed to help you:

- to understand the relationship between verbal and nonverbal codes.
- to articulate how perception and identity-management work.
- to comprehend and utilize effective ways of listening.
- to recognize the complexities of beginning, building, and ending relationships.

Course Evaluation Criteria

Your performance in this class will be evaluated according to the following criteria:

Experiential Learning Activities

Service-Learning Project:	25% total
Fieldnotes Journal & Lab Worksheets	5%
Class Presentation	5%
(This will be evaluated based upon feedback from your group, your peers, and myself.)	
Term Paper	15%

This will be evaluated based on two primary factors:

1. my evaluation of the quality of your application of course materials to your service-learning experience, and
2. your site supervisor's evaluation of your performance.

I will also take your self-assessment and your group's assessment of your work into consideration when evaluating your service-learning project.

Application Papers:	20%

Demonstrated Competency of Course Concepts & Materials

Midterm	20%
Final Exam	20%
Class Participation	15%

Your class participation is based upon your performance in the following areas:

- participation in class discussion, role playing, and other in-class activities;
- bringing examples of your service-learning experiences to class;
- the completion of other home-learning assignments (e.g., Personal Communication Profile).

Class Participation

Your class participation grade will be based upon my evaluation of your participation as well as a self-assessment of your classroom performance. I will evaluate the quality (as well as the quantity) of your participation in class discussions and involvement in the in-class activities. Your completion of home-learning assignments (e.g., personal communication profile) will also be evaluated as a part of your class participation.

Final Grades

Points will be totaled at the end of the semester, and your point total will be converted into a percentage; grades will then be computed according to the following conversion scale.

%	Grade		%	Grade	
93–100	A	4.00	66–68	D+	1.333
89–92	A–	3.667	63–65	D	1.000
86–88	B+	3.333	56–62	D–	.667
83–85	B	3.00	0–55	F	0.00
79–82	B–	2.667			
76–78	C+	2.333			
73–75	C	2.00			
69–72	C–	1.667			

Tentative Course Schedule

Spring Semester 2006

Date	Content & Assignment	Reading Due
Week One		
Tues. 1/10	Introduction to Course **Service-Learning Assignment** **Introduced**	Chapter 1 [pp. 5–15]
Fri. 1/13	Communication & Meaning **Service-Learning Preferences** **Submitted**	Chapter 2 [pp. 17–37]
Week Two		
Tues. 1/17	Communication & Meaning **Personal Profiles Due**	Chapter 2 [pp. 37–55]
Fri. 1/20	Interpersonal Communicating **Application Paper #1 Due** **(for Peer Review Exchange)**	Chapter 3 [pp. 57–70]
Week Three		
Tues. 1/24	Interpersonal Communicating & In-class Writing Lab **Application Paper #1 Peer** **Review Due**	Chapter 3 [pp. 70–84]
Fri. 1/27	Constructing Identities **Application Paper #1 Final** **Submission** **Service-Learning Agreement** **Form Due**	Chapter 4 [pp. 85–99]
Week Four		
Tues. 1/31	Constructing Identities	Chapter 4 [pp. 99–124]
Fri. 2/3	Perception	Chapter 5 [pp. 130–145]
Week Five		
Tues. 2/7	Perceptual Problems & **Application** **Paper #2 Due** **Review for Exam**	Chapter 5 [pp. 145–151]
Fri. 2/10	Mid-semester Exam	

Week Six		
Tues. 2/14	Return Exam, Revisit Core Course Concepts & Service-Learning Analysis Lab #1 **Fieldnotes Journal & Worksheet #1 Due**	
Fri. 2/17	Analytic & Empathic Listening Mid-semester Feedback	Chapter 6 [pp. 153–172]
Week Seven		
Tues. 2/21	No class—SL Group Preparation	
Fri. 2/24	Dialogic Listening	Chapter 6 [pp. 172–188]
Week Eight		
Tues. 2/28	Verbal Talk: Perception & Language	Chapter 7 [pp. 191–202] Reserve Case Study 1: "What's in a Name?"
Fri. 3/3	Guidelines for Effective Self-Expression & Rules for Self-Disclosure	Chapter 7 [pp. 202–216]
SPRING BREAK March 4th – March 12th		
Week Nine		
Tues. 3/14	Nonverbal Communication **Application Paper #3 Due**	Chapter 8 [pp. 217–247]
Fri. 3/17	Constructing Relational Systems: Relational Models as seen in Film	Chapter 9 [pp. 253–269] "When Harry Met Sally"
Week Ten		
Tues. 3/21	Models of Relational Development & Relational Turning Points AND	Chapter 9 [pp. 253–269] "When Harry Met Sally"
Fri. 3/24	Service-Learning Analysis Lab #2 **Fieldnotes Journal & Worksheet #2 Due**	
Week Eleven		
Tues. 3/28	Constructing Relational Systems: Friendships, Romantic & Family Relationships	Chapter 9 [pp. 269–289] & Reserve Case Study 25: "Parents, Children, People"

Fri. 3/31	Constructing Relational Problems: Betrayal, Deception, & Aggression	Chapter 10 [pp. 291–310] & Reserve Case Study 19: "Betrayal"
Week Twelve		
Tues. 4/4	Constructing Relational Problems: Codependence & Breaking Apart	Chapter 10 [pp. 310–313] Reserve Case Study 20: "If the Worst Had Come First"
Fri. 4/7	Defining Conflict & Understand Conflict Goals **Application Paper #4 Due**	Chapter 11 [pp. 315–342] & Alligator Story Exercise
Week Thirteen		
Tues. 4/11	Conflict Styles & Management	Chapter 11 [pp. 330–361] & Reserve Case Study 18: "Shallow Talk and Separate Places"
Fri. 4/14	**Service-Learning Presentations**	
Week Fourteen		
Tues. 4/18	Final Exam Review & **Individual Papers Due**	

Final Examination Period

April 21, 24–26 (w/ the exact time, date, and location to be determined by the Registrar).

SOURCE: Personal correspondence with Elise Dallimore, July 28, 2006. Used with permission.

After viewing the previous syllabi, the important thing to remember is that your syllabus must reflect the type of course you are offering and the focus of instruction. Students should not be in doubt about what to expect over the course of the semester. The last major issues we need to discuss regarding your choices in constructing the syllabus revolve around supporting materials and textbooks.

TEXTBOOK SELECTION AND SUPPORTING MATERIALS

It should be clear by now that logical fit serves as a primary principle for constructing a syllabus. That is, every choice you make to create a learning environment must have a logical fit and be reflected on the syllabus. We have talked about structure, learning outcomes, underlying teacher philosophy and understanding of the field, approach to teaching, assessment, marker courses, and organizational structure as interrelated pieces of a puzzle that must fit together in the end to create a pedagogically sound course. Selecting a textbook is actually your biggest responsibility because, for entry-level students, the text is the main tool they will rely on day after day to gain knowledge and pass the course. Let's be honest. One of the most frequently asked questions in the classroom is, "Will that be on the test?" Students are usually referring to readings assigned from the text, or something they *couldn't* find in the text! Students often mistake knowledge of the textbook content for knowledge of the course itself. A textbook, however, is only as good as the knowledge and skill of the textbook writer. How do you know how to select an appropriate text?

Many people use popularity as a criterion for selecting a textbook. What this means is that certain texts gain in use through popularity and thus drive the market. Frankly speaking, there are about five texts that top the charts in interpersonal communication. In alphabetical order they are *Inter-Act: Using Interpersonal Communication Skills* (Verderber, Verderber, & Berryman-Fink, 2006), *The Interpersonal Communication Book* (DeVito, 2006), *Interpersonal Communication for Everyday Encounters* (Wood, 2007), *Interpersonal Communication: Relating to Others* (Beebe, Beebe, & Redmond, 2005), and *Looking Out/Looking In* (Adler, Proctor, & Towne, 2005). If you conduct a content analysis of the most popular texts in any field, you will find that about 80 percent of the content is similar. Instructors expect certain theories and concepts (that is, "the accepted knowledge of the field") to be present in the text. The other 20 percent of textbook content varies based on author preference and knowledge and what a publisher wishes to do in a particular niche.

When selecting a textbook, consider the following checklist. You may not agree with all the criteria, but the list offers a starting point. Note that popularity is not my first criterion, but it does have a place in overall decision making. I developed this list from both experience and my work in synthesizing the literature on college teaching. The first criterion is the most important and implies that your view of interpersonal communication matches the view of the textbook author.

_____ The textbook meets the needs of the learning outcomes established for the course.

_____ The majority of chapters in the textbook will be used as required reading to support the learning environment.

_____ The textbook is well received by the students for its legibility and usefulness.

_____ The reading level is appropriate for students' average comprehension level—that is, it is neither too difficult nor too simplistic.

_____ The textbook contains activities, discussion questions, and other prompts that inspire the learning process.

_____ The textbook contains enough mainstream and current knowledge to get the student on par with other entry-level students across the communication field.

_____ The ancillary materials that come with the textbook are useful to your instruction.

_____ The textbook is affordable in the context of the textbook market and your university bookstore policies.

Once you have selected the textbook, you need to make decisions about other supporting materials. Most textbooks do not cover all the reading you need a student to do in order to achieve the learning outcomes. Note, for example, that on my syllabus, I indicate needed supporting materials such as texts on writing because it is a writing-intensive course; reserved readings to supplement the text; a course packet of materials for use in class; and supplies including a dictionary, index cards, and Scantrons for exams. Other supporting materials may include the publisher's overhead transparencies, DVDs of instructional materials, films to be viewed during or outside of class, materials for activities in class, and guest speakers. Note that technical supplies support instruction, but they are quite different from items such as movies. You must think on several levels about how materials support instruction. Index cards for use in class activities are part of the ease of instructional delivery, while movies are carefully selected because they assist in the delivery of concepts. It may take some time in the classroom before you know which supporting materials work best, and even then it is a constant responsibility to update materials (known as "currency") in order to relate to student knowledge and social positioning. For example, when it comes to romantic comedies that teach about gender, romance, and interpersonal communication, as much as my generation loved _When Harry Met Sally_, I find that today's students relate better to _Hitch_. Think about what works for you, your students, and the concept under study. Make a list of both technical and pedagogical supporting materials for yourself and your students, and then plug those materials into the syllabus as needed.

LEGIBILITY AND DESIGN

I will end this chapter with a note on syllabus legibility and design. Make your best effort to be clear, readable, and professional. Leave enough white space for students to see sections of the syllabus and make notes. I notice that a lot of instructors use a grid format to structure the daily calendar and assignments. I choose not to do that so that I can show units of the course in a clearer manner. I have seen any number of syllabi with cut-and-paste artwork that is cute, but may be distracting. Although the use of designs, cartoons, figures, and even photographs on a syllabus is up to the instructor, my advice is to present a professional document where graphics serve only to support the information given.

What new ideas do you want to try out in constructing or revising your interpersonal communication course syllabus? Make notes here:

_____

_____

3

Student Challenges and Problematics

Stepping into the classroom is the best part of my day. I love being with my students. Anything can happen in a given class period, from funny incidents to students turning on each other when they disagree over an issue. You just never know what *could* happen. I am not one who waits for the random act that leaves me standing there holding the bag, so to speak. As an experienced teacher, my job is to manage the classroom environment and the people in it so that we all work together in a productive and respectful manner. In this chapter we will examine some basic management issues and then move on to the challenges of disruptive students, nontraditional students, and co-cultural students.

CLASSROOM MANAGEMENT

The most basic aspect of classroom management is organizing people and space. We will talk about space first, but it is important to note that people are part of that space. A traditional classroom may have 25 to 35 students with movable desks—a luxury. This mobility allows you to configure the desks in rows, circles, or small groups to meet the needs of the instructional activity. If the seating arrangement is fixed because the tables or furniture are bolted to the floor, you may have to get creative by moving people rather than furniture, in order for students to get to know each other. But even in an auditorium with 100 people in the class, I have grouped students together to work. They will often sit on the floor or the stage if they are not comfortable doing group work in their seats.

Many communication professors are inclined to use circles because they believe circles promote face-to-face interaction. I have found them to be limiting, and those limits correspond to the number of people you are trying to fit into a circle in a fixed amount of space. In my experience 35 people don't fit in a circle very neatly. In order to make all the desks fit, students wind up with their backs shoved up against a wall, and there is no personal space between desks. The huge open space in the middle becomes dead space. Consequently, the teacher has difficulty sitting in a spot that allows him or her to maintain eye contact with all the students; also, there ends up being very little room for instructional equipment. If you need access to the board or multimedia, you wind up sitting near the equipment and getting up and down. If students are late to class, they must cut through the circle to find a seat and disturb whatever discussion is going on. You get the picture. Circles may be ideal for intimate discussion with small numbers of people, but they may not be the best arrangement for daily large-class interaction. Rows work best for me because they keep students facing the information on the board or screen, and I am able to make eye contact with each person in a quick and consistent manner. We break off into dyads or groups frequently, so students have the opportunity to have interpersonal contact with each other as well.

In an auditorium setting, I use a seating chart. Students pick a seat after about four class periods together. Each student writes his or her preferred name and seat number on a 3 × 5 card, and the teaching assistant draws up the chart. The TA can quickly take roll and I can learn the names of virtually everyone in the classroom. In a class of more than 100 students, the psychology of knowing students' names is an amazing teaching strategy. Students actually think you know them (even if you don't), and they are more inclined to come to class and participate. Names actually promote a positive communication climate and make the classroom seem more personal.

Teaching assistants are essential in a large class. My department allows one graduate teaching assistant to help me manage the classroom. I value this relationship as a team effort, and I treat my TA as a colleague right from the beginning. We start and end the semester going out to lunch together, something I believe in as an interpersonal ritual. We confer about every class session beforehand, so we each know what we are doing. I let the TA handle the media, attendance, folders for each student, and exam collation, as well as help with demonstrations. The TA normally teaches at least one class period and sometimes more if he or she is training to be a university professor. My TA and I talk about pedagogy all the time, and I share teaching knowledge with the TA throughout the semester. My TA also has office hours and answers a lot of procedural questions from students. The key to a successful relationship is anticipating each other. I strive for this with every TA because it means the classroom will manage itself once the teaching team knows what it is doing. See the box below for comments from Julia Wood, at UNC-Chapel Hill, who has her own system for working with TAs to manage the classroom.

Two other basic management devices are worth mentioning here. In a very old-fashioned manner, I pass out 3 × 5 cards on the first day of class and collect the following information from each student: name and preferred nickname, local address and phone, email, year in school and major, interests in communication and hobbies. This is an amazing amount of information to help me stay in contact with students and get to know them. I can also manage group or dyad composition by pairing students based on similarities or differences. If your university email system is restricted—that is, you may only contact students based on the university email address—the card contains back-up information. Over the years I have used phone numbers, email addresses, and postal addresses to communicate with students. I keep the cards right by my phone and computer at the office, and I use them frequently.

In a large class (to me, more than 35 is large), I ask each student to bring in a manila folder so I can file exams, assignments, Scantron forms, and other materials. I can carry folders to class with me using a portable file box on test days, or hand it off to a TA as we are preparing materials. This system works well and helps to manage paper and people.

FROM THE CLASSROOM: The Challenge of a Large Class

For years the biggest challenge for me has been teaching the class as a large class (80 to 150) with recitation sections. I used to teach classes of 20-30 in which I knew all of my students and knew many of them quite well. Although I learn the names of students in my large classes, I get to know only a handful of students in each class. That's frustrating to someone like me who believes that the best teaching and learning grow out of relationships.

My effort to meet the challenge has primarily focused on working closely with my teaching team (3 to 5 TAs who meet with recitation sections, which I also visit). I invest a great deal of energy in developing the TAs—a couple of hours every week for team meetings—so that they are effective in their section meetings and so that they develop as teachers in their own right. The professional, pedagogical development that I guide in team meetings is like teaching an extra course—I'm teaching them how to teach by working with them on everything from conceptualizing syllabi to debriefing activities. It's not a perfect solution. It doesn't eliminate the frustration I feel about not knowing all of my students personally. But it does ensure quality teaching in the course and it prepares a next generation of teachers.

Julia Wood
Lineberger Distinguished Professor of Humanities
University of North Carolina at Chapel Hill

SOURCE: Personal correspondence with author, April 27, 2006.

One more tip: my colleague, David Carlone, admits he is terrible at learning names. He takes a digital camera to class and snaps a photograph of each student. He then puts a name to a photo and studies this in order to learn names more quickly. If you are teaching an online course, this technique can also help everyone meet and get to know each other.

DISCUSSION MANAGEMENT

The Influence of Classroom Climate and Teacher Ethos

One of the most frequent complaints I hear from colleagues is that students disrespect each other during class discussion and need to be "managed" as people. I find more problems between me and individual students than I do among students. Nevertheless, all of this interaction needs to be organized and conducted in a respectful manner. There are three things a teacher can do to manage class discussion:

- First, set up a positive communication climate that is conducive to effective communication.
- Second, facilitate discussion using a procedure of fairness and effectiveness.
- Third, use discussion rules to minimize or eliminate racism, sexism, and other biased or inappropriate interaction.

Let's look at each of these issues in more detail. Note that we will explore discussion as an instructional strategy in Chapter 4.

Ever since Jack Gibb published his now-famous essay on defensive communication in 1961 (see Chapter 7) in the *Journal of Communication,* we have been aware of the fundamental characteristics of a supportive (positive) communication climate that facilitate effective group interaction. Using a series of pairs, Gibb demonstrated how people achieved better interaction if their communication was descriptive, problem-oriented, spontaneous, empathic, equality-oriented, and provisional rather than evaluative, control-oriented, strategic, neutral, superior, and certain. Many teachers of interpersonal communication use Gibb's pairs to teach about the communication climate within a dyad, so why not apply it to classroom climate as well? After all, the teacher's job is to teach and model interpersonal skills. I try very hard to model empathy even when a student is describing an opinion or life experience that I don't agree with or I think may be trivial. The older I get, the harder it is to stay calm and be patient, but I have to remember that if I invite students to give examples or share life experiences, I need to be ready for both immature and mature responses. If someone perceives you to be an empathic person, it will help that person to disclose appropriately, thus facilitating the learning process in an interpersonal communication course.

I find that a happy class is one where students are laughing, the teacher really does tell good jokes or can play off the humor set up in class, and people are just having fun as they learn. It turns out that research backs up the effectiveness of humor. Communication professors Melissa Wanzer and Ann Frymier (1999) found that teachers with a high humor orientation have a positive correlation with students' perceptions of learning. When students tell me that they *love* interpersonal communication and that they use what they learn in class all the time in their everyday lives, it tells me the class material is relevant, but it also tells me the students return day after day because they like coming to class. They *are* having fun. Something good is happening there, and part of that is the safe space that encourages positive and open communication.

One of the biggest dimensions of a positive communication climate is your own ethos (e.g., trustworthiness, competence, goodwill) as a teacher. Students develop a liking for you because of the ethos you project as a teacher and a person. Such liking then translates into student perceptions of learning, course value, and positive ratings of instruction (Comstock, Rowell, & Bowers, 1995; Moore, Masterson, Christophel, & Shea, 1996; Thweatt & McCroskey, 1998). Professors with high ethos are very much like the Aristotelian model (Kennedy, 1991) of moral character, embodied in speaker language and action. In contemporary research, teacher credibility has been translated into Albert Mehrabian's (1971) concept of immediacy and other positive teacher behaviors like caring (Teven, 2001; Teven & McCroskey, 1997). I have had students say to me over the years, "I wanted to do well in your class because it is you that spurred me on." Students respond to my ethos as motivation for their own work productivity.

Another instructor who projects ethos to students is Mark Orbe of Western Michigan University. He attracts students through his enthusiasm, knowledge, pleasant affect, respect for others, and inviting ways of teaching. He typifies the ethos of what is expected in an interpersonal communicator and students respond to that. His use of the African concept *dumela* (see Chapter 1) is a central component of his ethos because it embodies his own co-cultural theory (Orbe, 1998; Orbe & Bruess, 2005). *Dumela* is connected to the idea of affirming others based on interpersonal standpoints and simultaneously creating community. I've watched Professor Orbe in my own class; as a guest lecturer, he managed to create a positive communication climate through his own ethos within five minutes of walking into the room. The way he called out "dumela" to begin the class and then praised student comments energized the students and had them paying close attention. He is a role model for us all.

Student standpoint—that is, the sum of demographics, personality, and life experience—is something we cannot control. I do not know who the 35 people will be coming through the door and whether or not they will gel as a group. Generally, the group either gels within the first week or it doesn't. If the group gels (and it really is a mysterious dynamic), then the class members will relate well to each other throughout the semester. If the group doesn't gel, it's a disaster. I had this experience with a writing-intensive version of my interpersonal course recently. The majority of the students were nonmajors and had one goal: to get the W credit on the transcript. From the first day, there was no genuine concern for the course or for other students in the class. I picked up on the negative aura right away and asked if students would prefer a different seating arrangement. They chose a circle, but not everyone was happy with that. Many students sat silently and looked at the floor. When I put them in groups, they did better. Yet when it came time to role play and volunteer for an in-class activity, no one wanted to participate. By the third class period, I said to the class that we were in this together and needed some energy. Few students responded. This class caused me to lose sleep! What was wrong? Over the course of the semester, I tried every instructional strategy I could think of to draw them out. After poor grades on the first exam, I asked students to write me a one-paragraph response on the back of the exam about their performance. The most frequent comment was: "This class is not in my major, so I just didn't spend much time studying for the exam." A couple of communication majors emerged as the regular contributors (no surprise there), but the rest of the class just didn't seem to care. It was everything I could do to stay positive and try to keep the class going. In the end, I finally came to the conclusion that this was a class composition that didn't work. It never gelled. I was disappointed, but I had done my best to deliver a good class. The next semester, one of the students from that class enrolled in two more of my classes. When I saw him on the first day, I laughed and said, "Hey, you want to try another Natalle class after last semester?" He laughed too and said, "You know, that was the weirdest group of people I have ever been in class with. They just didn't want to be together." This same student clicked off interpersonal vocabulary and concepts right and left as they applied to the gender class we were in, so I know he learned in spite of the strange configuration of classmates. These things happen. Do your best, and try not to lose too much sleep.

FROM THE CLASSROOM: Setting the Tone

There is one thing that contributes to creating a positive climate from the first day of class that lasts throughout the semester. The instructor has to be sincerely excited about teaching and model excellent interpersonal communication skills. Students respect a good listener who exhibits a sense of fair-mindedness, respect, openness, and a collaborative spirit.

Marion Boyer
Instructor
Kalamazoo Valley Community College

SOURCE: Personal correspondence with author, April 26, 2006.

Facilitating Discussion

In *The Argument Culture* (1998), author Deborah Tannen opens with this premise: "This book is about a pervasive warlike atmosphere that makes us approach public dialogue, and just about anything we need to accomplish, as if it were a fight" (p. 3). She explores the idea that Americans are taught to be adversarial and seem to prefer debate over dialogue. In school we learn how to criticize and find loopholes, and by the time we are graduate students we engage in the deconstruction of every idea presented to us. Tannen encourages readers to rethink debate as a general communication approach and to learn the rules of engagement for dialogue as a more effective tool for building relationships. She invokes Amitai Etzioni's *The New Golden Rule* (1996) as a helpful source of rules for being an effective dialogic partner. I agree with both Tannen and Etzioni that exploring ideas and building a spirit of inquiry might be more useful than debating a correct answer, especially when it comes to interpersonal issues where there are different standpoints. To that end, good teachers need to have a degree of expertise in facilitation skills. Leading good discussions is an artful skill, and one that takes much practice to develop.

Education majors do receive training in facilitating discussion, but communication majors are assumed to be effective in all kinds of talk. This just isn't true. Our interpersonal texts include chapters on conversation management in dyads (e.g., DeVito, 2004; Verderber & Verderber, 2004), but why not go beyond that and train teaching assistants to manage discussion in the classroom? Although *conversation* and *discussion* are similar in that they both have a beginning, a middle, and an end and include turn taking, they are also distinct. Conversations, according to Verderber and Verderber (2004), "are locally managed sequential interchanges of thoughts and feelings between two or more people that are interactive and largely extemporaneous" (pp. 150–151). In contrast, "discussion occurs when a group of persons assemble in a face-to-face [or computer-mediated] situation and through oral [or written] interaction exchange information or attempt to reach a decision on shared problems" (Gulley, 1968,

p. 5). Note that *dialogue* (Bohm, 2004) is even something different from conversation and discussion because dialogue is technically seen as deep, empathic communication in which partners with profound differences are trying to come to an understanding. This is not usually the type of communication found in introductory interpersonal communication courses, even though the word *dialogue* is used frequently but incorrectly to refer to classroom discussion.

Students in an interpersonal communication class often mistakenly think that discussion is conversation. One of my biggest challenges is dealing with a constant revelation of personal experience that is trivial, not related to the concept at hand, and repetitive. References to talk shows abound. The "me too" syndrome is always at work in an interpersonal classroom—students want to share with each other that their lives are the same. I once had a Russian postdoctoral fellow who, after the first week of attending class with me, observed, "You know, American students like to hear themselves talk. They say anything, whether it's relevant or not. It's all about their personal experience. As much as I appreciate that freedom, why aren't they more interested in the concepts?" That wasn't the first time I've heard that type of criticism about American students, but hearing it about my own students woke me up to the fact that I could do a better job managing discussion. It isn't easy getting students to realize that social conversation and discussion achieve different goals. The latter is an instructional strategy that is characterized by the teacher's ability to facilitate the communication toward the learning goal.

Good facilitation skills are characterized by artful control. The teacher is guiding the class toward understanding while giving participants the opportunity to contribute to that exploration of the concept. The discussion needs to have

- an introduction of the concept,
- a call for contributions that involves possible ways of understanding the concept,
- links from discussion comments to the research base behind the concept (linking theory and practice), and
- closure on what was learned through discussion.

Recording key ideas or talking points on the board may be a running activity throughout the discussion, and students would be expected to take notes (something they may need to be reminded to do since notetaking does not occur to all students as an automatic activity).

From a procedural point of view, the discussion leader needs to

- move the progression of the discussion forward within the time limit allowed,
- give people an opportunity to speak,
- diplomatically cut off people who want to talk too much,
- draw out people whose faces indicate they want to comment even when their hands aren't raised,
- ask questions that probe,

- synthesize comments or point out differences, and
- summarize, come to closure, and transition to the next part of the class.

I actually facilitate better standing up because then I can see everyone. I can move around the room taking the energy to the person speaking at the moment, I can run to the board and jot down ideas (unless a student is doing that for the class), and my movement keeps everyone involved. However, if sitting gets the job done, do what is comfortable for you. Don't forget to take notes on what you wrote on the board.

If the discussion centers on relational dialectics, for example, then the teacher needs to have knowledge of, at the very least, the textbook. To me that is not enough to be a good discussion leader because the leader has to anticipate the questions that will arise from discussions that quickly carry the class beyond the textbook. The teacher needs to have read the key work on relational dialectics (see Chapters 6 and 7), including Leslie Baxter and Barbara Montgomery's *Relating* (1996) and William Rawlins's *Friendship Matters* (1992). The teacher needs to be prepared to discuss the dialectical tensions in relationships, how those tensions manifest themselves in relational life, and how communication assists in the negotiation of dialectical tension. This knowledge is in addition to general facilitation skills! Every time you lead discussion, you bring your knowledge to bear on the discussion process itself. The deeper your knowledge, the better the discussion.

Online discussions, called *conferencing,* occur through discussion lists or bulletin board systems. Computer expert Susan Barnes (2003) argues that teachers facilitate rather than control discussion in computer-mediated communication (CMC). In fact, she says students are actually in charge of the discussion because the teacher can no longer dominate it. The teacher is responsible for training the students on the system, setting up the rules for discussion (e.g., topics for discussion, number of postings per week), and reinforcing network etiquette policies.

Rules for Discussion

The last discussion management technique to use is a kind of rule system that promotes smooth process and enhances the quality of discussion content. Students (and sometimes teachers) can be dominant and try to do all the talking. Even worse are people who exhibit rude or disrespectful treatment of others. If you use a rule system, it can be presented on the first day of class and included in the syllabus, or the class can make the rules and the instructor can distribute them later.

What would a printed set of rules look like? Following is a sample set that could serve as a model if you want to compose your own for more effective classroom discussion. This sample comes from a set of rules I composed to help first-semester, first-year students survive a gendered-relationships class. I think the division of content and process guidelines will help a less-experienced student see that effective discussion considers both types of rules. I present this set of rules as it might appear on a classroom handout.

CST 207 INTERPERSONAL COMMUNICATION
HOW TO ENGAGE IN CLASS DISCUSSION

Classroom discussions require a different kind of speech from what you might be used to when talking with friends. To get the most out of discussion as a learning tool, the following guidelines will assist you in your communication choices.

Content Guidelines

1. Class discussions are generally not open forums. Rather, they have the purpose of serving as a learning tool. Through group conversation, participants learn more about required reading assignments and the way theoretical matter connects to students' lives. So come to discussion prepared! Complete the reading and have questions or reactions to the material that might serve as helpful discussion.
2. Think about the content of discussion and the flow of ideas so you can make a meaningful contribution. Add ideas that extend what is being talked about, or offer your perspective as a way to clarify the issues. If you disagree with what's being advocated, back up your reasons for disagreeing with material from the reading assignments.
3. Let the facilitator (usually the professor) keep the group moving forward in its ideas and themes, but don't be afraid to ask questions or make connections from previous class discussions.
4. Stay away from thoughtless comments that are sexist or racist or demean a speaker because of his or her background or beliefs. Think before you speak, and develop a tolerance for diversity!

Process Guidelines

1. Take turns and be respectful of others when they have the floor. Only one person at a time can be heard.
2. Listen when others are speaking. Engaging in conversation with your neighbor means you can't hear the speaker. Then you will get confused and eventually lost. As you listen, evaluate the ideas of the speaker so you can react thoughtfully.
3. Take notes to keep up with your own and others' ideas. This may help you come back to an important point later and make a valuable contribution.
4. Do not shout each other down. Respectful tone of voice is expected.
5. Do not curse or use slang terms that border on distasteful or disrespectful. There simply is no place in the classroom for this type of vocabulary.
6. Assume we are all doing our best to understand material and make contributions.
7. Everyone should speak in a discussion. Give quiet people a chance to say something by not dominating the floor.
8. Stay alert and open-minded to ideas. This is a great way to learn something new!

Computer-mediated discussion also requires rules. In her excellent book, *Computer-Mediated Communication,* Susan Barnes (2003) includes netiquette (network etiquette) rules in her list of acceptable use policies. These rules can be adapted for effective online discussion and help reduce flaming (unchecked and aggressive hostile comments). Check your own university's or college's acceptable use policy to be sure you comply when creating a list of netiquette rules. I synthesized Barnes's rules and my own university policy to create this rule set. Note that a negative approach, such as "do not," is the most common policy language.

NETIQUETTE POLICY

Students are expected to refrain from the following CMC (computer-mediated communication) behavior:

1. Harassing others through language, frequency, or message size.
2. Altering others' message content with intent to deceive.
3. Disguising sender identity/email header information.
4. Using profane or vulgar language.
5. Sending impolite or otherwise abusive messages.
6. Revealing personal contact information of other students or faculty without their permission.
7. Discussing or revealing illegal or unlawful activities.

Tolerance and Diversity of Views

So far we have discussed the ideas of how communication climate, including teacher ethos, influences student willingness to engage in discussion; procedures for facilitating discussions; and rules for the engagement of process and content in discussion. In today's classroom, discussion takes place among students who hold different political and social views that can create problems of racism, sexism, homophobia, ageism, and other forms of intolerance.

Students with little or no knowledge of difference often find it difficult to discuss diversity issues, especially when they are asked to consider thinking about and perceiving the world in ways other than what they are familiar with; their sense of knowledge and safety become threatened. This is especially true of first-generation college students who may have limited experience outside their own small communities and have grown up with people more similar to than different from themselves. Even a decade ago, our textbooks did not really consider diversity issues very well. It was up to the teacher to try and bring these issues to the class and moderate the heated discussion that usually ensued. Today our textbooks do discuss racist, sexist, and heterosexist language (see, e.g., DeVito, 2004). Cultural considerations and viewpoints of all types—from Caucasian to African-American, from male to female, from gay to straight—not only regularly appear now (see, e.g., Trenholm & Jensen, 2004), but they all have credibility in the classroom as well. In spite of this progress, however, many students still find it uncomfortable talking about these topics or recognizing the validity of others' viewpoints. Lately, conservative students have been directing vocal complaints at instructors whom they claim have a liberal bias against their points of view on religion, politics, and relationships. Indeed, it is a challenging time to be caught in the so-called "culture wars" (Rosen, 2003), especially in the interpersonal communication classroom. Hence, it is important to conscientiously include a tolerance policy in the list of general discussion rules. The expectation of tolerance should be explicitly expressed for students—see, for example, Content Rule #4 presented in the box on page 65.

Tolerating diverse viewpoints is as much about power as it is about what ideas may be in control in a classroom and how we respect others as human beings. Lynn Weber Cannon, sociologist and professor of women's studies at Memphis State University, was the expert who tuned me in to the assumptions, goals, and outcomes of meeting diversity in the college classroom. In a workshop I took with Professor Cannon in 1989, I learned some valuable ideas about how to approach the concept of diversity, and I use this information to facilitate discussion and enforce rules. Here are my condensed notes from that 1989 workshop. This information is for you, the teacher, to keep in mind.

THE ASSUMPTIONS BEHIND MEETING DIVERSITY IN THE CLASSROOM

- The teacher-student relationship is a social relation in which power is vested in teachers by virtue of their middle-class position in the social structure.
- In small group settings such as classrooms, powerless people are less likely to talk, have their ideas validated, and be perceived as making significant contributions to group tasks.
- Material about race, class, gender, and so forth is emotionally charged, as well as intellectually challenging.
- People want to learn about each other (despite their fears).

GOALS AND OUTCOMES OF MEETING DIVERSITY IN THE CLASSROOM

The broadest goal of the course is to empower students and:

- to promote understanding and an open appreciation of diversity in American life.
- to treat every student as a unique human being, to appreciate every one of them, and to treat them equally (but certainly not the same).
- to develop a classroom environment in which the traditional racism, sexism, and classism in the university and in society are not replicated.
- to enhance the expression of diversity among students in the work they do.
- to deal with a wide range of authentic feelings among learners: discomfort, frustration, excitement, and satisfaction.

When promoting tolerance in the classroom, we also need to incorporate it into our teaching approach to facilitate good discussion and to explore our students' range of experiences in dealing with diversity issues.

General Techniques for Classroom Management

To be honest, I get very few complaints on my student evaluations about being too liberal, losing control of discussions, or not being able to handle delicate subject matter. I use a range of communication techniques in class to meet the many student opinions and to encourage respectfulness in discussion. I announce that I am not a trained counselor and will not entertain personal dilemmas as class discussion. I state plainly that self-disclosure should be something that would not embarrass the individual making the disclosure. I do not self-disclose too much in class as a purposeful strategy to keep the focus on the concepts as they relate to the lives of the students and to model *appropriate* disclosure as an interpersonal skill. For example, I would not disclose personal information about my husband or walk into class and reveal the content of a conflict over a personal issue. Knowing too much about the teacher can lead to gossip, which may not be healthy for the department as a whole. It's not about me, it's about the students. Research in communication and social psychology (see, e.g., Cayanus, 2004; Goldstein & Benassi, 1994; Wambach & Brothen, 1997) supports the idea that teacher self-disclosure needs to be appropriate (not too much or too little) as an instructional strategy to promote student participation and positive regard for the teacher. Jacob Cayanus of West Virginia University (2004) recommends the following:

- use positive self-disclosure rather than reveal negative assessments of yourself;
- ensure that the disclosure is relevant to the course material;
- vary the topics of disclosure;
- vary the timing on disclosure; and
- use an appropriate amount of self-disclosure.

If you model such rules for self-disclosure, students likely will follow.

Using humor works for me in the classroom, and when students start breaking rules in both discussion and general responsibility, I say things like, "Okay, everybody, we are falling off the wagon here with our [fill in the blank with the behavior]" (personal disclosure, getting to class on time, etc.). These friendly reminders help bring students back in line as a group. If students curse or start talking about their sex lives, I bring them back with statements like "No cursing. Come on, we are communication students," or "Let's not go there. That's too much for me to handle." All of this works well if you are firm, consistent, and nice about it.

The big problems are the mean comments from one student to another, or the dominating students who need your attention outside of class. After 30 years of teaching, I am known as a no-nonsense teacher. I am a direct person, and I am not afraid to shut down a person who is genuinely challenging me or his or her peers for control of the class. I've had overbearing males drop my class after the first day or two, when they realized they would not be the one in charge. At the same time, I've had students who would not stop talking to the point that I've had to call them in my office or write them a note. These students tend to get angry and have a great deal of difficulty finding a balance of how much to contribute. I know that I've taken hits on my teaching evaluations as a result. Although I have not developed a surefire way to discipline a student without some kind of negative fallout, I stand fast. My job is to teach competent interpersonal communication. If I have been too harsh or gotten too angry in class, I make a public apology. I am not above making errors or getting emotional myself. It is my responsibility to recognize the error and make amends when appropriate as part of competent communication. Students appreciate that.

When a student gets out of control (for example, yelling at me in class about a grade or work responsibilities with group projects), I let the student cool down and see if he or she will contact me in my office to talk things over. If there is no follow-up, I ask the student to come see me. I always start by recognizing something positive about our teacher-student relationship and say, for example, "We are both good people. I don't know what happened yesterday in class, but let's try to talk so we can understand and then decide what to do." At the end of the discussion, I will shake a student's hand or hug him or her and say, "I'm glad we talked. Let's do our best from now on." My experience is that we get back on track and the rules are followed.

Course Policies as General Classroom Rules

In reviewing the course syllabi of other interpersonal communication instructors, I see that many professors embed or spell out general classroom rules of student responsibility. Attendance policies, for example, are rules that dictate the consequences of lateness or absence from class. Turning in homework late, missing exams, and not completing course requirements usually carry rule-bound penalties. The university honor code is a set of rules for ethical student behavior. All of these rules help the teacher manage people and course activities so work is completed on time and the learning process can progress within the time allotted for the course. What happens when students break the rules? The teacher's responsibility is to enforce the rules, ensuring fairness to all students, and to maintain the integrity of the course. Over the years I have had many students earn grades that do not reflect their intellectual capabilities because they could not work within the rule system. As much as I hate to see grades drop over penalties, it truly is not fair to other students who do come to class and complete work on time. I stick to my rules knowing that students will need to abide by work policies once they get into the working world.

If only the rule systems worked so smoothly in every class! That is not the case, however, when we begin to consider our students as individuals with complex lives. Most student dilemmas arise from issues outside the classroom. As professors, one thing we could all do better is to try and understand our students as, for example, first-year students away from home for the first time, or adult students with jobs and families, or perhaps students who struggle with depression. In the next section we will confront common student challenges and consider some effective responses.

STUDENT CHALLENGES

I used to worry most over fair grading and the occasional cheater. Every once in a while a more troubling personal and serious problem, such as pregnancy or a violent dating partner, would arise. Now I worry about a whole generation of students who often seem less prepared for adult social interaction and behave inappropriately in the college classroom. My colleagues and I joke about which will drive us to retirement first: the workload or the bizarre student behavior. Maybe media-effects theorist George Gerbner (1990) is right in his observation that the media violence that surrounds us has cultivated a "mean world syndrome" that begets more aggressive people. This has certainly trickled down to the classroom, and student dilemmas take up more time than I wish to spend on problem solving. On a regular basis I confront everything from students cursing or bullying each other in class to students talking back to me to students expecting that their personal problems excuse them from work deadlines. On rare occasions students have threatened me to the point at which I have feared for my personal safety. As I was writing this chapter, I spoke to our Dean of Students, Jen Day Shaw, about today's students and some of the issues they face. She said to me, "Issues students are bringing to the classroom seem to have increased in intensity and number. In talking to my colleagues nationally, they confirm that this is a universal experience" (Shaw, personal correspondence, April 25, 2006). Clearly there's a lot we need to be prepared for as classroom teachers, and particularly as teachers, of interpersonal communication, because it is in an interpersonal classroom that such dilemmas are likely to be self-disclosed or come to public attention.

Difficult or Disruptive Students

We have been reading about and researching the phenomenon of "difficult people" since family therapist Virginia Satir published *peoplemaking* in 1971 (see Chapter 7). A search of titles in my university library catalog produced more than a dozen books aimed at organizational and classroom environments where I could get advice for dealing with difficult coworkers or students. Interpersonal trainer Robert Lucas (2005) offers 176 tips for difficult classroom situations, including such topics as people who speak English as a second language right along with the more expected categories of difficulty: clowns, experts, agitators, monopolizers, poor listeners, and latecomers, among many others. To give advice on every type of problem student you will encounter is almost impossible because people act out in many different ways, depending on the situation. Classroom management techniques actually curb a lot of disruption because rules and a positive communication climate keep most people in order. I also find that the following three practices go a long way toward preventing difficult behavior:

1. knowing people's names and something about them helps to acknowledge them as people (some students simply crave confirmation),
2. inviting students to take advantage of my office hours, and
3. being firm when I correct a student.

These techniques also prepare me to handle difficulties that arise unexpectedly.

I recall a student who was a real fan of mine in the first class we took together, but in the next class she became a completely difficult person and started disrupting by wearing sunglasses in class, refusing to speak in group activities, and either handing in incomplete work or missing deadlines altogether. In class I politely but firmly asked her to remove the sunglasses so we could see each other. I encouraged her to make contributions to her group (because she really was bright and had much to offer). Her disruptions continued throughout the semester, and I asked her to visit me in my office. I confronted her and said, "Something is wrong. You are not the same person this semester and it is affecting your work and your relationships with others. Can I help?" She said simply, "I'm going through a lot." I couldn't get any more out of her, and she remained defiant and distant in class. Her research supervisor said the same was happening with their work together. As faculty, we remained open and offered assistance. She finished the semester with poor grades, but graduated. The faculty were sorry we couldn't do any more to help. Although the class suffered some because of her disruptive behavior, no one blamed me or themselves, since we all had tried to bring her around. As a class we learned that patience and tolerance are part of a response, but that enforcing the rules and moving ahead also need to happen for the good of all. You will have to deal directly with difficult students, because if you don't, other students will resent it and judge you negatively on teaching evaluations for losing control of the class. Reading books is a starting point for dealing with difficult people, but I suggest you confer with your peers as well. I often find that faculty can compare observations and take collective action as an effective way to help a student in difficulty.

Ethical Considerations and Problem Students

Ethical communication is speech that is honest, morally intact, and aimed at honoring the relationship and its goals. Many questions arise about the ethics of communication in the classroom on a daily basis. For example, is it ethical to shut down someone in class discussion for dominating? Here the issue is more a separation of the behavior from the person. What I want to curb is the domination, not the self-worth of the person. It is certainly ethical to not call on someone who always has a hand up or to say, "Let's hear from some quiet people today," as you are trying to facilitate turn taking. There may even come a point when you have to pull a student aside and ask him or her to simply

---

FROM THE CLASSROOM: The Most Common Interpersonal Communication Problem between Professor and Student

Having different perceptions of appropriate classroom behavior is the most common interpersonal problem between professors and students. Unclear expectations are definitely an issue. Faculty are not clear in their syllabi and during the first few sessions of class, of expectations for behavior and consequences of not abiding by the guidelines. The faculty most successful at working with difficult students recommend spending the first day of class discussing what type of learning environment will be established for the class and get buy-in from students by providing an opportunity for students to contribute to the discussion of a good classroom environment. In addition, they address problem behavior immediately directly with the student and document the conversation. That way, if the behavior escalates, action can be taken immediately. At UNCG, the Disruptive Behavior in the Classroom Policy might be invoked. Oftentimes, the initial conversation with the student might yield information about personal issues that are influencing the disruptive behavior, which allows the faculty member to refer the student to an office like ours that can work with getting the student assistance.

> Jen Day Shaw
> Dean of Students
> University of North Carolina at Greensboro

SOURCE: Personal correspondence with author, April 25, 2006.

---

control the behavior in question. Be aware that students can get angry and bad behavior can escalate. Keep notes on problem students because you may need to solve bigger issues later. Note the box above from my own Dean of Students about bad behavior in general.

Similar problems arise regarding student communication to professors through email. Beyond acceptable-use policies, students now engage in a variety of Internet behaviors that could be considered unethical. Journalist Jonathan Glater (2006) hit the nail on the head in a *New York Times* article that described everything from flaming a professor to demanding information or attention to criticizing the course and peers to general immaturity in requests. When students write me threatening or bizarre email messages, I retain a copy of the message and report it to my department head. On one occasion, we discovered during a faculty meeting that one student had threatened several of us in different classes, so the Dean of Students was made aware of the situation. I wrote to the student and said that email seemed to be a source of misunderstanding rather than clarity and that she should come to my office to communicate about assignments. She never came to my office but she did complete her work, and that was the end of the problem for me. Such situations are very uncomfortable, and I do worry about them. I wonder if the student will escalate the verbal aggression into physical violence. Threats (face-to-face or online) are as far as anything has ever gone in my 30 years in the classroom, however.

At my institution there is a pamphlet titled "Students in Distress: A Guide for Faculty and Staff" that is published by the Division of Student Affairs. The pamphlet is very helpful and contains a list of indicators (academic, emotional, physical, and safety risk) to look for if you suspect a student is having diffi-culty. There is also a list of ways to help, including the following points:

- Take these signs seriously.
- Meet privately with a student in distress.
- Specifically point out signs you've observed.
- Listen to the student's response.
- Refer.
- Follow university procedures.
- Recognize an urgent situation.
- Set expectations.
- Respect confidentiality.

Finally, the brochure has a list of relevant offices, contact names, and phone numbers. Find out whether your institution has such a brochure. Keep a copy with your other important resources. Always remember that if you are not a certified counselor, you must refer any troubled student to an expert. You may not legally dispense advice. The university attorney and Dean of Students are there to help, so enlist their aid as appropriate.

I want to turn now to two different types of students who may challenge you in creative ways rather than through the type of difficulty just discussed. The nontraditional or adult student is part of a growing population across the country. Such students are, indeed, different from the more traditional 18- to 24-year-olds. The other type of student you may face is the one who comes from a different cultural background, someone we might refer to as *co-cultural*. For example, if you are a Caucasian, heterosexual man, a co-cultural student in your class might be an African-American lesbian. Not only will you have to negotiate those different standpoints in your teacher-student relationship, you may have to mediate between and among co-cultural students as they interact and disagree on their opinions of topics under study.

Nontraditional or Adult Students

Adult students earning undergraduate degrees are defined at UNC Greensboro as being 24 years of age or older; they comprise about 17 percent of our total student population. According to researcher Marian Houser (2004), age usually is the defining characteristic of an adult learner. At UNCG, most of the adult students are between 24 and 30 years old, and then the age drops significantly, although we do have one 70-year-old student on record! We have been respon-sive to adult students by providing an Office for Adult Students, a Web site, a chance to communicate in person or in advice chatrooms, a slate of activities, and tips on childcare and parking. Although the Office of Adult Students works with their clients to solve practical problems as adults return to school, the classroom teacher often faces both interpersonal and practical issues that challenge the student and his or her peers in negative ways.

The challenges of teaching adult students run the gamut, and your experience may vary based on the type of institution where you teach. For example, community colleges as a general pattern have more adult students enrolled than do four-year colleges in undergraduate courses. In my classroom, if there is an adult student in the class (and there is usually only one or two), I have found that a woman will more likely make herself known than will a man. That student will talk more, be perceived by younger students as a "mom," will be more stressed over earning an A, will spend more time in my office asking about assignments, will dominate class activities by taking on self-appointed leadership roles, and will get less out of the class because she has disproportionate life experience to the material being taught. While younger students are learning to put vocabulary on life experience and looking ahead to the future, adult students—particularly parents—are more likely reflecting on past experiences. This generational difference can cause some conflict, but it is manageable, and each group can actually learn from the other.

Occasionally, adult students who are also parents may miss class when their child is sick or when there are activities at their child's school that require the parents' attendance. These students may wish to be excused when family matters take them away from class. Too, these students may make a special request more often to fax or email assignments rather than turn them in at the requested time or in class. To avoid setting up double standards that traditional college students may potentially resent, I try to be fair under the circumstances and often work with adult students on a one-on-one basis to negotiate school requirements, given the reality of family life. I have observed that many adult students will put a lot of pressure on themselves to succeed at the same time that they express a lack of confidence in their academic ability because they've been out of school for so long.

The challenges of teaching a class comprising both traditional and adult students put me in the position of mediator: I find myself having to remind people to be respectful of each other. I have to reassure adults that they can succeed (even when they make the top grades in class), and that even though their enthusiasm is wonderful, they should not get carried away with contributions to class discussion. Although I have to be humane in recognizing that adult students *do* have different needs and face challenges that require some flexibility, I am also responsible for holding adult students accountable to general class rules. At times I also have to remind younger students to be respectful of their older peers. It's quite a balancing act! I try to capitalize on the interpersonal experiences of adult students as evidence that theories and concepts presented in the text and in class are leading us somewhere. Marian Houser writes in an article in *Communication Teacher* (2004) that nontraditional students do have different needs and suggests the following effective strategy: "Create a positive learning environment and a non-threatening communication climate where adults feel as if they are part of the learning community.

Some ways to do this are to have students interview each other, break students into groups, encourage support networking, and get to know students yourself" (p. 80). These are good suggestions and should help you mix students together for effective learning.

If you are a younger instructor, it's quite possible you may face some difficulty with nontraditional students as the result of an age differential. I've known teaching assistants who have occasionally reported that adult students appear to talk down to them or show disrespect. One of my colleagues, who is in her mid-twenties, reported that an older student talked to the point of dominance, stayed after class every session, and then started interrupting her in lecture to "teach" the class himself. When he received a C on the first major assignment, he confronted her. She explained the grading rubric to him and outlined some suggestions for improvement. All of this was done in a calm and respectful manner. After the confrontation, he stopped staying late and interrupting lectures, but she did have to keep working on the dominance problem. Many instructors may have to consider a more firm and professional tone as a strategy for dealing with nontraditional students who challenge authority.

Co-Cultural Student Populations

Today's diverse college classroom is comprised of many students from a variety of backgrounds. Mark Orbe's (1998) concept of co-cultural communication recognizes that two people from different cultural standpoints will come together and experience automatic power imbalances and a struggle for dominance based on the differences in standpoints. Think back to the example of the Caucasian, heterosexual, male teacher and the African-American lesbian student—note that the two partners in this interpersonal relationship are quite different. How do you negotiate the differences in this relationship to ensure that learning is mutual? It takes a diverse number of communication strategies and cultural knowledge to achieve this negotiation. Orbe describes 26 different co-cultural strategies. They are worth studying to help you familiarize yourself with what your students do and with what you might be doing to communicate with students who are culturally different from you.

My own experiences have forced me more than once to negotiate my position as a Caucasian woman in a variety of co-cultural relationships. In each case I had to use my knowledge, experience, or outside resources to figure out communication strategies that would help me cross a cultural gap rather than have a relational breakdown. For example, I taught a nontraditional Mexican man who did not have enough English language skill to understand the vocabulary of the course. In this case, I knew enough Spanish to be able to converse with him in two languages. In another instance, I taught a Japanese exchange student who failed every exam and wrote me emails apologizing for being "so stupid," even though she needed to pass the class to enroll the following semester. With only a reading knowledge of Japan, I sought out a Japanese colleague to advise me on the teacher-student relationship in Japan so that I could approach the student without scaring her. There are many types of co-cultural interactions that include people one wouldn't ordinarily think of as differing in their status or level of power. Even first-generation college students come to school without the same knowledge as students of college-educated parents (Orbe, 2004). Those students may feel powerless and uninformed, yet they need to be assimilated into the education system so they are successful. Consider any resources you may have on campus, such as a multicultural resource center or an office for African-American student affairs, for example, where you can get training, tap into resources, or seek advice in your quest to communicate effectively.

As instructors, we need to stay alert every day to the possibilities of both success and failure when cultural differences meet in the classroom. As Afrocentric theorist Molefi Asante wrote many years ago under the name Art Smith (1973), "normalization" will not occur in interracial relationships (and, by extension, co-cultural relationships) until we are willing to communicate, we make ourselves mentally and physically accessible, we appreciate that the task of communication has the potential to be difficult, and we attempt to be authentic by presenting a self that isn't masked in facade.

CONCLUSION

Student challenges will inevitably arise in an interpersonal communication course. Classroom management is an issue of controlling space, people, and discussion. It helps teachers stay organized and move forward in an orderly manner to accomplish course goals and have fun at the same time. It also helps to control student disruption and other similar behaviors. For the deeper problems, we need to remember that we are teachers, not counselors, and we need to rely on outside help when student needs go beyond the classroom. We also need to remember that we live in an ever-changing world of student demographics and standpoints. The ability to adapt to and empathize with students will help us make the most out of the classroom experience.

4

Structural Challenges and Problematics

Every introductory interpersonal communication course has inherent structural challenges that are unique to the course. In this chapter we explore five of those challenges: development of instructional strategies, balancing theory and practice, teaching the vocabulary of the discipline, use of technology, and service learning. Sorting out best practices connected to each of these areas can only strengthen the framework of your course and make your teaching more effective.

INSTRUCTIONAL STRATEGIES

An *instructional strategy* is a teaching method that facilitates learning and helps an instructor achieve course objectives. Recall from Chapter 2 that instructional strategies are one piece of the larger puzzle that is the structure of your course. There must be logical connections among the course objectives, instructional strategies, evaluation procedures, organization of course content, and syllabus. Common instructional strategies in an introductory interpersonal course include reading texts and research articles; lecturing; class, small-group, and online discussions; case-study analysis; tutorials; team teaching, in-class or laboratory activities; film viewing and analysis; fieldwork (interviewing a family member or conducting a relationship analysis); journaling; service learning; student presentations; guest speakers; and workshops. Choosing the most effective teaching style is part of the overall instructional strategy.

A new teacher may start with the primary pedagogical decision of how to balance lecturing and activities. However, developing an effective set of teaching methods is actually more complicated than that. Education professors Keith Prichard and McLaren Sawyer (1994) argue that selecting teaching methods comes down to a fairly complex set of decisions that includes at least six factors: knowledge of the research on the psychology of teaching, one's prior role models, the personality of the instructor, the teaching philosophy of the instructor, outside influences on the academy (such as the public mood on political correctness), and the teaching context (such as a small- versus a large-enrollment course).

Regarding the first factor, what we know about students' learning styles today is that most tend to be visual learners with short attention spans. As one reviewer of this book commented, "Every year it seems like I have to work harder and be more creative in order to keep my students interested." Another reviewer reminded me that when selecting instructional strategies, it might be helpful to consider the typological preferences (e.g., Myers-Briggs Type Indicators®) or learning styles (e.g., Kolb's learning style inventory) of both the teacher and the students. For example, teachers who are strong extroverts may have to consider how best to relate to students who are more introverted when it comes to discussions.

Factor five from Prichard and Sawyer concerning outside influences relates to how the surrounding political or religious environment can affect one's teaching decisions. I live in the "Bible Belt" of America, so it was a big decision for me to start talking about gay and lesbian families when the textbooks didn't have much on that topic in the chapter on family relationships. I initially inserted the topic in a mini-lecture that introduced the textbook chapter. I always give a quick statistical look at the current status of the American family. Students then often nod, "yeah, that's me" when they recognize a family configuration that describes them. This sets the stage for students to talk and contribute examples of communication from a diverse range of family relationships. Most texts now include something about gay and lesbian families, which adds credibility to the topic and diffuses some of the controversy in the teaching decision.

The teaching context may include the fact that many communication courses now play a central role in "communication across the curriculum" programs. Speaking and writing-intensive courses require a course structure and instructional strategies that help students use speaking and writing both as literacy skills and as tools for expressing their thoughts. You may have to build into the course exercises or assignments that achieve particular objectives for communication-intensive courses. At my institution, teachers can attend workshops and receive assistance with those decisions; find out if your institution offers help as well.

Locating Instructional Strategies

New teachers will initially find instructional strategies in the textbook and the accompanying instructor's manual. For an interpersonal course, this implies two things: first, students will be expected to read chapters and then come to class and discuss them (most likely in a lecture-discussion format). Second, instructors will probably engage students in class activities that will enable them to practice or realize how a concept works, I still do this as a successful set of instructional strategies after 30 years in the classroom. If students are buying a text, they expect to use it. I use the text every day as part of my delivery of instruction. I may say, "Let's look at the chart on confirming and disconfirming language in our text so we can talk about how that works in our relationships." Or, "Tonight I want you to take the love styles test in the text so we can talk about that in our next class period." We use information, assessments, and text activities as part of the overall instructional strategy. Why is this good for new instructors as well as old hands? Entry-level students want the reassurance of a textbook, and reading a book is a primary way of learning in our educational system. Reading and discussing a text, followed by an in-class exercise, is probably the most common instructional strategy in an interpersonal communication course. One of my students, Michelle Lewis, put it well when she said, "Exercises and activities have really helped me learn the material. The role playing and skits helped the material become more of a 'real life' situation. For me, I was able to take the activities and reflect back on my relationships" (personal correspondence, June 15, 2006).

In addition to the text and instructor's manual, most instructors keep files of activities and assignments they've collected over the years from observing other classes, attending convention panels or workshops where these strategies are presented (e.g., G.I.F.T.S., or great ideas for teaching speech, are common at communication conferences), culling issues of *Communication Teacher,* talking to colleagues around the country, and modifying activities from their own days as students. Instructors might also go online and get activities from Web sites, although caution is recommended. Recently, an alumna sent me a Johari Window email that is circulating on the Internet. She fondly recalled us studying this concept and doing a class exercise. When I looked at what she sent, it wasn't the Johari Window at all! The item was a personality test and something that didn't look anything like Joseph Luft's (1969) ideas in *Of Human Interaction* (see Chapter 7).

What works among all these possible strategies? Many things do—that's for sure. You will probably engage in trial and error as you get comfortable and reflect on some of the factors outlined by Prichard and Sawyer (1994) just discussed. I can tell you that interactive strategies that involve energy, student participation, and fun are what draw students to the material. If they are having fun and learning at the same time, they will keep coming back.

During the course of a semester my students are involved in at least eight to ten activities requiring a response on a 5 × 8 card, three to five role plays, one case study, three to five small-group discussions, five to six charts on the board to be filled in, six to ten demonstrations or quick practices, and three to five additional scales or assessments. This is in a class that meets twice a week for 16 weeks. There is something active going on every day in addition to lectures, discussions, and other forms of instructional delivery. As topics develop, I bring in newspaper clippings and create additional in-class activities to address breaking topics.

Getting Students to Read

Reading assigned chapters in the textbook is the most common instructional strategy employed by instructors, yet one of their biggest concerns is that students come to class without having read the assigned material from the text or the reserved reading list. I experience this syndrome all the time. What happens then? A punitive approach is to give quizzes or to ask students who didn't read to leave the class. More motivational approaches include asking each student to bring a 5 × 8 index card to class with a reaction to the reading or an application of a concept from his or her own life. Jump ahead to Chapter 7 and look at the section on reading resources efficiently. Material from that section could be used to compose a handout to help students better comprehend the textbook. I have done this for first- and second-year students, and it has proven useful.

During class I ask students what they think of the reading. This is a consistent practice for me because I want to emphasize for students the relationship between reading and thoughtful class discussions. Students who do not read simply do not participate as well in class, nor do they perform at high levels on exams. A show of hands in my own classes reveals that anywhere from one- to two-thirds of the students have not read on any given day. It is hard to ignore the fact that students do not read before coming to class, so we need to be proactive in confronting this reality.

English professor and writing expert John Bean demonstrates how critical thinking, writing, and reading all intersect when we teach students to solve problems actively rather than passively. In his book, *Engaging Ideas* (1996), Bean advises teachers on how to help students read. In addition to the standard suggestions of showing students how to take notes in the margins of a book and prepare cards with thesis statements from the reading, he offers the following tips:

- Develop student interest in readings by discussing in advance problems or issues that may then be addressed in the reading.
- Create reading guides if the texts involve cultural codes or knowledge of difficult vocabulary and then discuss those items after the reading is done.
- Ask students to keep a "reading log" in which they make journal-like entries with ideas and responses triggered by the reading. Use those responses to launch class discussions.
- Provide one or two questions students must respond to after doing the assigned reading. Use the answers in class discussion.
- Ask students to summarize in their own words particularly difficult passages.

Note that all of these strategies could employ 5×8 cards that are then handed in for you to review. By helping students to read better, there is every expectation that other aspects of learning, such as discussions and completion of assignments, will also improve.

Team Teaching

Team teaching is an instructional strategy that is well suited to an interpersonal communication course, but we do not use it often enough because of economic reasons. Instructor teams could serve as the model of an effective dyad. Note that having a teaching assistant is not necessarily team teaching, unless the TA is a true part of shared instruction for the course. One successful instructor team is Steven McCornack and Kelly Morrison, a husband-and-wife team at Michigan State University; together they teach an entry-level course that enrolls almost 650 students a semester. I can't even imagine what it takes to be skillful enough to pull that off, but they both love it. One key to success in team teaching is really knowing your co-teacher well and sharing a similar teaching philosophy. After a while, the team will grow and become a kind of synchronized whole. Here's what the MSU team has to say:

Kelly

I really enjoy team-teaching this course. It is truly beneficial to have two seasoned lecturers in there because while one is talking the other can be observing the class to gauge understanding and decide whether or not a concept needs to be explained again or clarified with an additional example. The most challenging aspects are making sure that it doesn't seem to the students that one person is more knowledgeable than another (i.e., one person is the "lead" and the other the "assistant"), especially when gender roles come into play. It is also challenging to team teach if you get in a fight right before lecture, or disagree with something they are saying or the way they are presenting an idea. (Personal correspondence, June 6, 2006.)

Steve

It's great *fun* to teach with such an excellent co-instructor, with whom I share so much history. We can "play off" each other quite a bit. But it's also a challenge. Even though there are large points of agreement and "deals" struck in advance regarding how things should and will be covered, when it comes to the particulars everyone has their own unique view of things, and it's frequently the case that one or the other of us thinks, "well, that's not *quite* how I would have explained it." Team teaching is like playing in a band. You know what your potential is, but that potential is fully realized only on certain occasions. (Personal correspondence, June 1, 2006.)

If team teaching is an instructional strategy you want to employ, investigate the policies and attitudes toward this unique approach. Be sure you have a compatible partner who is willing to commit to team teaching for more than one semester. It takes time to perfect this strategy.

Instruction on the First Day of Class

What impression would you like to make on the first day? How will the first day of your interpersonal communication course set the tone for the rest of the semester? The first day of class gets a lot of attention from pedagogy experts. Wilbert McKeachie's famous book, *Teaching Tips* (1969), discussed what to do on the first day, and we are still getting advice (e.g., Friedrich & Cooper, 1999) on how to overview a course and present ourselves to meet the expectations of students. Graduate assistant supervisor Katherine Hendrix (2000) even provides a helpful checklist of behaviors to perform on the first day, from identifying yourself (yes, some people forget to introduce themselves!) to staying after class for a few minutes to answer questions or greet students who wish to speak to you. If you are new to teaching, or you just want to refresh your memory on the technical procedures of what to do, say, and bring to class, Hendrix's guide is a good source.

The first day of class is important in demonstrating to students what to expect from your instruction. In communication courses, a common first day schedule is to hand out the syllabus, conduct an icebreaker activity so students can get to know one another, and end the class early. Many instructors do not want to start any content because there are absences, adds and drops, and general jockeying for the line-up of a final roll sheet. Students are excited the first day, or lost, or hung over, and generally not expecting to do any cognitive work. I think it's a waste of time not to cover any content because, in spite of all the logistical problems just mentioned, I want to show students that we are serious, that there is *great* content in the course, and that we need to get started!

Some professors do not pass out the syllabus on the first day. If the syllabus has been posted online, the professor may direct the students to the posting and answer questions on the second day of class or through email. A colleague of mine who refrains from handing out the syllabus on the first day does so because he wants to shake things up and not be predictable. For the most part, however, professors do pass out and discuss the syllabus. I do so because many students at my school commute and work full-time. Some are trying to balance their course load and need to see a syllabus to decide if it is the right time to take this course. I certainly respect that and let the students know what to expect through a syllabus. I try not to spend more than 20 minutes on logistics.

I spend the next 25 minutes introducing students to the five assumptions that point toward the key concepts underlying our study of interpersonal communication: communication is the basis of relating, empathy, understanding self and other, making communication choices, and consequences of choices. This sounds boring, but it is not. It is a fascinating, sincere, and intelligent set of ideas that sets us up for both the philosophical and the practical units in the course curriculum. The course and my efficacy as an instructor get overviewed in this way.

The last 30 minutes of class is the icebreaker, where students pair off in dyads, get to know each other, and name a characteristic of an effective interpersonal relationship based on their knowledge and experiences. They then introduce each other to the rest of the class and we make the list of characteristics (e.g., honesty, trust, good listening). We have fun meeting one another and talking about the list as it is generated. The list, along with the initial assumptions, are then used during the next class period to launch our discussion of definitions and are further used in an exercise the following week in which students build their own models of the interpersonal communication process. In fact, the material from the first day is still being referred to on the last day of class as everything comes full circle. Everything is strategic about the first day and is designed to set the pace, introduce content, establish my credibility, and let students introduce themselves. The classroom climate is established by the end of the class period, expectations are laid out, and we all have a good idea of whether the class is going to work. Much of the time we leave the first class on a high note and look forward to a good semester together. We are connected at that point and the awesome responsibilities of teaching and learning together begin. For me, the first day is very exciting, and I always look forward to meeting new students and persuading them to be just as enthusiastic about interpersonal communication as I am.

A note on impression management on the first day: dress for success. If you are trying to model effective communication, dressing to honor the professional nature of the classroom is appropriate. Students scrutinize every move you make and every piece of clothing you wear. Try to minimize clothing choice as something that could be negative or could bias the way students relate to you.

On the first day, wear your best smile and be your most open. Use that day to create the kind of learning community that reflects your overall philosophy of interpersonal communication. For example, Professor Bill Rawlins of Ohio University establishes a sense of community from the first day forward. Professor Rawlins is well-known in interpersonal communication circles as a kind, soft-spoken, and philosophical person. He's a big believer in dialogue as the best approach to negotiating the partnership of a dyad. Rawlins creates a classroom environment around the Aristotelian notion of civic friendship. From the first day, he encourages students to be who they are (the Buberian notion of the authentic self; see Chapter 6) and to thrive on the unique insights each person will bring to the classroom. He says, in effect, "We are a political community where we grow together in the freedom to be different from each other" (personal conversation, June 12, 2006). In this community, Rawlins and his students spend the semester studying interpersonal communication in a safe environment (psychologically, emotionally) in which he asks his students to be who they are apart from all the distractions of the world around them. This is accomplished through his ability to suspend judgment and welcome all students in dialogue about the issues at hand.

BALANCING THEORY AND PRACTICE

Regardless of years of experience, instructors overwhelmingly talk about the challenge of trying to balance theory with practice in the interpersonal communication classroom. Three reasons explain why we struggle with this so much:

1. The "touchy-feely" approach to teaching in the early 1970s has left us with a bad reputation for being without content (that is, theory);
2. Students recoil at the idea of getting too involved with theory because it seems difficult; and
3. Textbooks seem to emphasize skills and practice over in-depth examinations of theory.

I try to find a balance by selecting particular theories that I want to spend more time on because they are important to a student's knowledge and understanding of the interpersonal communication process. In my class the theories that fit this category include (see Chapter 7 for sources on these theories) the following:

- social exchange/equity,
- attribution,
- uncertainty reduction,

- rules,
- negotiation of self,
- relational dialectics,
- stage theory,
- communication competence,
- gendered conversational style,
- conflict management, and
- intercultural communication theories.

Depending on the depth I go into, students receive extra information in lecture, handouts in their course packets with information and suggested readings, or reserve readings. These theories get played out in assignments and class activities, and I use them as often as possible when answering questions or engaging in discussion. My goal is to develop critical thinking and problem-solving skills about relationships that involve a theoretical frame of reference. In looking at my syllabus (see Chapter 2), it is easy to see how theories such as those just mentioned become the way of talking about and seeing the world in our class.

Making consistent references to theory is a strategy that also demonstrates to students that an educated individual has the critical thinking skills and the appropriate communication knowledge to approach the world as a reality that needs some kind of an explanation. Theory is the tool that helps us solve problems, enjoy a higher quality of life, and understand behavior and attitudes in our relationships with others. In a short period of time, I hear students discussing theory among themselves, or they come to class telling me how they applied uncertainty reduction, for example, to a situation in their own lives. This shows me that a "mind-map" is beginning to form in their heads as a coherent way to approach real-world relationships. Above all, we approach the study of the interpersonal communication process with cognitive, behavioral, and emotional intelligence. The balance of theory and practice is the manifestation of that intelligence.

Colleagues tell me that stories and examples work best in helping students understand how to put theory into practice. My students also report that examples are one of the best ways they learn. So for every concept I teach in class, I give an example. For every theory there must be a scenario or story. Students may be invited to add their own examples in discussion. One important key here is to use excellent examples and stories that students can relate to. For example, when we discuss attribution theory, I tell a hypothetical story about an old man living in a student neighborhood and a problem with the trash cans. At least half the students will start smiling, and as the story starts to unfold some will even say, "That's my neighbor." This story works because so many of my students live in a neighborhood adjacent to campus that is a mix of senior citizens and students. There *are* problems with trash cans and parking spaces and efforts to communicate for an effective neighborly relationship. The students quickly "get" attribution because the story is realistic and familiar. Many of them also start thinking about treating their neighbors in a kinder way as a result of seeing how attribution theory explains an unpleasant situation.

One caution about stories: do not let students get the upper hand. One of my colleagues, Jessica Delk, who has only been teaching the introductory course for a couple of years, expressed frustration with students telling stories from personal experience and losing sight of the theoretical idea under study. She summed it up: "I do find this tie back to theory to be problematic and not where they [the students] want to focus their energy" (personal correspondence, October 4, 2004). Although we all want students to participate and share the responsibility of linking theory to real life, the teacher must control the amount of storytelling and the linkage to theory. This takes skill in facilitation and discussion leadership, as discussed in Chapter 3.

There are alternatives to stories and examples. To explore uncertainty reduction theory, I ask students to analyze a case study in groups of four to six people for about 15 to 20 minutes. The case accomplishes a lot more than just "practicing" theory because the content of the case involves an interracial relationship that gets students talking about cultural issues and how racism and uncertainty might be related. As an instructional strategy, the case study demonstrates the complex nature of explanation and choice making. Students can also learn from each other and participate actively in figuring out answers to problems. Note that the students also have in hand an information sheet on uncertainty reduction theory with references to the textbook and some recommended reading. I also let the students know that the case is about a former communication major who told this scenario in a focus group I was conducting. Here is the case as it appears on the worksheet handed out in class (see the box on page 86).

Chapter 6 explores the theory that serves as the basis for my course. The readings are all recommended and made available to my students. In an introductory course, not all students will grasp theory well as they read primary sources, so I do a fair amount of interpreting with my students. Sometimes they complain about reserve readings (after all, they say, they bought a textbook, so why read more than that?), but I tell them to get what they can and to look forward to their communication theory course for a continued exploration of several of these theoretical ideas. These students are in transition from lower-order knowledge and application to higher-order synthesis and evaluation, to use the language of Bloom's Taxonomy (see Chapter 2). A little dose of primary source reading is not a bad thing!

I invite you now to think about five theories that constitute primary components of the theoretical perspective of your course. Next, browse Chapter 7 for any resources that might be appropriate for you to review as possible sources to recommend to your students. How can you integrate these selected theories more tightly into the thinking and practice of your students?

A CASE STUDY IN UNCERTAINTY IN WORKPLACE RELATIONSHIPS

Scenario (based on a true story):

A young African-American male (Eric) arrives at his job at the restaurant where he waits tables. His hair is perfect because he spent almost an hour styling it. His Caucasian manager (Jim) takes one look at him and says, "Go in the restroom and put some water on that hair to calm it down." Eric is dismayed and then very angry. He can't put water on his hair! "Fixing" this style would take a while and he tells Jim so. Jim dismisses Eric from his shift, and the waiter loses an evening of pay. Within another week Eric (who is very good at his job) quits, complaining that his manager's lack of understanding feels like racism.

Analyze this scenario as a case of uncertainty. Remember, there is no one correct answer in case analysis. Rather, we are using a real-life situation to reflect on possible communication choices for ourselves.

1. What type of cognitive and/or behavioral uncertainty exists for both Eric and Jim?

2. What constraints (role, rules, situation, language, etc.) may be adding to the level of uncertainty?

3. Is racism a viable explanation for the situation, or does uncertainty reduction theory work better?

4. What strategies would you advise both Eric and Jim to use for more effective workplace communication?

VOCABULARY

Teaching the vocabulary of interpersonal communication is as challenging as balancing theory and practice. The common complaint is "There is just so much vocabulary!" This is true. There are about 350 entries in the glossary of my own textbook, and we use just about all of them over the course of a semester. I would estimate 50 to 75 core vocabulary terms that I expect students to have as a working vocabulary when talking about interpersonal communication. The idea of professional jargon versus common sense is one of those tensions that students need to negotiate. My colleague, Jennifer Baker, put the problem in perspective for me:

> [A difficult pedagogical issue is] helping students to understand that learning about interpersonal communication is the same thing as learning, say, about microbiology. Since they [students] communicate everyday and have relationships, when we talk about things, they think they understand them, and then freak out when they don't do well on the tests. There are terms, theories, ideas

that they have to associate with the experiences they have had with communication and relationships. Getting them to understand this, and then discuss or write, using the theories and terms, I think is the most difficult for them to understand and then apply. (Personal correspondence, October 21, 2004)

Jennifer's statement helps explain those students who complain, "I already know all this stuff." The academic use of terms is quite different from the lay use of terms. The academic vocabulary is a more precise way to understand the nuances of interpersonal communication. For example, a *transaction* in lay terms is usually a quick business deal in a store or at a bank. But a *transaction* in interpersonal communication vocabulary is deep, shared meaning where partners in a dyad reciprocate behavior. Students have to be told this, but once they begin to use academic vocabulary properly, it changes the way they perceive and act in their relationships.

In an introductory class, it is common to test students' understanding of vocabulary on exams. I use a matching section of 20 vocabulary terms on each major exam to test students on basic vocabulary. So learning the vocabulary terms also helps prepare them for upper-level courses. I need students to be comfortable with such terms as *dyad* and *dialectics,* so I don't mind testing for this as part of their overall assessment of learning. Given how much vocabulary there is, posting vocabulary lists online for students to access and study is a useful technique. During review sessions for exams, and time permitting, a fun activity to play is vocabulary *Jeopardy:* Divide the class into two teams. Read definitions and ask students to call out the answers in the form of questions. For example:

> Instructor: Behaviors that gain the agreement of your partner, persuading him or her to do as you wish. For example, promising dinner if your roommate will help you move some furniture.
>
> Student: What is a compliance-gaining strategy?

We can play *Jeopardy* for 15 minutes, awarding points to teams, and get the review done in a hurry. Students love the competition, but they also get a sense of what vocabulary is important for the exam, thus enabling them to continue studying on their own. The game also provides much-appreciated levity to the classroom.

For me, the biggest challenge in teaching vocabulary is showing students why it is important. I tell them that if they can name an experience, then they can take the next step, which is to talk about that experience in an intelligent manner. This is where we can separate "everyone communicating and having relationships" from "educated people who can communicate with knowledge and make strategic choices for more effective relationships." There is a significant difference.

TECHNOLOGY AND INSTRUCTION

Technology serves as both an instructional strategy and a course structure, depending on your use of it. If you are using technology as an instructional strategy, it supports the course in a different manner than if you are teaching an online (distance education) course; in the latter case the course and the technology are inseparable. *Low-technology* courses are those in which you can sit in a circle with a small group and get into a discussion that is so meaningful you don't want class to end. High-technology courses are those with constant audio-visual stimulation, including film clips, PowerPoint slides, overheads, Web sites, and sound stimulation. Notice that talking about technology in this manner is more about how technology helps you deliver instruction. If you have more than ten students in a class, you may need some level of technology to deliver information about interpersonal communication concepts. For example, PowerPoint slides work well to deliver key points during a lecture. A scene from a film could demonstrate particular relational concepts such as *metacommunication* and conflict-management strategies. Web sites are also helpful. MySpace, Facebook, and Friendster, among others, provide a basis for talking about Internet friendships and the pros and cons of Internet self-disclosure in relationships. Students want to talk about the role of technology in their relationships, so it is appropriate to use the Internet as a resource. On an interesting metacommunication level, four students in an interpersonal class of mine told me they use MySpace as a way to talk about our class. As they discussed class issues, they were also developing friendships. For an instructor the question is, what function does technology serve in teaching about relationships and the communication process? Instructors may have different levels of comfort using technology in the instructional process, but students often expect some technology to be integrated into the course.

Other instructional strategies that are linked to technology include online discussions and the use of Blackboard or WebCT to post notes, assignments, or activities required for the course. Reserve readings are now frequently electronic as well, so students either read journal articles on a computer screen or print copies to bring to class. As more students wish to take notes using their laptop computers, or as universities require students to own laptops, it is expected that instructors will welcome laptops into the classroom. This poses a particular problem for interpersonal communication instructors, given the preferred mode of face-to-face interaction and the frequent rearranging of desks for activities. The instructor cannot see a student's face when a computer screen hides it therefore, a laptop acts as a nonverbal barrier to interaction. Students often engage in other activities on their laptops, such as surfing the Internet, completing other assignments, or checking email, and become disengaged from the class. The clicking sound of keyboards is a distraction for those not using computers. For all of these reasons, an interpersonal communication instructor may need to formulate a policy about the use of laptops and put it in the syllabus.

Distance learning or online courses are now in place for teaching interpersonal communication courses entirely over the Internet. The few syllabi that I have seen for online courses all share a similar structure: students read from a textbook, engage in several online discussions, take tests, and turn in term papers or other written assignments. I have not yet tried teaching an online course, and honestly, they go against my philosophy of developing teacher-student relationships in face-to-face settings. Yes, I am somewhat old-fashioned here, but even my students are weary of technology. Most of our students *want* to be face-to-face, and that makes sense given that they love communication enough to have majored in it. I think your own decisions really do revolve around making decisions about how technology of any kind is an appropriate component of your instructional scheme. Do what works for you, what you can competently handle, and what delivers instruction in the most appropriate manner for the concepts under study.

If your institution asks you to develop an online interpersonal communication course, be sure to utilize campus resources. At my school there is a team that assists the instructor to mount the course on the Web once it is designed. So far, there is not as much flexibility for changing course structure once the course is in place for the semester. The future of online courses truly is in the making.

SERVICE LEARNING

Service learning is an instructional strategy that has gained popularity in the last ten years in communication studies. Endorsed by the National Communication Association (NCA) and linked to both Campus Compact and the American Association for Higher Education, service learning is generally defined as "a pedagogy that addresses both our obligations as 'institutional neighbors' in the communities in which our campuses are located and our historic role of preparing students for participation in civil society" (Droge & Murphy, 1999, p. 3). James Applegate and Sherry Morreale, both NCA advocates for service learning, see it as "what happens when students are afforded the opportunity to practice what they are learning in their disciplines, in community settings where their work benefits others" (1999, p. x). There is also a form of critical service learning (Artz, 2001) where a student's service to community is seen as a political act involving a transformative experience between student and community members that helps build social capital (Putnam, 2000) using communication and social action.

In my own communication department, we have a commitment to service learning involving 20 to 40 hours spent in the community by each student enrolled in a service learning course. Our introductory interpersonal communication course is not designated as service learning; rather, we engage it through a communities course, a research methods course, and an intercultural communication course. In conducting research for this book I did not find service learning to be a widespread instructional strategy in the introductory interpersonal communication course. There may be two reasons for this: first, the majority of courses are taught with a skills-based approach that requires basic practice of competencies best done in familiar dyadic contexts (e.g., family, friendship, romance). Second, the maturity level of the traditional introductory student may not be at a point where service in the community is the best use of his or her time and effort. Service learning is a serious commitment that may require advanced cognitive skills, knowledge sets, and higher levels of maturity that are more suited for and expected from juniors and seniors.

That is not to say that service learning shouldn't be employed in introductory interpersonal communication courses. Depending on the approach of the course, service learning may be a very appropriate strategy. A course that employs service learning as one instructional strategy rather than the overall structure of the course may work out well to provide a community or field experience that puts theory into practice. A good example is the service learning component Tasha Souza (1999) developed using a social constructionist perspective. She wanted her students to use dialogue as a way to see how communication creates relationships and social reality (the basic concept of social constructionism). Her students went out into the community to preselected sites for a four-hour experience and then each wrote up a six-page paper that interpreted the communication process he or she engaged in with community members. In particular, students wrote about negotiating selves, perception, expressing self, dialogic listening, and verbal/nonverbal process. Professor Souza's evaluation of the strategy revealed its usefulness in helping students apply interpersonal concepts in the real world, understand the concept of agency in the communication process, and see the value of service learning as a contribution to community.

If you are thinking about service learning as an instructional strategy, consider the following questions:

- Does service learning as an instructional strategy fit with the objectives of the course?
- Do I want to incorporate service learning as one strategy or as the entire approach to the course?
- Does my institution have a service learning office that could help with arranging service sites and meeting any legal obligations as students travel off campus?
- Are there enough community sites (e.g., homeless shelters, schools) where interpersonal relationship building would be at the core of student activities?
- Do I need resources for supervision of student learning and site visitation?
- What specific assignments (journals, papers, etc.) would be appropriate as an assessment of the learning accomplished through community service?

Finally, plan ahead if you are going to employ service learning. There is a lot of legwork that needs to be done as you prepare the course. Consult the NCA Web site (www.natcom.org); select the pull-down menu labeled *Education* and then click on *Service Learning*. You might want to attend state, regional, or national workshops to help with the preparation of service-learning instruction. If you are a novice teacher, perhaps team teach with a more experienced instructor before going out on your own. All in all, service learning can be one of the most profound learning experiences a college student will ever participate in, so it is worth thinking about how the introductory interpersonal course could contribute to such an experience.

SUMMARY

This chapter brought up issues about structuring an interpersonal course to successfully deliver its content. There is no one best way to do this, so your challenge is to build instruction that works for you and your students. Use variety, have fun, and get students involved. It's clear that we are way beyond the days of lecturing as the primary method of instruction. Effectiveness in teaching, at least in the introductory interpersonal communication course, is a balance of methods, a balance of theory and practice, a balance of responsibility between teacher and student, and, ultimately, a balance between the teaching and learning processes.

5

Evaluation and Assessment

This chapter focuses on the most difficult aspect of an interpersonal communication course: administering tests and evaluating student progress. The dilemma of grading students is that most of their relating happens outside of class, where we are not present to observe them, thus making it difficult to track competency development. The course has to set up tangible assignments and measurement instruments that enable each student to analyze, apply, and evaluate his or her own performance in relationships. We are often left with knowledge and comprehension as the primary cognitive abilities that we can measure with any degree of certainty. In order to test students' analytical and evaluative skills, instructors need to create both hypothetical and real-world situations; these work fairly well. In addition to giving examinations, assignments that support the learning objectives of the course need to be constructed and graded, and an overall grading system needs to be developed. Further, with most institutions under the mandate of statewide assessment or accrediting procedures, program assessment compliance is now the responsibility of many individual instructors. This chapter examines program assessment procedures and what can be learned under the guidance of the National Communication Association (NCA). It should be noted that evaluation is not based solely on one type of grading, but that learning objectives, general feedback, student evaluation, a grading system, and program assessment are all interconnected. Although I will separate topics for purposes of discussion, keep in mind that everything in this chapter happens as a systemic process.

COURSE STRUCTURE AND LEARNING OBJECTIVES

Recall from Chapter 2 that the syllabus serves as the structural template for the course; learning objectives support the aim and direction of the course. For an introductory course, my best advice is to keep it simple. I tell my students:

> The emphasis of the course is on the practical application of concepts and strategies. In addition to gaining knowledge through lecture and reading, students will increase awareness of relational messages through skill-based activity, discussion, and a relationship analysis.

Following are the learning objectives and, in square brackets, the evaluation measures I use to ensure that those objectives are being met:

GENERAL OBJECTIVES

Upon completion of this course, the student should be able to

1. define and use a vocabulary of relational communication terms
   [evaluated by quizzes, exams, model exercise, and relationship analysis];
2. apply major theoretical concepts in the field of relational communication to real-world relationships
   [evaluated by model exercise, relationship analysis, exams, and in-class
   exercises];
3. analyze his or her own role in interpersonal relationships in a family,
   professional, friendship, interracial/intercultural, or intimate context
   [evaluated by relationship analysis, exams, and class discussions];
4. apply both practical and theoretical knowledge to increase his or her own
   competency in relational communication skills
   [evaluated by in-class exercises, class discussions, quizzes, exams, and
   competence diary]; and
5. evaluate the effectiveness of an interpersonal relationship
   [evaluated by relationship analysis, class discussions, and in-class exer-
   cises].

At the introductory level, much of this course is about building knowledge
of vocabulary, concepts, and theories. The skills, or *competencies,* are limited
because students are just learning to name behaviors and try out some of the
skills in their lives. I include a lot of application questions on my exams so that
students can demonstrate how a concept should work in a given situation. The
hope is that if a student can apply a concept in a hypothetical situation, he or
she will be able to apply that concept in a real-life situation. We can't be there
in everyday life to evaluate each student's actual competence, so we can at least
use exams to determine whether the student is competent and prepared. My
course is typical of most such courses in schools across the country. Even
though we emphasize knowledge and skills, most of us spend more time evaluating through exams rather than actual observation of skills.

Interpersonal communication course syllabi collected from institutions
across the country revealed that performance on exams accounts for anywhere
from 25 to 75 percent of the course grade, with about 60 percent as the average. These statistics indicate that we seem to value examinations as a primary
form of student evaluation. In rare instances there are no exams. Instead, students may be evaluated on the work they do in journals, group activities, presentations, projects, movie analyses, class discussions, portfolios, or other
learning measures. Ultimately, the goal is to conduct an overall assessment of
the student's learning process.

At this point, I want you to see that learning objectives, evaluation measures,
and the grading system need to be aligned so that the proper weight for each component reflects what you are doing in the course. If your course is speaking intensive, writing intensive, service learning, or any other marker type of course, include
that as part of the learning objectives and evaluation. I have writing intensive
incorporated into the syllabus in Chapter 2, so use that for guidance as needed.

GRADES AND GRADING SYSTEMS

Grading has become more objective over the years. It is no longer acceptable to simply award big red As on papers and exams. Nor can an instructor just add up grades without letting students know what the system is. Students place enormous value on grades (way more than most teachers) and grade point averages (GPAs). I recently sat through a faculty senate session at my university where student government representatives were arguing vehemently for 4.0+GPA calculations to reflect the *real* value of an A+. I have to confess, I am not impressed with that sort of thing—partly because grade inflation is rampant in the American higher education system and partly because I am tired of the constant "I have to make an A in your course" mentality in students. Communication courses are particularly subject to this because students have built a mythos about communication as the "easy" major. I do respect that grade inflation is real and student complaints about grades do happen, so we need to be concerned as teachers about what is fair, objective, and appropriate. Most teachers also now use *criterion-referenced* grading systems, in which each student must meet objective criteria set for the course, rather than *norm-referenced* grading systems, in which students are graded against each other.

I suggest you reexamine your university or college policy on grades located in the bulletin or catalog produced by your school. This macro-policy will describe the grading system, the criteria and/or meaning of each grade, and the implications for grades. Procedures for registering complaints about grades should also be mentioned in the policy, as well as in student handbooks and faculty policy manuals. Familiarize yourself with university or college expectations before you create your own grading system and stay within the protocol specified.

The majority of grading systems I have seen for introductory interpersonal communication courses are based on points. All graded activities in the course are listed and assigned a point value. The following is the point system I use in my course. The actual number of things a student has to do at this level is relatively small, and the items are weighted here to show their relative importance in the overall assessment scheme. Roughly two-thirds of the class material is evaluated by examinations and one-third is activity-based through in-class and out-of-class assignments and exercises.

Quizzes	2 @ 25 pts.	50 pts.	Weight = 13%
Exams	2 @100 pts.	200 pts.	Weight = 54%
Homework		70 pts.	Weight = 20%
Model exercise = 15			
Relationship analysis = 50			
Competence diary = 5			
Class participation and exercises		50 pts.	Weight = 13%
Total		370 pts.	

Students work to earn as many points as possible; the final grade represents some percentage of the total points possible. Most people use a ten-point scale, where 90 to 100 percent of the points earned is an A; 80 to 89 percent of the points earned is a B; and so forth. Not every school requires a particular scale. My school requires the posting of + and − grades because they are calculated into the student's GPA, so the grading scale on my syllabus reflects that. It is also easier to use points when deductions off final point totals are necessary. For example, attendance policies may include point deductions for absence or tardiness. All things considered, points are understood by students and reduce grade complaints because there isn't much to dispute unless a technical error has been made in the grade calculation.

I work hard to set appropriate criteria for student success and to maintain the integrity of the grading system. Admittedly the negative side to grading is that grades may not reflect what the student actually learned. We evaluate student performance at given moments throughout the semester, but we all know that a student having a "bad semester" may perform below his or her academic capability. Until we invent another system, we maintain the current one.

You also should keep a grade book. Many people prefer computer-generated spreadsheets and post grades for students on Blackboard or other electronic systems. I have tried using both old-fashioned grade books and Excel spreadsheets. Note, however, that the computer is not necessarily more effective and may require more time to input data. The tradeoff is the automatic calculations and ability to cut and paste information to send to students. Other professors prefer that students track their own grades and provide space on the syllabus for recording such information. My university requires electronic posting of the final grade, which allows instructors to post grades quickly and students to access their grades on their own.

Whether you are grading assignments or exams, you need to set up performance expectations in the instructions you give to students, and then set up the grading criteria to reflect those expectations. For example, performance expectations range from the length of the assignment to the type of evidence or supporting material to be used to content. I found that passing out the grading rubric does not necessarily increase the number of As or improve the overall quality of work. Some students will still wait until the night before to type up an assignment or study for an exam. Regardless, it is advisable to maintain the integrity of the grading system by giving information out beforehand. The following are general tips for grading that I have learned over the years and that have proven effective.

Tips for Grading

- Blind grade whenever possible to eliminate bias.
- Use a rubric or set of criteria to ensure consistent grading across papers or exams.
- Use an ink color that contrasts with the ink/print on the document so the comments and marks can be seen. (Students generally dislike red in spite of its visibility; you make the call.)
- Grade one item at a time for consistent application of grading criteria.
- Grade through a set of items or categories and then take a break.

- Shuffle exams periodically so as not to recognize a student's style or fall into an order of grading.
- If writing is important to the presentation of ideas, correct grammar and punctuation.
- Invite the student to come see you if the grade is a D or an F and you detect problems.
- Make comments and notes in the margins. Students expect and appreciate individualized feedback.
- Spend time grading in proportion to the weight of the assignment.
- Return assignments and exams to students as soon as possible.
- Ask students to wait 24 hours before registering a grade complaint.
- Provide a summary of class performance along with the individually graded assignment so students can consider their individual performances in the context of class performance.

EVALUATING CLASS AND HOMEWORK ASSIGNMENTS

Class and homework assignments should measure the progress of a student toward achieving the course's learning objectives. I have my own students engage in assessments, exercises, and class discussions as the major forms of activity. Most of this activity involves skill building (e.g., a reflective listening exercise) and application (e.g., constructing Johari Windows for a relationship the student is part of). During class discussion we talk about topics such as strategies for building a positive communication climate in a dyad or conflict management strategies in content and relational conflict situations. I am more global about this type of participation and look for consistency, knowledge/application, and maturity as the student engages me and his or her peers. I use 5 × 8 index cards or assessment sheets from a course packet for most exercises and collect them at the end of the hour. I acknowledge the work with a check system (✓, ✓+, ✓−), write feedback on every item, and return it during the next class period. The plus and minus indicate evaluation, while the comments give both evaluation and feedback on their ideas and performance. I keep notes on class contributions such as frequency and quality of contributions. At the end of the semester, I work out points based on how many items were completed in class over the semester and balance the rest for class contributions. For 50 points worth of class work my grade book might look like this: class exercises 8 @ 3 points = 24 points; discussion participation then gets the other 26 points. There is a degree of subjectivity here that requires the instructor to use a general rubric for assigning discussion points. For example, in looking at my criteria above, the 26 points would break down as follows:

23–26 points	Student makes a class contribution 28 or more times in a 32-class semester.
	Student demonstrates excellent knowledge of the concepts and appropriate application.

	Student makes mature/adult contributions in both content and metacommunication.
20–22 points	Student makes a class contribution 25–27 times in a 32-class semester. Student demonstrates knowledge of the concepts and appropriate application with some misunderstanding at times. Student makes mature/adult contributions in both content and metacommunication the majority of time.
18–19 points	Student makes a class contribution 22–24 times in a 32-class semester. Student shows misunderstanding of knowledge or incorrect application of concepts several times over the semester. Student is mature/adult in contributions most of the time with some breaking of class rules for in-class behavior.
15–17 points	Student makes a class contribution 19–21 times in a 32-class semester. Student consistently shows misunderstanding or incorrect application of concepts. Student frequently breaks class rules and demonstrates immature behavior.
13–14 points	Student makes class contributions less than half the time in a 32-class semester. Student has little to no knowledge of concepts and cannot apply concepts. Student consistently breaks class rules, demonstrates immature behavior, and disrupts learning process.
12 points	Student attends class.

Experts such as Rebecca Rubin (1999) advise caution when evaluating participation because it is too subjective and you might penalize a student whose personality you do not like. I disagree with the idea of not evaluating participation in an interpersonal communication class because the pedagogy is based in active participation. We communicate to learn!

Now is a good time to bring up a philosophical issue about evaluation. The traditional way of evaluating students is through a *performance-based* approach—that is, the final grade assesses how well the student performed on course criteria. A newer approach is the *learning-based* philosophy, where the teacher attempts to track the student's cognitive development and maturity as he or she progresses through the course. In his study on teaching excellence teacher Ken Bain (2004) describes how the best teachers use a learning-based approach, where grades are used to communicate with students rather than rank students' performances:

> Learning entails primarily intellectual and personal changes that people undergo as they develop new understandings and reasoning abilities.... Evidence about learning might come from an examination, a paper, a project, or a conversation, but it is that learning, rather than a score, that professors try to characterize and communicate. (p. 153)

I have developed a kind of hybrid approach that combines both performance and learning approaches. Looking back at the rubric for evaluating participation is a good example of the hybrid philosophy: there are rewards for numbers of contributions, but the change in learning is evident in the criteria for mature contributions and demonstration of internalized learning. I do look at performance and penalties because students need to continue in that mode after college. In the working world, performance evaluations are common practice. On the other hand, this is the student's education, and my job is to help each one learn to be a more competent thinker, a problem solver, and, in the case of the introductory interpersonal course, a more competent relational partner who can use effective communication strategies. I spend a lot of time listening to students in order to perfect the way I teach so that the learning process is the best it can be. I use participation to gauge learning and development over the semester rather than just give points for speaking up. I do not use extra credit, something that Bain asserts may reflect little on learning and a lot on racking up points. I also spend a lot of time trying to get students to move away from their tendencies to think and act in discrete chunks of knowledge (that is, what is necessary to memorize for a test) and move toward a more holistic thinking and behavioral process. I design essay test questions that take a student in the direction of the big picture (example: What is the transactional philosophy and how might its implementation contribute to the overall health of an interpersonal relationship?). I look for this type of thinking and behaving in student participation throughout all course activities.

EVALUATING MAJOR CLASS ASSIGNMENTS

It is useful to use a rubric to evaluate major class assignments because you can create and refine the rubric over time as you continue to use the assignments, and a rubric standardizes evaluation, making it a process that can be applied objectively to all students. According to J. Worth Pickering, assessment director at Old Dominion University, a rubric is a "standardized scoring guide that identifies important criteria and levels of success for each criterion. A rubric describes qualitative as well as quantitative differences" (2006). The most common rubric in our field is the NCA Competent Speaker Speech Evaluation

Form. In an entry-level interpersonal communication course, the one activity for which we have a discipline-wide rubric is conversation (Spitzberg, 1995). The Conversational Skills Rating Scale is available through the NCA corporate office. For the most part, you will need to create your own rubric for each major assignment. This is tricky and takes some practice. If you are new at constructing rubrics, look for opportunities to attend assessment workshops, and ask colleagues for help. Meanwhile, two useful Web sites to help you get started are RubiStar, http://rubistar.4teachers.org/index.php, and Stylus Publishing, http://styluspub.com/resources/introductiontorubrics.aspx. Stylus is the publisher of the primer called *Introduction to Rubrics* (Stevens & Levi, 2005), which you may want to order if your library doesn't have a copy.

My students conduct a relationship analysis as their major class assignment and spend about two-thirds of the semester working on it. In this assignment, each student analyzes and evaluates a variety of communication processes in a current relationship in which he or she is a partner. A common alternative to an assignment like this might be to log activities in a journal intended to chart a student's interpersonal communication development over the course of the semester. My colleague Chris Poulos assigns an in-class partnership project to his students in which they are asked to pair off and develop a dyad using the skills and concepts being taught. These partnerships allow Professor Poulos to teach core skills and to make his own observations of student interpersonal communication. His students all turn in a ten- to twelve-page essay at the end of the partnership to document the assignment. This is a major part of his course and is weighted at 200 points. On the next page is a box containing a completed rubric, with a sample set of points a student might earn on the assignment.

EXAMINATIONS

Test Construction

Examinations are a typical component of most courses and they serve to evaluate each student's performance at given points in the semester. They are only one type of measurement of a student's overall learning. New teachers, graduate assistants, or teachers participating in a standardized course created by the department may use tests provided by senior teachers, a departmental test bank, or the instructor's manual that accompanies a textbook. If you are not subject to a testing policy or use of particular standardized tests, then you probably create your own. Test construction, like the creation of learning objectives, is a highly technical process and one that most people cannot do well without some kind of instruction. Because constructing and testing an exam for reliability and validity are difficult, it is not recommended that you constantly create new exams. Having a template with interchangeable items that can be switched out or added works well. I also use all types of test questions, from true/false to essays, because the entry-level course typically has younger students who are making the transition from straight objective type questions such as multiple choice to the more interpretive type questions such as essays.

CST 207 POULOS   NAME _____

EVALUATION RUBRIC: Partnership Evaluation Exercise

Scoring:

10 — **Excellent:** Surpasses criteria in terms of complexity and depth—e.g., several examples, thorough consideration, ingenuity. Demonstrates the writer's ability to produce and synthesize complex ideas.

9 — **Very good:** Surpasses criteria in one or more areas in regard to complexity and depth. Demonstrates the writer's ability to produce and synthesize complex ideas, draw on evidence from texts, films, lectures, and discussions. Evidence of minor weaknesses.

8 — **Good:** Meets the listed criteria, offering minimal examples and sufficient evidence of analysis. Demonstrates evidence of the writer's ability to support key ideas, but does not show the highest level of synthesis and complexity.

7 — **Average:** Shows superficial execution of listed criteria. Demonstrates that the writer possesses average ability to support ideas, synthesize information, or analyze issues thoroughly.

6 — **Poor/lowest passing grade:** Does not sufficiently meet listed criteria. Shows several errors in reasoning, little development of ideas, few examples or details, and little evidence.

5 — **Unacceptable/failure:** Fails to meet listed criteria. Shows serious errors in reasoning, little or no development of ideas, and/or few or no details and evidence.

Criteria:

9   *Completeness:* The author offers a direct, specific, detailed, and complete answer to the question or assignment. The author thoroughly explores the theory/concept/theme being examined.

8   *Clarity/Coherence:* The author offers a clear, readable, and compelling presentation of ideas/insights in response to the question or assignment. The various parts of the paper "stick together"—i.e., the paper is marked by an orderly or logical relation of parts that affords comprehension or recognition.

7.5 *Support:* The author supports his/her story/argument with clear examples from everyday communicative life, practical knowledge, class discussions, etc., and provides textual support from course texts, films, class lectures, etc.

9   *Application:* The author carefully explores and explains how the theory/concept/theme under examination applies to his/her and others' communicative lives.

8   *Professional Presentation:* The author writes a polished paper with no grammatical, spelling, or typographical errors. Citations are made in appropriate style format (APA, MLA), and a reference list/bibliography is provided.

41.5 TOTAL POINTS ÷ 5 (CATEGORIES) = 8.3 (AVG) = 166/200 POINTS = B-LETTER GRADE

I am helping students go from comprehension to synthesizing and evaluating in their critical thinking skills, and the exams reflect this progression. Also, different types of questions work efficiently to measure different types of knowledge—for example, matching questions for vocabulary terms and multiple choice for application of concepts.

It takes a while to fine tune quizzes and exams, so I could not possibly teach test construction skills here. I will offer two pieces of advice: first, a test should have integral links to course learning objectives, the knowledge set under study, and the appropriate levels of Bloom's Taxonomy (Bloom, 1956; Krathwohl, 2002; see discussion in Chapter 2). If those three items are not aligned, then there isn't much point in using an exam as part of the overall assessment of a student's learning. Second, if you cannot take a course in test construction (and I highly recommend it), then teach yourself the basic philosophy and mechanics by reading the sources in this chapter's reference list by L. B. Curzon (2004, chapters 29 & 30), Rebecca Rubin (1999), and Neil Salkind (2006). These three sources provide explanations of basic terminology; how to consider reliability and validity; how to write test items of all types, including true/false, multiple-choice, matching, short-answer, and essays; how to format; tips on grading; and the pros and cons of the many decisions you need to make when constructing an exam that is right for your course. I suggest buying the textbook used in the test construction course taught in your teacher education program and perhaps even asking the professor of that course for some advice. A text that has helped me is *Measurement and Evaluation in Teaching* (Gronlund & Linn, 1990). Such a text will take you through the entire process of linking your learning objectives to the test you are constructing to long-term appraisal of your test.

Preparing Students

Students should begin their own preparation for quizzes and tests by knowing from the first day of class exam policies and dates for testing, as published on the syllabus. I remind students of the big concepts to expect on a test ("You will need to synthesize your own view of the transactional philosophy and be able to articulate that on the first quiz.") so they are not surprised. Several days before the exam I conduct an in-class review in which I list on the board the types of questions (T/F, matching, etc.) and the point values for each of the question types. I give examples of sample questions that might be in each section of the test. I put Bloom's Taxonomy on the board and show what types of cognitive skill go with different sections of the test. For example, because of the sheer volume of vocabulary, I include a matching section of vocabulary terms and definitions. Students know that we are into knowledge and comprehension levels of ability there. Multiple-choice questions test a student's ability to comprehend and apply concepts. By the time we reach the essay portion of the exam, they see that they need to be prepared to analyze, synthesize, and evaluate theories such as social exchange, uncertainty reduction, and attribution in interpersonal situations. We then talk about how to study for different types of test questions. I also show students how to use the syllabus as a template for content and progression of thought about concepts as they study. We look at the end-of-chapter reviews in the textbook for a quick overview of the reading. I ask if there are concepts that need clarifying or holes in their notes that need filling. I remind students to bring their Scantron forms and No. 2 pencils, along with a pen if they prefer that for the essays. I tell them of my availability through office hours or email for last-minute questions. I then ask each student to pair up with their study-buddy, if they have one, and make sure they have their contact information and study plans in order before leaving the class.

Test Administration

The basic protocol for administering tests is designed to provide an atmosphere conducive to test taking and to minimize cheating. Students do cheat when given the opportunity. I found this out the first year I taught, and research over the years consistently supports that finding—and that students cheat a lot. My favorite discovery in the past couple of years is the way students store vocabulary and information in their cell phones and then attempt to access that with their cell phones in their laps during tests. In a class with a large enrollment, the task of monitoring cheating is the number one concern. Below, Kelly Morrison of Michigan State University talks about cheating in her team-taught course, which enrolls just over 650 students, with only one teaching assistant assigned to the team.

FROM THE CLASSROOM: Cheating in the Large Enrollment Course

I think the biggest logistical challenge is actually conducting the exams in the allotted amount of time with the allotted amount of space with very few proctors. Cheating is typically occurring and we catch what we can, but I know we are missing a lot. It would be nice to be able to break into smaller sections, but we don't have the resources/proctors to do it. One of the strategies we use for dealing with cheating (people who are looking at other people's exams) is that we announce we will move you if you are looking at someone else's test, or if we think someone is looking at your test—this way it is less face threatening in a large group. We also now don't let students leave the room once they have a test (before I started doing this I had students go into the bathrooms with their cell phones).

Kelly Morrison
Michigan State University

SOURCE: Personal correspondence with author, June 6, 2006.

To reduce cheating during exams:

- Seat students one seat apart in a row and make students move desks to increase space.
- Ask students to put all personal belongings under their desks, with only their writing instruments and Scantron/computer forms on the desktop.
- Ask students to put cell phones on a table in the front of the classroom and provide sticky notes for the students to label their phones with their names.
- Provide the paper for the exam so students do not need to have extra paper on their desks. (Both blue books and laptop computers can come pre-loaded with information.)
- Walk around the room during the exam and walk very close to any student you suspect is cheating. If the room is too small for movement, scan it with your eyes and smile if you make eye contact with a student.
- Do not leave the room; it is recommended that students not be allowed to leave during the exam either. If you do allow students to leave the room, then let only one student at a time go to the restroom.
- Do not get caught up in conversation with students turning in exams. Maintain quiet and order for those still writing.
- If students reveal cheating by other students or you catch students cheating, follow the policies on your syllabus to take action.
- Don't let students keep exams. After going over the exam results, students should turn exams back in; be sure that all exams are returned.

If you administer exams through the computer, ask your campus testing center how to put safeguards in place. The university should have procedures in place if students go to a center to take exams.

Other procedural items include giving time checks and bringing extra pencils and Scantron/computer forms to class. Give instructions if necessary and be available to clarify any questions a student may have (some still don't read the printed directions on an exam and then ask questions about what to mark on the Scantron form versus the test paper itself). If you have a blind student, a student with a hand in a cast, a student who needs extra time because of a learning disability or English as a second language, or any other logistical issue, make arrangements to proctor that exam elsewhere and agree in advance to a plan with the student. Are you feeling anxious and paranoid as you read all of this protocol? Don't be. Go into the room early on test days, be organized, be friendly and calm in attitude, and be helpful to students. All of this relieves stress for everyone. I tell my students that exams should actually be great days because it is their opportunity to shine and "show me their stuff." They usually laugh, but I do think being positive about taking exams is a good approach.

Grading Tests and Debriefing Students

Follow the tips described earlier in the chapter to be consistent, efficient, and fair when grading an examination. Prepare scoring keys before you start grading, and make notes on the way students interpret short-answer and essay questions. If you locate errors, go back and correct every test item just to be fair. Double check the computer for scoring errors. Score all parts of the exam in sections. Add numbers and arrive at a grade when you are fresh and thinking clearly. If you are constructing a new exam or trying out new items, conduct an item analysis. Computer-scored exams can sometimes provide item analyses, but if you need to do it yourself, you might consult a source like Neil Salkind (2006), who provides formulas for computing difficulty indices, discrimination indices, and reliability and validity checks.

I spend time handing back exams (during the last 20 to 30 minutes of the next class period) and going over everything. Class performance information is put on the test analysis form I give back so students can see how they performed as both individuals and as a class. In spite of criterion-referenced grading, students engage in a lot of social comparison and want to know where they stand in relation to their peers. I tell students that I blind grade. I also say that I will not argue questions or grades from individual students in front of the whole class. Any student with a grade dispute should come to my office for private consultation. This debrief includes providing correct answers, letting students know which items the class had difficulty with, and why a given correct answer is what it is. Note privately those items for information on what to reteach if students appear not to have met your learning goals. For short essays, I always praise four to five people who met the criteria by saying something like, "John, Megan, Keshia, Joel, and Hollie did a great job on this essay. Megan, why don't you read your answer to us so we can hear what the question was looking for in a good response?" In this way, students hear their classmates meeting the expectations of the exam question and can rethink their own strategies for the next exam.

Because I collect the exams after the debrief, I give each student a test analysis form to fill out and keep in their notebook. Students are also invited to come to my office at any time and visit their exams on file. If a student clearly indicates poor test-taking skills, I put a note on his or her exam inviting an office visit to strategize. We then go over missed items and talk about different ways to think in the privacy of a tutorial session. If a student flat out fails an exam (sometimes I know why and sometimes I don't), I will put a personal note to this effect: "I know this isn't your best work. Come see me and we will strategize." Or, if there were challenging circumstances outside the classroom, I might write, "I know you've had a tough time lately. You will do better next time. Come see me if you need help." In each case, there is an acknowledgment of a problem, a show of empathy, and an invitation to help the student improve. Finally, I ask the student to set a goal if he or she wants to make a different grade on the next exam and to record what to work on in preparation for the next exam. A sample of an analysis form the student keeps is shown below, with actual information from a test given in class.

CST 207 EXAM 1 ANALYSIS

Name: _____   **Class Performance:**

                                         n=33
Grade: T/F & Mult. Choice ____ out of 45   Range = 36–94
        Matching   ____ out of 20   Average = 78 Median = 80
        Essay   ____ out of 35   Grade cutoff: 90–100 =A [5]*
                                                        80–89 =B [13]
                                                        70–79 =C [8]
Total   ____ out of 100   60–69 =D [5]
                                                        59–below=F [2]

* The number in brackets equals the number of people in our class who made this grade. You can see that the overall performance of the class was good and, in fact, a nice bell curve. These are good grades overall, and everyone is in good shape.

Tips for the entire class: Most of the problems were on the essays and vocabulary. On the essays, read the question carefully and provide a relevant answer. Rather than telling me everything you know about a topic, answer with the essential information. Draw conclusions and answer all parts of the question. Take time to write coherent sentences that are grammatically correct. This class has a good imagination, so combine your creative examples with solid theory and you'll do great on the next exam. See Dr. Natalle if you need help, want something clarified, or just plain need to talk about your test performance if it was not your usual grade.

What areas or test strategies are you going to work on to improve your score on the next exam?

ASSESSMENT

Program Assessment

In Chapter 2 I spent time discussing assessment as a nationwide phenomenon. In some ways the assessment movement is modeled after the way high schools are mandated to test for student learning. In higher education the pressure is on from state legislators to assess whether students are learning what we say we are teaching them. In a communication studies program, the interpersonal communication course *may* play a role in a department's systematic assessment program. I say *may* because introductory courses are not necessarily sites for measuring student learning. Senior-level and capstone courses are more likely a part of assessment, but if you only have one interpersonal communication course, you may be required to participate.

My point in the earlier discussion was to show how course learning objectives relate to assessment learning outcomes. I want to extend that discussion just a bit in this chapter, but before you read further, you might want to revisit the pages on assessment in Chapter 2 (pp. 36–37). Then review the NCA Web site's assessment resources to familiarize yourself with their perspective, at www .natcom.org. The NCA site is very informative and provides a thorough crash course in a short period of time. I highly recommend that you spend the time to gain both knowledge and context on the topic. Finally, if you want to gain some historical grounding for the way the communication discipline responded to the assessment movement, read Bill Christ's edited anthology, *Assessing Communication Education* (1994). This was the first comprehensive resource guide produced in this discipline and it covers all the important topics.

The NCA has a list of suggested interpersonal communication competencies that majors should be proficient in if they expect to function effectively beyond college. I have reprinted both sets of the basic interpersonal competencies (Tables 2 and 3) from the NCA Web site. Basic skills from Table 2 would be a mark of general education achievement in speaking and listening in interpersonal contexts. Basic skills from Table 3 are those that we would expect college graduates to use as part of their professional communication and in their citizenship. These skills may be included in both entry-level and advanced-level interpersonal communication courses. You may want to think about the competencies from three perspectives: what you need to assess as

Essential Interpersonal Skills from Table 2 of the NCA Competencies for College Students (Jones, 1994)

III. INTERPERSONAL AND GROUP COMMUNICATION SKILLS

A. SITUATION ANALYSIS
1. Recognize when another does not understand their message.
2. Identify and manage misunderstandings.
3. Recognize when it is inappropriate to speak.

B. RELATIONSHIP MANAGEMENT
1. Manage conflict.
2. Allow others to express different views.
3. Effectively assert themselves.

C. INFORMATION EXCHANGE
1. Listen attentively to questions and comments from other communicators.
2. Ask questions effectively.
3. Answer questions concisely and to the point or issue.
4. Give concise and accurate directions.

D. CONVERSATION MANAGEMENT
1. Be open-minded about another's point of view.
2. Convey enthusiasm for topic through delivery.

Basic Skills from Table 3 of the NCA Competencies for College Graduates
(Rubin, 1995; Rubin & Morreale, 1996)

IV. RELATING SKILLS

A. **Students can (a) develop, maintain, and nurture interpersonal and small group relationships with others; (b) fulfill their own interpersonal needs; and (c) manage conflict while respecting all interactants' rights.**

B. **Students can respond to others' attempts to build relationships and reciprocate by self-disclosing, focusing on the other, empathizing, and displaying affinity.**

C. **Specifically, students can:**
1. achieve interpersonal goals (giving/seeking inclusion, affection, and control).
2. identify conflict situations.
3. respect others' rights and stand up for one's own rights.
4. feel and convey empathy to others.
5. build relationships with others.
6. describe others' viewpoints.
7. describe differences in opinion.
8. express their feelings to others when appropriate.
9. perform social rituals (introductions, telephone answering, greetings, farewells).
10. maintain conversations by taking turns, managing the interaction, reciprocal conversation, self-disclosure, and altercentrism.
11. receive affinity (e.g., compliments) from others.
12. work on collaborative projects in teams.
13. keep group discussions relevant and focused.

---

part of your communication program; whether your learning objectives for your course dovetail with the standards of expectation developed by our professional organization, and which assignments in your course may serve both as evaluation measures of student progress and as vehicles for assessing student accomplishment of program learning outcomes. Very often, administrators appreciate that course instructors are taking into consideration a discipline-specific set of skills endorsed by the profession.

In sum, program assessment may play a role in how you set up learning objectives and choose evaluation measures for your interpersonal communication course. It's a good idea to consult with your department head and university or college assessment office to ensure that you comply with the institution's assessment plan. Guidance from the National Communication Association can help you match your school's learning outcomes with professional expectations developed by the discipline and as outlined in the tables above.

Teacher Assessment

We are a performance-behavioral-oriented discipline, and as professional communicators, we are expected to model what we teach. However, performance without content is not good teaching, and we do need to assess ourselves as teachers. Typically we are assessed by means of student evaluations, peer evaluations of teaching, formal mentoring, self-assessment, and alumni evaluations. Each type of evaluation may be used or weighted differently in your overall performance evaluation.

I think our discipline has done a good job of addressing this issue and our literature reflects a range of good sources, from Katherine Hendrix's (2000) mention in her teaching assistant training guide to Anita Vangelisti's (1999) comprehensive chapter on assessing teaching process. Pamela Cooper and Cheri Simonds are now on the seventh edition of their book, *Communication for the Classroom Teacher* (2003), an excellent source for motivating new teachers to practice the kind of interpersonal skills that lead to positive teacher evaluations. *Communication Education* has also published consistently on the implications of teacher behavior on student evaluations of teacher performance, including teacher immediacy (Moore, Masterson, Christophel, & Shea, 1996), teacher caring (Teven & McCroskey, 1997), teachers' aggressive communication (Schrodt, 2003), and halo effects of teacher behavior (Feeley, 2002). Communication research reveals that competent relating produces high teaching evaluations, yet it takes hard work to get to the point where you are not either worrying over your own performance evaluations or teaching to the items on the teaching evaluation forms. To that end, I like the advice that Kalamazoo Valley Community College professor Marion Boyer gives to new teachers of interpersonal communication:

> *Be* the interpersonal communicator the textbooks describe. Every movement, gesture, expression, sentence, glance of yours should model what is best practice in interpersonal communication. You're their human textbook. Then, be aware that you, too, have much to learn. Interpersonal communication is a process, and we're all evolving. Let the students know you're willing and eager to evolve right along with them. (Personal correspondence with author, April 26, 2006)

This is healthy advice that should help you grow and earn high evaluations for good teaching.

SUMMARY

This chapter examined the topics of student evaluation measures such as assignments and examinations, grading, and program and teacher assessment. Much of the preparation needed for success is technical in nature, such as learning to conduct reliability checks on your own exams, so we could only take a surface look at best practices. We also considered the challenges of the evaluation and assessment process. We will now turn to Part II for a look at readings and resources.

II

Resources and Readings

6

Theoretical Foundations and Readings

Every teacher of interpersonal communication should walk into the classroom with some knowledge of the field. Ideally, that instructor will have used that knowledge to formulate a mental map that synthesizes theory and practice and that serves as a guide to his or her approach to teaching the course. In general, every interpersonal communication course needs to be grounded in an instructor's knowledge of the theory of the discipline, not the details of the textbook in use. In this chapter we will explore the larger, more philosophical issues of teaching through the lens of theory. We will also discuss mind mapping and model building, as well as read excerpts from readings that ground my own thinking and teaching.

Too often, the novice interpersonal communication instructor will be handed a textbook with the following directive: "Teach interpersonal communication next semester." Because many texts use a skills-based approach, the new teacher may mistakenly assume that delivering instruction is only a matter of devising class exercises to implement interpersonal skills. The text is considered the extent of knowledge required, and as long as the instructor is one step ahead of the student in the reading, everything will be fine. Nothing could be further from the truth. The well-prepared instructor is the one who enters the classroom having read the most current theory on interpersonal communication. Each time a student asks a question, or a point of discussion arises from the textbook, the well-read instructor will be able to respond with a depth of knowledge that results in a richer intellectual experience. Overall, an instructor who can balance communication theory and skills will be able to facilitate the student's ability to think about and take action in interpersonal relationships.

In this chapter you will find a brief history on the theory of interpersonal communication, followed by five abridged readings that show how theory links to the design of an interpersonal communication course. Although the readings and ideas presented here reflect my course and syllabus, know that when mapping your own course, you can take it in any of several directions.

A BRIEF HISTORY OF INTERPERSONAL COMMUNICATION THEORY

One of the reasons you have so many choices in how to create a personal map of the field is because the history of interpersonal communication theory is so diffuse. Prior to the 1960s, we didn't have many communication departments because our study of communication was split between mass media studies and rhetorical studies, both of which were housed in established departments such as journalism and English. Although interest in interpersonal communication is clearly evident in other disciplines before the 1960s—for example, through the work of scholars such as sociologist Erving Goffman, nothing really coalesced until the humanist movement of the 1960s. Social movements of the period (e.g., the anti-war and women's movements) and social practices (e.g., the "free love" associated with communes, hippies, and Woodstock) produced communication structures such as encounter groups and the slogan "Let it all hang out!" that led to the general idea that the more we self-disclosed the healthier our relationships would be. Even John Lennon and Yoko Ono were known to be practicing primal screams as a way to let out emotion and learn to relate to each other. Much of the social action in the United States influenced early courses in interpersonal communication from the late 1960s through the mid-1970s, where exercises in trust and disclosure garnered the reputation for communication as a "touchy-feely" discipline. I know this because I lived through this time period as a college student and have grown up with the development of the field. I participated in encounter groups and fell back into the arms of a classmate with my eyes closed as I learned to trust others. These were not my favorite activities, but they were certainly a reflection of the times.

Humanistic approaches to studying and theorizing about interpersonal communication have benefitted from philosopher-scholars such as Martin Buber (1970), psychotherapists such as Virginia Satir (1972), Carl Rogers (1961), and R. D. Laing (1969), and popular writers such as Leo Buscaglia (1982) and Robert Fulghum (1989). Note that this historical path evolved simultaneously from several sites: popular culture, social movements, philosophy, theology, therapeutic counseling, and group dynamics. Today the humanistic approach has given way to a more phenomenologically based, interpretive approach. That is to say, narratives of personal experience are often the starting point for interpreting interpersonal communication process.

As the humanistic movement influenced our thinking, so too did social scientists from various disciplines contribute to our expanding knowledge of interpersonal communication. Anthropology, sociology, and social psychology all influenced the communication field. Certainly, experimental social psychology has been the dominant scientific influence. Doctoral degrees in communication were first awarded in the 1960s, but by the 1970s and solidly in the 1980s, scholars were developing their own theories in, for example, social cognition (Uncertainty Reduction Theory) and nonverbal communication (Expectancy Violations); interpersonal communication became the focus of much of their teaching and research. Most of the theories on relationship, cognition, process, communicator characteristics (personality), emotion, language, and interpersonal influence come from hypothesis testing. If you examine the annotated bibliography in Chapter 7, you will see that the balance tips toward social science. This is the research that dominates our textbooks. For more in-depth treatment and a more social-scientific perspective of the history and themes in the development of interpersonal communication theory, I recommend the first chapter in the *Handbook of Interpersonal Communication* (Knapp & Daly, 2002).

Another influence on the development of interpersonal communication theory is interpretation. Interpretation bases its approach on the general notion that human beings communicate within realities they create for themselves. The significance of self-identity and life in general arises from the dyadic relationships in which we engage. An interpretivist studies conversation, the stories from the life experiences of relational partners, and the general patterns of social interaction that are attached to the roles we perform. Generally, interpretive theory lets us tease out how communication helps us to construct interpersonal realities and what the communication process contributes to relational meaning. In some ways interpretive theory has taken precedence over humanistic theory because interpretivists also study dialogue, self-actualization, and other humanistic concerns. And although the theory is considered newer than humanism and science, you can certainly detect in it strong roots in sociology—from George Herbert Mead's theory of symbolic interaction developed in *Mind, Self and Society* (1934) to Erving Goffman's work in self presentation (1959) to Peter Berger and Thomas Luckmann's *The Social Construction of Reality* (1966). If you want to read in greater depth on the history of interpretive theory in the context of interpersonal communication, consider the first two chapters in Wendy Leeds-Hurwitz's *Social Approaches to Communication* (1995).

Now let us turn from this historical overview of interpersonal communication theory to a discussion of how the theory is generally organized. Both history and issues of theory construction are intertwined; looking at interpersonal communication theory from both perspectives will help you crystallize your own point of view of the field and, subsequently, the decisions you make as an interpersonal communication instructor.

BASIC FOUNDATIONS IN INTERPERSONAL COMMUNICATION THEORY

Theory Is Organized Systematically

Although some theorists disagree, the field of communication is organized according to paradigms for inquiry into communication processes that include both practical (appropriate problems, methods, evidence, goals) and philosophical components (epistemology, ontology, axiology). I teach three major paradigms: social scientific, rhetorical, and interpretive. Some theorists (Farrell, 1987) prefer a broader organization of two paradigms: social scientific and humanistic. Others (Craig, 1999; Cushman & Kovacic, 1995) see conceptual approaches, or traditions, rather than strict paradigms. Craig's (1999) seven traditions include rhetorical, semiotic, phenomenological, cybernetic, sociopsychological, sociocultural, and critical. Yet others (Miller, 2002) use the term *perspective* rather than *paradigm* and then group theories by process and context. A recent treatment of communication as perspective (Shepherd, St. John, & Striphas, 2006) challenges the reader to look at 27 different perspectives (e.g., relational, constructive, raced, autoethnographic) to figure out where his or her thinking lies regarding communication process. No matter how you see the communication field organized, all types of organizational typologies group categories of theories in order to better understand the big picture.

The historical development of the field and the components of paradigms are linked. Interpersonal communication processes have historically been researched and theorized through the social science paradigm using both quantitative and qualitative methods of study. In the past decade, interpretive approaches (Carter & Presnell, 1994) have been integrated into our understanding through work in stories (Bochner, 1994) and performance (Taylor, 2000). Our knowledge of the interpersonal process also comes from psychiatry/clinical psychology, sociology, anthropology, social and cognitive psychology, and communication, thus securing interpersonal communication as an interdisciplinary field. As a teacher, then, always try to see where ideas are coming from in order to understand the logic and point of view of the author's work you are using. The more you understand the origin and intersection of ideas in the field, the better you will be at delivering those ideas to your own students.

Teaching Needs a Range of Theory

It is important to understand that interpersonal communication knowledge comprises a range of theory. In our teaching, we may have preferences for certain approaches or paradigms, but we also need to acknowledge the array of theories available. Then, as communication theorists John Nicholson and Steve Duck (1999) advise, "have a vision of the destination for the course or a plan for the blind date" (p. 87). But, how do you achieve that vision or make a plan to get through the blind date known as teaching? I think you have to start with a lot of background reading and a basic understanding of how interpersonal communication theory works. In reading theory over a long period of time, I have observed the following characteristics about the field:

1. Interpersonal communication theories build off and intersect with other communication theories.
2. Interpersonal communication theory construction is embedded in pivotal historic works that have had surprisingly lasting influence.
3. Messages, communicators, behaviors, and the interpretation of meaning within the context of the dyad continue to be key foci of interpersonal communication theory.
4. Interpersonal communication benefits from both scientific and humanistic/interpretive modes of theorizing.

If you keep these observations in mind, you will be in a better position to make decisions about what you think belongs in an undergraduate introductory interpersonal communication course. It would be a wise exercise to match your behavioral objectives or learning outcomes for your course with the readings that best help you accomplish those objectives or outcomes.

Theory Informs Course Content and Structure

In Chapter 2 we studied the construction of a syllabus. Look now at my syllabus (pp. 26–33), keeping in mind our discussion of theory. Notice that the course is more heavily based on social science theory, where students are taught normative patterns of behavior from scientific testing of variables related to interpersonal communication. This is especially true of the material in Unit II, on relationship cycles, Unit III, on competence, and Unit IV, on dyadic context and competence. Why is social science such a successful way to study and theorize interpersonal communication? I have come to understand several answers to this question over the years.

First, we tend to socialize ourselves into roles (e.g., Goffman, 1959) and appropriate behaviors as we organize and maintain society. This social construction (Berger & Luckmann, 1966) process means that normative patterns of behavior will keep us stable, maintain cohesion, and allow society to be ongoing. Further, social cognition theories (Canary, Cody, & Manusov, 2003; Roloff & Berger, 1982) explain how dyadic partners use rational thinking processes in their attempts to understand behavior and make good decisions when interacting with others. Social science helps to account for patterns and, in a way, suggests what we should be doing in dyads to stay competent.

Second, most people want both to enjoy healthy relationships and to feel "normal." People are interested in finding out if their friendships, family relationships, and work relationships are pretty much like everyone else's. This "social comparison" approach is the notion that normative patterns allow us to explain, predict, and control ourselves as we achieve functional and emotional goals through participation in dyads. Science helps us discover those patterns. This is why theories such as social exchange, uncertainty reduction, expectancy violations, social penetration, attraction, and conflict negotiation are so useful to students.

However, for all the value of science, humans are emotional and spiritual animals who need to account for more primal means of connecting. We also engage in a search for the meaning of self and life. In Unit I of my course we set up the notion of a philosophy of relationships. I argue to students that we cannot be competent in our dyads until we take a point of view toward relationships in general. Although I loosely term this philosophy "transactional," I draw from a range of humanistic literature when talking about notions of confirming our humanity (Buber, 1970) and disclosing the self (Jourard, 1971). Let me also note that authors such as Sidney Jourard (1971), Carl Rogers (1961), and Virginia Satir (1972) were trained in psychiatry or clinical psychology, but the books they wrote for public consumption are highly compassionate, humanistic considerations of interpersonal relating and communicating. We can say the same thing for interpretive researchers in communication such as Arthur Bochner (1994) and William Rawlins (1992).

FIVE ESSENTIAL READINGS

In the section that follows, I provide you with five essential readings that undergird my own course. Watzlawick, Bavelas, and Jackson (1967) and Buber (1970) are the foundation for the first part of my course, where the self is explored and the transactional philosophy is set up. Knapp and Vangelisti

(1992) provide the framework for the second unit, on the relationship cycle. Wiemann (1977) was my original reading for the second half of the course on competence, and Baxter and Montgomery (2000) represent ways to reconsider both the linear nature of the relationship cycle and the skills-only notion of competence. These five articles are rooted in psychiatry, theology, and communication. Within communication we can see a quantitative social science method (Knapp & Vangelisti, 1992; Wiemann, 1977) and an interdisciplinary method that looks at philosophy, interpretation, and qualitative social science (Baxter & Montgomery, 2000). Indeed, I can see all four characteristics of interpersonal communication theory stated above, and I feel pedagogically solid about the range of theory that serves as the basis for my course.

Please note that I introduce each reading with a brief headnote to provide some historical context about the importance of the piece and a note on how I use the reading in my course.

Paul Watzlawick, Janet Beavin Bavelas, and Don D. Jackson

Some Tentative Axioms of Communication

No other book has had more influence on the teaching of interpersonal communication than The Pragmatics of Human Communication *(1967), and the "axioms" appear consistently in both theoretical essays and textbooks. Psychiatrists Paul Watzlawick, Janet Bavelas, and Don Jackson formed a research team at Stanford University (and became known as the Palo Alto Group) to observe the relational dynamics of patients undergoing counseling at the medical center. Their observations and analysis still provoke discussion today. Following in the footsteps of Jurgen Ruesch and Gregory Bateson (1951), the authors used a systems approach to develop a pragmatic or behavioristic view to understand dysfunctional interpersonal communication within family contexts. Using observations from therapeutic intervention in unhealthy dyads, the team then offered principles to characterize healthy communication. In spite of this controversial approach, it is important to see the principles or axioms as the structural components of a worldview on interpersonal communication as a systemic process.*

The five axioms described in the following reading comprise the heart of Chapter 2 in the book and are claimed to be the "properties of communication." In my teaching, I refer to the axioms throughout the course as basic truisms of everyday relationships. This essential reading by Watzlawick, Bavelas, and Jackson provides us with the theoretical ideas that underpin the basic concepts of what we talk about in interpersonal communication courses: communication codes, relational structure, intention, message types, interaction sequences, and basic functions that communication serves in a dyad. In some ways they provide a kind of macro-structure to our thinking about all types of interpersonal relationships, and students internalize the axioms as part of their core knowledge.

2.1 INTRODUCTION

The conclusions reached in the first chapter generally emphasized the inapplicability of many traditional psychiatric notions to our proposed framework and so may seem to leave very little on which the study of the pragmatics of human communication could be based. We want to show next that this is not so. However, to do this, we have to start with some simple properties of communication that have fundamental interpersonal implications. It will be seen that these properties are in the nature of axioms within our hypothetical calculus of human communication. When these have been defined we will be in a position to consider some of their possible pathologies in Chapter 3.

2.2 THE IMPOSSIBILITY OF NOT COMMUNICATING

2.21

First of all, there is a property of behavior that could hardly be more basic and is, therefore, often overlooked: behavior has no opposite. In other words, there is no such thing as nonbehavior or, to put it even more simply: one cannot *not* behave. Now, if it is accepted that all behavior in an interactional situation has message value, i.e., is communication, it follows that no matter how one may try, one cannot *not* communicate. Activity or inactivity, words or silence all have message value: they influence others and these others, in turn, cannot *not* respond to these communications and are thus themselves communicating. It should be clearly understood that the mere absence of talking or of taking notice of each other is no exception to what has just been asserted. The man at a crowded lunch counter who looks straight ahead, or the airplane passenger who sits with his eyes closed, are both communicating that they do not want to speak to anybody or be spoken to, and their neighbors usually "get the message" and respond appropriately by leaving them alone. This, obviously, is just as much an interchange of communication as an animated discussion.

Neither can we say that "communication" only takes place when it is intentional, conscious, or successful, that is, when mutual understanding occurs. Whether message sent equals message received is an important but different order of analysis, as it must rest ultimately on evaluations of specific, introspective, subject-reported data, which we choose to neglect for the exposition of a behavioral-theory of communication. On the question of misunderstanding, our concern, given certain formal properties of communication, is with the development of related pathologies, aside from, indeed in spite of, the motivations or intentions of the communicants....

2.23

The impossibility of not communicating is a phenomenon of more than theoretical interest. It is, for instance, part and parcel of the schizophrenic "dilemma." If schizophrenic behavior is observed with etiological considerations in abeyance, it appears that the schizophrenic tries *not to communicate*. But since even nonsense, silence, withdrawal, immobility (postural silence), or any other form of denial is itself a communication, the schizophrenic is faced with the impossible task of denying that he is communicating and at the same time denying that his denial is a communication. The realization of this basic dilemma in schizophrenia is a key to a good many aspects of schizophrenic communication that would otherwise remain obscure. Since any communication, as we shall see, implies commitment and thereby defines the sender's view of his relationship with the receiver, it can be hypothesized that the schizophrenic behaves as if he would avoid commitment by not communicating. Whether this is his purpose, in the causal sense, is of course impossible of proof; that this is the effect of schizophrenic behavior will be taken up in greater detail in s. 3.2.

2.24

To summarize, a metacommunicational axiom of the pragmatics of communication can be postulated: *one cannot* not *communicate.*

2.3 THE CONTENT AND RELATIONSHIP LEVELS
OF COMMUNICATION

2.31

Another axiom was hinted at in the foregoing when it was suggested that any communication implies a commitment and thereby defines the relationship. This is another way of saying that a communication not only conveys information, but that at the same time it imposes behavior. Following Bateson (*132*, pp. 179–81), these two operations have come to be known as the "report" and the "command" aspects, respectively, of any communication. Bateson exemplifies these two aspects by means of a physiological analogy: let *A, B,* and *C* be a linear chain of neurons. Then the firing of neuron *B* is both a "report" that neuron *A* has fired and a "command" for neuron *C* to fire.

The report aspect of a message conveys information and is, therefore, synonymous in human communication with the *content* of the message. It may be about anything that is communicable regardless of whether the particular information is true or false, valid, invalid, or undecidable. The command aspect, on the other hand, refers to what sort of a message it is to be taken as, and, therefore, ultimately to the *relationship* between the communicants. All such relationship statements are about one or several of the following assertions: "This is how I see myself…this is how I see you…this is how I see you seeing me…" and so forth in theoretically infinite regress. Thus, for instance, the messages "It is important to release the clutch gradually and smoothly" and "Just let the clutch go, it'll ruin the transmission in no time" have approximately the same information content (report aspect), but they obviously define very different relationships. To avoid any misunderstanding about the foregoing, we want to make it clear that relationships are only rarely defined deliberately or with full awareness. In fact, it seems that the more spontaneous and "healthy" a relationship, the more the relationship aspect of communication recedes into the background. Conversely, "sick" relationships are characterized by a constant struggle about the nature of the relationship, with the content aspect of communication becoming less and less important.…

2.33

…The reader will have noticed that the relationship aspect of a communication, being a communication about a communication, is, of course, identical with the concept of metacommunication elaborated in the first chapter, where it was limited to the conceptual framework and to the language the communication analyst must employ when communicating about communication. Now it can be seen that not only he but everyone is faced with this problem. The ability to meta-communicate appropriately is not only the *conditio sine qua non* of successful communication, but is intimately linked with the enormous problem of awareness of self and others. This point will be explained in greater detail in s. 3.3. For the moment, and by way of illustration, we merely want to show that messages can be constructed, especially in written communication, which offer highly ambiguous metacommunicational clues. As Cherry *(34,* p. 120) points out, the sentence "Do you think that one will do?" can have a variety of meanings, according to which word is to be stressed—an indication that written language usually does not supply. Another example would be a sign in a restaurant reading "Customers who think our waiters are rude should see the manager," which, at least in theory, can be understood in two entirely different ways. Ambiguities of this kind are not the only possible complications arising out of the level structure of all communication; consider, for instance, a notice that reads "Disregard This Sign." As we shall see in the chapter on paradoxical communication, confusions or contaminations between these levels—communication and metacommunication—may lead to impasses identical in structure to those of the famous paradoxes in logic.

2.34

For the time being let us merely summarize the foregoing into another axiom of our tentative calculus: *Every communication has a content and a relationship aspect such that the latter classifies the former and is therefore a metacommunication.*

2.4 THE PUNCTUATION OF THE SEQUENCE OF EVENTS

2.41

The next basic characteristic of communication we wish to explore regards interaction—exchanges of messages—between communicants. To an outside observer, *a series of communications can be viewed as an uninterrupted sequence of interchanges.* However, the participants in the interaction always introduce what, following Whorf *(165),* Bateson and Jackson have termed the "punctuation of the sequence of events." They state:

> The stimulus-response psychologist typically confines his attention to sequences of interchange so short that it is possible to label one item of input as "stimulus" and another item as "reinforcement" while labelling what the subject does between these two events as "response." Within the short sequence so excised, it is possible to talk about the "psychology" of the subject. In contrast, the sequences of interchange which we are here discussing are very much longer and therefore have the characteristic that every item in the sequence is simultaneously stimulus, response and reinforcement. A given item of A's behavior is a stimulus insofar as it is followed by an item contributed by B and that by another item contributed by A. But insofar as A's item is sandwiched between two items contributed by B, it is a response. Similarly A's item is a reinforcement insofar as it follows an item contributed by B. The ongoing interchanges, then, which we are

here discussing, constitute a chain of overlapping triadic links, each of which is comparable to a stimulus-response-reinforcement sequence. We can take any triad of our interchange and see it as a single trial in a stimulus-response learning experiment.

If we look at the conventional learning experiments from this point of view, we observe at once that repeated trials amount to a differentiation of relationship between the two organisms concerned—the experimenter and his subject. The sequence of trials is so punctuated that it is always the experimenter who seems to provide the "stimuli" and the "reinforcements," while the subject provides the "responses." These words are here deliberately put in quotation marks because the role definitions are in fact only created by the willingness of the organisms to accept the system of punctuation. The "reality" of the role definitions is only of the same order as the reality of a bat on a Rorschach card—a more or less over-determined creation of the perceptive process. The rat who said "I have got my experimenter trained. Each time I press the lever he gives me food" was declining to accept the punctuation of the sequence which the experimenter was seeking to impose.

It is still true, however, that in a long sequence of interchange, the organisms concerned—especially if these be people—will in fact punctuate the sequence so that it will appear that one or the other has initiative, dominance, dependency or the like. That is, they will set up between them patterns of interchange (about which they may or may not be in agreement) and these patterns will in fact be rules of contingency regarding the exchange of reinforcement. While rats are too nice to re-label, some psychiatric patients are not, and provide psychological trauma for the therapist! (*19,* pp. 273–74)

It is not the issue here whether punctuation of communicational sequence is, in general, good or bad, as it should be immediately obvious that punctuation *organizes* behavioral events and is therefore vital to ongoing interactions. Culturally, we share many conventions of punctuation which, while no more or less accurate than other views of the same events, serve to organize common and important interactional sequences. For example, we call a person in a group behaving in one way the "leader" and another the "follower," although on reflection it is difficult to say which comes first or where one would be without the other....

2.44

Thus we add a third metacommunicational axiom: *The nature of a relationship is contingent upon the punctuation of the communicational sequences between the communicants....*

2.5 DIGITAL AND ANALOGIC COMMUNICATION

2.52

In human communication, objects—in the widest sense—can be referred to in two entirely different ways. They can either be represented by a likeness, such as a drawing, or they can be referred to by a name. Thus, in the written sentence

"The cat has caught a mouse" the nouns could be replaced by pictures; if the sentence were spoken, the actual cat and the mouse could be pointed to. Needless to say, this would be an unusual way of communicating, and normally the written or spoken "name," that is, the word, is used. These two types of communication—the one by a self-explanatory likeness, the other by a word—are, of course, also equivalent to the concepts of the analogic and the digital respectively. Whenever a word is used to *name* something it is obvious that the relation between the name and the thing named is an arbitrarily established one. Words are arbitrary signs that are manipulated according to the logical syntax of language. There is no particular reason why the three letters "c-a-t" should denote a particular animal. In ultimate analysis it is only a semantic convention of the English language, and outside this convention there exists no other correlation between any word and the thing it stands for, with the possible but insignificant exception of onomatopoeic words. As Bateson and Jackson point out: "There is nothing particularly five-like in the number five; there is nothing particularly table-like in the word 'table' " (*19*, p. 271).

In analogic communication, on the other hand, there *is* something particularly "thing-like" in what is used to express the thing. Analogic communication can be more readily referred to the thing it stands for. The difference between these two modes of communication may become somewhat clearer if it is realized that no amount of listening to a foreign language on the radio, for example, will yield an understanding of the language, whereas some basic information can fairly easily be derived from watching sign language and from so-called intention movements, even when used by a person of a totally different culture. Analogic communication, we suggest, has its roots in far more archaic periods of evolution and is, therefore, of much more general validity than the relatively recent, and far more abstract, digital mode of verbal communication.

What then is analogic communication? The answer is relatively simple: it is virtually all nonverbal communication. This term however, is deceptive, because it is often restricted to body movement only, to the behavior known as kinesics. We hold that the term must comprise posture, gesture, facial expression, voice inflection, the sequence, rhythm, and cadence of the words themselves, and any other nonverbal manifestation of which the organism is capable, as well as the communicational clues unfailingly present in any *context* in which an interaction takes place.

2.53

Man is the only organism known to use both the analogic and the digital modes of communication. The significance of this is still very inadequately understood, but can hardly be overrated. On the one hand there can be no doubt that man communicates digitally. In fact, most, if not all, of his civilized achievements would be unthinkable without his having evolved digital language. This is particularly important for the sharing of information about *objects* and for the time-binding function of the transmission of knowledge. And yet there exists a vast area where we rely almost exclusively on analogic communication, often with very little change from the analogic inheritance handed down to us from our mammalian ancestors. This is the area of *relationship*. Based on Tinbergen (*153*) and Lorenz (*96*), as well as his own research, Bateson (*8*) has shown that vocalizations, intention movements, and mood signs of animals are analogic communications by which they define the nature of their relationships, rather than making denotative statements about objects. Thus, to take one of his examples, when I open the refrigerator and the cat comes, rubs against my legs, and mews, this does not mean "I want milk"—as a human being would express it—but invokes a specific relationship, "Be mother to me," because such behavior is only observed in kittens in relation to adult cats, and never between two grown-up animals. Conversely, pet lovers often are convinced that their animals "understand" their speech. What the animal does understand, needless to say, is certainly not the meaning of the words, but the wealth of analogic communication that goes with speech. Indeed, wherever relationship is the central issue of communication, we find that digital language is almost meaningless. This is not only the case between animals and between man and animal, but in many other contingencies in human life, e.g., courtship, love, succor, combat, and, of course, in all dealings with very young children or severely disturbed mental patients. Children, fools, and animals have always been credited with particular intuition regarding the sincerity or insincerity of human attitudes, for it is easy to profess something verbally, but difficult to carry a lie into the realm of the analogic.

In short, if we remember that every communication has a content and a relationship aspect, we can expect to find that the two modes of communication not only exist side by side but complement each other in every message. We can further expect to find that the content aspect is likely to be conveyed digitally whereas the relationship aspect will be predominantly analogic in nature....

2.55

To summarize: *Human beings communicate both digitally and analogically. Digital language has a highly complex and powerful logical syntax but lacks adequate semantics in the field of relationship, while analogic language possesses the semantics but has no adequate syntax for the unambiguous definition of the nature of relationships.*

2.6 SYMMETRICAL AND COMPLEMENTARY INTERACTION

2.62

...Symmetrical interaction, then, is characterized by equality and the minimization of difference, while complementary interaction is based on the maximization of difference.

There are two different positions in a complementary relationship. One partner occupies what has been variously described as the superior, primary, or "one-up" position, and the other the corresponding inferior, secondary, or "one-down" position. These terms are quite useful as long as they are not equated with "good" or "bad," "strong" or "weak." A complementary relationship may be set by the social or cultural context (as in the cases of mother and infant, doctor and patient, or teacher and student), or it may be the idiosyncratic relationship style of a particular dyad. In either case, it is important to emphasize the interlocking nature of the relationship, in which dissimilar but fitted behaviors evoke each other. One partner does not impose a complementary relationship on the other, but rather each behaves in a manner which presupposes, while at the same time providing reasons for, the behavior of the other: their definitions of the relationship (s. 2.3) fit.

2.63

A third type of relationship has been suggested—"metacomplementary," in which *A* lets or forces *B* to be in charge of him; by the same reasoning, we could also add "pseudosymmetry," in which *A* lets or forces *B* to be symmetrical. This potentially infinite regress can, however, be avoided by recalling the distinction made earlier (s. 1.4) between the observation of behavioral redundancies and their inferred explanations, in the form of mythologies; that is, we are interested in *how* the pair behave without being distracted by why (they believe) they so conduct themselves. If, though, the individuals involved avail themselves of the multiple levels of communication (s. 2.22) in order to express different patterns on different levels, paradoxical results of significant pragmatic importance may arise (s. 5.41; 6.42, ex. 3; 7.5, ex. 2d).

2.64

The potential pathologies (escalation in symmetry and rigidity in complementarity) of these modes of communication will be dealt with in the next chapter. For the present, we can state simply our last tentative axiom: *All communicational interchanges are either symmetrical or complementary, depending on whether they are based on equality or difference.*

2.7 SUMMARY

Regarding the above axioms in general, some qualifications should be re-emphasized. First, it should be clear that they are put forth tentatively, rather informally defined and certainly more preliminary than exhaustive. Second, they are, among themselves, quite heterogeneous in that they draw from widely ranging observations on communication phenomena. They are unified not by their origins but by their *pragmatic* importance, which in turn rests not so much on their particulars as on their *interpersonal* (rather than monadic) reference. Birdwhistell has even gone so far as to suggest that

> an individual does not communicate; he engages in or becomes part of communication. He may move, or make noises...but he does not communicate. In a par-

allel fashion, he may see, he may hear, smell, taste, or feel—but he does not communicate. In other words, he does not originate communication; he participates in it. Communication as a system, then, is not to be understood on a simple model of action and reaction, however complexly stated. As a system, it is to be comprehended on the transactional level. (*28*, p. 104)

Thus, the impossibility of not communicating makes all two-or-more-person situations *interpersonal*, communicative ones; the relationship aspect of such communication further specifies this same point. The pragmatic, interpersonal importance of the digital and analogic modes lies not only in its hypothesized isomorphism with content and relationship, but in the inevitable and significant ambiguity which both sender and receiver face in problems of translation from the one mode to the other. The description of problems of punctuation rests precisely on the underlying metamorphosis of the classic action-reaction model. Finally, the symmetry-complementarity paradigm comes perhaps closest to the mathematical concept of *function*, the individuals' positions merely being variables with an infinity of possible values whose meaning is not absolute but rather emerges only in relation to each other.

Martin Buber

First Part from *I and Thou*

*Theologian Martin Buber is the person the field looks to for spiritual and philo-
sophical wisdom about interpersonal communication. His work has enjoyed
many years of respect from a readership diverse in religious and spiritual
thought. In Buber's classic book* I and Thou *(1937/1970), the reader is
guided through the idea that people see themselves as an "I" and then relate to
others as either "it" or "you." When individuals use the "I–It" approach to
relationships, they are indicating they are not invested in each other. When they
use the "I–You" approach, they are indicating they value each other as human
beings.*

*The following excerpt introduces the idea of a relational world, but one that
has three spheres to balance: nature, human, and spirit. Buber's conceptualization of three spheres of activity demonstrate the human and spiritual intercon-
nectedness of people within nature; people thus fully realize "self" and "other" by
approaching a dyad with a sense of wholeness. This reading emphasizes the importance of relationships in that they provide confirmation for our value as human
beings; thus, I deem it essential to the way I approach my students and my course.*

*That I teach my class from a transactional perspective, where the emphasis
is on reciprocity and full participation, makes Buber's underlying philosophy of
wholeness obvious. Buber's ideas help me to teach the concept that we must be
whole people (physically, spiritually, emotionally, intellectually) as we interact
with others because this is how we actualize ourselves, or become mature, in
interpersonal relationships. Most importantly, we cannot fully realize ourselves
as human beings alone—we need the help of others. In reading other literature
about humanistic perspectives on relationships, such as symbolic interaction,
you will find that Buber's influence is undeniable; he is, therefore, a touchstone
in our field.*

The world is twofold for man in accordance with his twofold attitude.

The attitude of man is twofold in accordance with the two basic words he
can speak.

The basic words are not single words but word pairs.

One basic word is the word pair I-You.

The other basic word is the word pair I-It; but this basic word is not changed
when He or She takes the place of It.

Thus the I of man is also twofold.

For the I of the basic word I-You is different from that in the basic
word I-It.[1]

*

---

[1] In the first edition the next section began: "Basic words do not signify things but relations." This
sentence was omitted by Buber in 1957 and in all subsequent editions.

128

Basic words do not state something that might exist outside them; by being spoken they establish a mode of existence.[2]

Basic words are spoken with one's being.[3]

When one says You, the I of the word pair I-You is said, too.

When one says It, the I of the word pair I-It is said, too.

The basic word I-You can only be spoken with one's whole being.

The basic word I-It can never be spoken with one's whole being.

*

There is no I as such but only the I of the basic word I-You and the I of the basic word I-It.

When a man says I, he means one or the other. The I he means is present when he says I. And when he says You or It, the I of one or the other basic word is also present.

Being I and saying I are the same. Saying I and saying one of the two basic words are the same.

Whoever speaks one of the basic words enters into the word and stands in it.

*

The life of a human being does not exist merely in the sphere of goal-directed verbs. It does not consist merely of activities that have something for their object.

I perceive something. I feel something. I imagine something. I want something. I sense something. I think something. The life of a human being does not consist merely of all this and its like.

All this and its like is the basis of the realm of It.

But the realm of You has another basis.

*

Whoever says You does not have something for his object. For wherever there is something there is also another something; every It borders on other Its; It is only by virtue of bordering on others. But where You is said there is no something. You has no borders.

Whoever says You does not have something; he has nothing. But he stands in relation.

*

We are told that man experiences his world. What does this mean?

Man goes over the surfaces of things and experiences them.[4] He brings back from them some knowledge of their condition—an experience. He experiences what there is to things.

---

[2] *stiften sie einen Bestand.* The locution is most unusual, and *Bestand* in any applicable sense is very rare. Buber intends a contrast with "that might exist" (*was...bestünde*).

[3] *Wesen:* see page forty-six.

[4] *Der Mensch befährt die Fläche der Dinge und erfährt sie.* Both *erfährt* in this sentence and *erfahre* in the preceding paragraph are forms of *erfahren,* the ordinary German equivalent of the verb, to experience. The noun is *Erfahrung.* These words are so common that it has hardly ever occurred to anyone that they are closely related to *fahren,* an equally familiar word that means to drive or go. *Befahren* means to drive over the surface of something. The effect of the German sentence is to make the

But it is not experiences alone that bring the world to man.

For what they bring to him is only a world that consists of It and It and It, of He and He and She and She and It.

I experience something.

All this is not changed by adding "inner" experiences to the "external" ones, in line with the non-eternal distinction that is born of mankind's craving to take the edge off the mystery of death. Inner things like external things, things among things!

I experience something.

And all this is not changed by adding "mysterious" experiences to "manifest" ones, self-confident in the wisdom that recognizes a secret compartment in things, reserved for the initiated, and holds the key. O mysteriousness without mystery, O piling up of information! It, it, it!

*

Those who experience do not participate in the world. For the experience is "in them" and not between them and the world.

The world does not participate in experience. It allows itself to be experienced, but it is not concerned, for it contributes nothing, and nothing happens to it.

*

The world as experience belongs to the basic word I-It.

The basic word I-You establishes the world of relation.

*

Three are the spheres[5] in which the world of relation arises.

The first: life with nature. Here the relation vibrates in the dark and remains below language. The creatures stir across from us, but they are unable to come to us, and the You we say to them sticks to the threshold of language.

The second: life with men. Here the relation is manifest and enters language. We can give and receive the You.

The third: life with spiritual beings. Here the relation is wrapped in a cloud but reveals itself,[6] it lacks but creates language. We hear no You and yet feel addressed; we answer—creating, thinking, acting: with our being we speak the basic word, unable to say You with our mouth.

But how can we incorporate into the world of the basic word what lies outside language?

---

reader suddenly aware of the possibility that *erfahren* might literally mean finding out by going or driving, or possibly by traveling. But by further linking *erfahren* with *befahren* Buber manages to suggest that experience stays on the surface.

In the original manuscript this point was elaborated further in the sentence immediately following upon this paragraph; but Buber struck it out: "Thus the fisherman gets his catch. But the find is for the diver."

[5] This locution echoes the Passover Haggadah which contains a famous song in which each stanza begins: One is…, Two are…, Three are…, etc.

[6] *sich offenbarend*. A few lines earlier, *offenbar* was translated as manifest. The adjective, unlike the verb, generally has no religious overtones.

In every sphere, through everything that becomes present to us, we gaze toward the train[7] of the eternal You; in each we perceive a breath of it;[8] in every You we address the eternal You, in every sphere according to its manner.

*

I contemplate a tree.

I can accept it as a picture: a rigid pillar in a flood of light, or splashes of green[9] traversed by the gentleness of the blue silver ground.

I can feel it as movement: the flowing veins around the sturdy, striving core, the sucking of the roots, the breathing of the leaves, the infinite commerce with earth and air—and the growing itself in its darkness.

I can assign it to a species and observe it as an instance, with an eye to its construction and its way of life.

I can overcome its uniqueness and form so rigorously that I recognize it only as an expression of the law—those laws according to which a constant opposition of forces is continually adjusted, or those laws according to which the elements mix and separate.

I can dissolve it into a number, into a pure relation between numbers, and eternalize it.

Throughout all of this the tree remains my object and has its place and its time span, its kind and condition.

But it can also happen, if will and grace are joined, that as I contemplate the tree I am drawn into a relation, and the tree ceases to be an It. The power of exclusiveness has seized me.

This does not require me to forego any of the modes of contemplation. There is nothing that I must not see in order to see, and there is no knowledge that I must forget. Rather is everything, picture and movement, species and instance, law and number included and inseparably fused.

Whatever belongs to the tree is included: its form and its mechanics, its colors and its chemistry, its conversation with the elements and its conversation with the stars—all this in its entirety.

The tree is no impression, no play of my imagination, no aspect of a mood; it confronts me bodily[1] and has to deal with me as I must deal with it—only differently.

One should not try to dilute the meaning of the relation: relation is reciprocity.

Does the tree then have consciousness, similar to our own? I have no experience of that. But thinking that you have brought this off in your own case, must you again divide the indivisible? What I encounter is neither the soul of a tree nor a dryad, but the tree itself.

---

[7] *Saum* means hem or edge, but this is surely an allusion to Isaiah 6:1.

[8] *Wehen:* literally, blowing (of a breeze or wind), wafting.

[9] *das spritzende Gegrün:* the noun is a coinage.

[1] *Er leibt mir gegenüber* ... *Leib* means body; *leibt* is most unusual and means literally: it bodies—across from me or vis-à-vis me. Locutions that involve *gegenüber* abound in this book. A few lines below, in the first sentence of the next section, we find *Stehe ich* ... *gegenüber,* in the following section, *gegenübertritt* and *des Gegenüber* and—a variant—*entgegentritt.* Cf. p. 45.

*

When I confront a human being as my You and speak the basic word I-You to him, then he is no thing among things nor does he consist of things.

He is no longer He or She, limited by other Hes and Shes, a dot in the world grid of space and time, nor a condition that can be experienced and described, a loose bundle of named qualities. Neighborless and seamless, he is You and fills the firmament. Not as if there were nothing but he; but everything else lives in *his* light.

Even as a melody is not composed of tones, nor a verse of words, nor a statue of lines—one must pull and tear to turn a unity into a multiplicity—so it is with the human being to whom I say You. I can abstract from him the color of his hair or the color of his speech or the color of his graciousness; I have to do this again and again; but immediately he is no longer You.

And even as prayer is not in time but time in prayer, the sacrifice not in space but space in the sacrifice—and whoever reverses the relation annuls the reality—I do not find the human being to whom I say You in any Sometime and Somewhere. I can place him there and have to do this again and again, but immediately he becomes a He or a She, an It, and no longer remains my You.

As long as the firmament of the You is spread over me, the tempests of causality cower at my heels, and the whirl of doom[2] congeals.

The human being to whom I say You I do not experience. But I stand in relation to him, in the sacred basic word. Only when I step out of this do I experience him again. Experience is remoteness from You.

The relation can obtain even if the human being to whom I say You does not hear it in his experience. For You is more than It knows. You does more, and more happens to it, than It knows. No deception reaches this far: here is the cradle of actual life.

*

This is the eternal origin of art that a human being confronts a form that wants to become a work through him. Not a figment of his soul but something that appears to the soul and demands the soul's creative power. What is required is a deed that a man does with his whole being: if he commits it and speaks with his being the basic word[3] to the form that appears, then the creative power is released and the work comes into being.

The deed involves a sacrifice and a risk. The sacrifice: infinite possibility is surrendered on the altar of the form; all that but a moment ago floated playfully through one's perspective has to be exterminated; none of it may penetrate into the work; the exclusiveness of such a confrontation demands this. The risk: the basic word can only be spoken with one's whole being; whoever commits himself may not hold back part of himself; and the work does

[2] *Verhängnis* means, and has been consistently translated as, doom; *Schicksal,* as fate.

[3] *Es kommt auf eine Wesenstat des Menschen an: vollzieht er sie, spricht er mit seinem Wesen das Grundwort...* Henceforth, *Wesenstat* and *Wesensakt* are translated "essential deed" and "essential act"; but the meaning that is intended is spelled out here.

not permit me, as a tree or man might, to seek relaxation in the It-world; it is imperious: if I do not serve it properly, it breaks, or it breaks me.

The form that confronts me I cannot experience nor describe; I can only actualize it. And yet I see it, radiant in the splendor of the confrontation, far more clearly than all clarity of the experienced world. Not as a thing among the "internal" things, not as a figment of the "imagination," but as what is present. Tested for its objectivity, the form is not "there" at all; but what can equal its presence? And it is an actual relation: it acts on me as I act on it.[4]

Such work is creation, inventing is finding.[5] Forming is discovery. As I actualize, I uncover. I lead the form across—into the world of It. The created work is a thing among things and can be experienced and described as an aggregate of qualities. But the receptive beholder[6] may be bodily confronted now and again.

*

—What, then, does one experience of the You?
—Nothing at all. For one does not experience it.
—What, then, does one know of the You?
—Only everything. For one no longer knows particulars.

*

The You encounters me by grace—it cannot be found by seeking. But that I speak the basic word to it is a deed of my whole being, is my essential deed.

The You encounters me. But I enter into a direct relationship to it. Thus the relationship is election and electing, passive and active at once: An action of the whole being must approach passivity, for it does away with all partial actions and thus with any sense of action, which always depends on limited exertions.

The basic word I-You can be spoken only with one's whole being. The concentration and fusion into a whole being can never be accomplished by me, can never be accomplished without me. I require a You to become; becoming I, I say You.

All actual life is encounter.

"Form" *Gestalt.* One might consider leaving this word untranslated because *Gestalt* has become familiar in English; but the associations of Gestalt psychology might be more distracting than helpful, and *Gestaltung* (below: "forming") needs to be translated in any case.

[4] actual: *wirklich;* acts: *wirkt;* act: *wirke.* Earlier in the same paragraph, actualize: *verwirklichen.* In English "real" and "realize" would sometimes be smoother than "actual" and "actualize"; but it is noteworthy that the German word *wirklich* is so closely associated, not only by Buber but also by Nietzsche and Goethe before him, with *wirken, Werk* (work), *Wirkung* (effect), and *wirksam* (effective). Cf. p. 45f.

[5] *Schaffen ist Schöpfen, Erfinden ist Finden. Schaffen* can mean to work or to create; *schöpfen* means to create. *Erfinden* is the ordinary German word for invent, and *finden* means to find.

[6] *dem ... Schauenden. Schauen* is a way of looking that in this book is not associated with experiencing, with objects, with It. It has generally been translated "behold."

John M. Wiemann

Explication and Test of a Model of Communicative Competence

John M. Wiemann originated the research on interpersonal communication competence from a scientific perspective, and his work set the stage for others (e.g., Spitzberg & Cupach, 1984) to continue the work of discovering competency skills in individual communicators. During a 1992 NCA conference panel, Wiemann extended his original ideas to include the following: competence is interactive rather than linear; competent people are integrated with competent relationships; functions of behaviors may be more important than individual skills; and relationships should be honored with appropriate behavior. Wiemann has continued to experiment with and theorize about interpersonal communication competence and has arrived at the notion that competence exists in the dyad itself (O'Hair, Friedrich, Wiemann, & Wiemann, 1995). Consequently, I now teach that competence in interpersonal dyads needs to be contextualized—that is, a friendship may require a different kind of competence from, say, a romance. This may be why individuals are more successful in some types of relationships than others.

When I first read the following article, it was shortly after this groundbreaking model came out in Human Communication Research. *He explicitly addresses interpersonal communication behaviors that indicate effectiveness, and he clusters those behaviors into five factors: affiliation/support, social relaxation, empathy, behavioral flexibility, and interaction management. In the excerpt that follows, the empirical procedures and statistical analysis have been edited out so the reader can more easily see the theoretical framework Wiemann constructed and tested.*

Wiemann's work is an excellent example of empirical approaches to understanding the actual behavior that communicators engage in as they actively participate in relationships. This is the type of information students very much want to know about: appropriate, skill-based behavior.

Abstract. This research investigated the concept of communicative competence. A definition and a five-component model of communicative competence is proposed. Interaction management, empathy, affiliation/support, behavioral flexibility, and social relaxation are identified as components of competence, with interaction management playing a central role. In an experiment designed to partially test the model, 239 Ss were assigned to evaluate a confederate's role-played communicative competence in one of four interaction management treatment conditions. Results indicated a strong, positive, linear relationship between interaction management and communicative competence. Positive correlations between competence and other components of the model were observed. The competent communicator is thus described as empathic, affiliative and supportive, and relaxed while interacting; he is capable of adapting his behavior as the situation within an encounter changes and as he moves from encounter to encounter. The manner in which the interaction is managed contributes, in part at least, to his fellow interactants' perceptions of his competence.

It must be the nature of man to first examine those things which are exotic in his environment. Only later, after the exotic has been dealt with, does he take note of the "normal" conditions of his day-to-day life. Such seems to be the case, at least, in the study of man's communication behavior. In spite of the pervasiveness of everyday face-to-face interaction, it has received comparatively less study than most other rhetorical situations. While communication scholars have at their disposal a wealth of research on, for example, effective persuasion or interviewing there is very little dealing with effective or "good" conversational behavior.

Though research may fail us in this regard, "common sense" does not. It is a fact of our everyday experience that there are some people with whom we would rather converse than others. While most of us can easily identify these "desirable" conversational partners, it is probably more difficult to specify why they are more desirable. The implication is that certain sets of behaviors are more desirable than others in any given specific situation. Further, it is problematic for the interactant to determine which behaviors afford him the best chance of bringing off an encounter in such a way that all participants will evaluate it positively.

PURPOSE AND RATIONALE

The purpose of this study was to explore the substructure of everyday social conversation which allows for judgments of competent conversation behavior in the context of initial interactions.

While many people might label the behavior discussed here as "ordinary" social grace, behavioral scientists have dealt with this phenomenon under the rubrics *social skill, interpersonal effectiveness, interpersonal competence,* and *communicative competence.*[1] Because the primary concern here is with communicative behavior, the term "communicative competence" (CC) is used. A little reflection will lead one to believe that such behavior is anything but ordinary.

The importance of communicative competence in everyday conversation lies in the role that such conversation plays in the development of the social identity of the members of any society. While a conversational encounter can serve many functions, its primary function is the establishment and maintenance of self and social identities of the participants (Goffman, 1959, 1967; McCall & Simmons, 1966). The competent communicator, therefore, is in a better position to present and to have accepted his own definition of himself and others. To the extent that identities are the product of negotiation among participants in an encounter, communicative competence must be viewed as a *dyadic* concept. It is not *necessarily* competent to force one's self/situation definition on others. Such force, while possible, generally does not take into account the needs of other participants. Thus, *effectiveness* in an intrapersonal sense—that is, the accomplishment of an individual's goals—may be

incompetent in an interpersonal sense if such effectiveness precludes the possibility of others accomplishing their own goals. Since the competent communicator arrives at a self/situation definition through a process of interpersonal
negotiation, the definition reached may not be exactly the same as the definition either participant had in mind when the encounter began. But, if the participants are competent, they should be able to arrive at a definition that is the
"best possible" for both.

Consequently, even the highly Machiavellian communicator can be judged
as competent if he is able to maintain social relationships *over time* that are
mutually satisfactory for all concerned. This dyadic notion of CC has seldom
been made explicit in past writing on the subject, but does seem to be part of
the underlying reasoning of previous approaches to competence.

Approaches to the Study of Competence

The concept of competence in face-to-face interaction has been influenced by
three main schools of thought which can be characterized as: (1) the human
relations or T-group approach (Argyris, 1962, 1965; Holland & Baird, 1968;
Bochner & Kelly, 1974), (2) the social skill approach (Argyle & Kendon, 1967;
Argyle, 1969), and (3) the self-presentation approach (Goffman, 1959, 1961,
1963, 1967; Weinstein, 1966; Rodnick & Wood, 1973).

While each of these approaches differs from the others in some ways, their
similarities are more striking than their differences—differences more of
emphasis than of kind. All three approaches characterize competence in terms
of "effectiveness." For example, Bochner and Kelly (1974) define competence
as "a person's ability to interact effectively with other people" (288). Taking a
social skill approach, Habermas (1970) states that "communicative competence means the mastery of an ideal speech situation" (p. 138). Argyle (1969),
using the terms *social competence* and *social skill* synonymously, suggests that the
concept carries "the assumption that some people are better at dealing with
social situations in general than others are" (p. 330). Each approach is briefly
discussed below, with emphasis on its contribution to the understanding of
competent communication behavior, and with an eye to constructing a model
of CC.

The self-presentation approach: In his seminal work dealing with self-presentation, Goffman (1959) describes man as an actor who must play various roles
(in both the theatrical sense and the social psychological-role theory sense) to
various audiences (i.e., those co-present in any face-to-face encounter). Goffman's work, in particular, leads to the conclusion that competence is a dyadic
construct. He views encounters as "situational constraints" on an interactant's
communicative behavior. It is the person's *duty* to play an appropriate role at
any given time, for it is through each person's role enactment that particular
situations are defined, thus creating and reinforcing social reality.

The competent communicator, in Goffman's sense, is one who is aware of the
sacred quality of encounters as demonstrated by (1) his presentation of appro-

priate faces and lines (that is, social identities his fellow participants can support without jeopardizing their own faces and lines) and (2) his support of the faces and lines presented by others. Additionally, the competent person is adept at helping others "save face"—for example, helping to maintain the other's identity when it is threatened by a *faux pas* (Goffman, 1967; see also Garfinkel, 1972).

Snyder (1974) concludes that these self-presentation skills are differentially distributed through the population. That is, some people are better at self-presentation than others and thus are more effective in social situations.

The T-group approach: Bochner and Kelly (1974), expanding previous work by Argyris (1962, 1965), propose three criteria against which CC can be judged: "(1) ability to formulate and achieve objectives; (2) ability to collaborate effectively with others, i.e., to be interdependent; and (3) ability to adapt appropriately to situational or environmental variations" (288). Five skills which would allow a person to meet these criteria are: (1) empathy; (2) descriptiveness, i.e., the manner in which feedback is given and received; (3) owning feelings and thoughts, i.e., the assumption of responsibility for one's feelings and thoughts; (4) self-disclosure; and (5) behavioral flexibility, i.e., the ability to recognize the behavioral choices open in a given situation and the capacity to relate in new ways given the present combination of participants, situation, and the history of the relationship (Bochner & Kelly, 1974).

The social skill approach: In a more explicit model than either of the other approaches, Argyle (1969), suggests that social behavior can be studied in much the same way that motor skills are studied. He defines "skill" as an "organised, coordinated activity in relation to an object or a situation, which involves a whole chain of sensory, central and motor mechanisms. One of its main characteristics is that the performance, or stream of action, is *continuously under the control of the sensory input*" (p. 180, emphasis added). The specific dimensions of CC discussed by Argyle are: (1) extroversion and affiliation, (2) dominance-submission, (3) poise-social anxiety, (4) rewardingness, (5) interaction skills, (6) perceptual sensitivity, and (7) role-taking ability.

A Model of Communicative Competence

Based on these three approaches to communicative competence, a tentative identification of its behavioral dimensions can be undertaken. To this point, I have dealt with previous attempts to define competence that have in common the equating of competence with "effective" communication. All, however, suffer from imprecision and/or the confounding of communicative and noncommunicative (e.g., personality traits) elements.

Based on literature dealing with face-to-face conversational encounters, a definitional model of communicative competence composed of the following five dimensions was developed: (1) affiliation/support, (2) social relaxation, (3) empathy, (4) behavioral flexibility, and (5) interaction management skills.

In general, this model suggests that the competent interactant is other-oriented to the extent that he is open (available) to receive messages from others, does not provoke anxiety in others by exhibiting anxiety himself, is empathic, has a large enough behavioral repertoire to allow him to meet the demands of changing situations, and, finally, is supportive of the faces and lines his fellow interactants present. The competent person's interaction management skills allow him to realize (present) this other-orientation. Competence, however, does not mean that the interactant is completely selfless, i.e., completely other-oriented. In spite of this other-orientation, he is successful in accomplishing his own goals in any given interaction. This notion of mutual satisfaction with the self/situation definition leaves open the possibility that one interactant may be able to persuade the other to accept a specific definition—such persuasion is well within the bounds of competent communication *if* the outcome is functional for the long-term maintenance of the social relationship.

To illustrate this point, consider the stereotypic used car salesman—the person often held up as the example of high Machiavellianism. In his relationships with customers, our salesman may or may not be considered competent, depending on the measures of sales competence used. If "cars sold" is the measure, then the means to that end make little difference. But, if "repeat customers" or "new customers referred by old customers" are used as measures, then the means by which sales are made become important because relationships with customers *over time* become important. The point is that, regardless of the measure of competence used, cars are sold; the manner in which the salesman is evaluated, however, will determine whether or not he is considered competent at this profession.

The same case can be made for communicative behavior in the social sphere. A person can always have his way in a relationship and be judged effective only if the end (i.e., having his way) is considered of primary importance. But if the maintenance of the relationship is paramount (or if it is considered the "end" in and of itself), then the manner in which relational decisions are made is critical. The competent communicator is the person who can have his way in the relationship while maintaining a mutually acceptable definition of that relationship.

This notion of competence becomes especially meaningful when the temporal aspects of relationships are considered. If a relationship is to be (or has been) in existence for some period of time, then individual acts generally become less significant than the aggregate of relationally oriented acts (Altman & Taylor, 1973). The person who is considered "effective" by the "I had my way" criterion is really incompetent if the relationship is terminated because the other party in it could not live with a self-definition of "loser." In many cases, a person is considered pathological if his communicative behavior across situations is of the "I must get my way" variety.

From this description, communicative competence can be defined as *the ability of an interactant to choose among available communicative behaviors in order that he may successfully accomplish his own interpersonal goals during an encounter while maintaining the face and line of his fellow interactants within the constraints of the situation.*

Each of the dimensions of CC can be defined according to discreet, molecular behaviors (as opposed to configurations of behaviors), all readily observable in face-to-face encounters by "normal," (i.e., untrained) interactants. Following is a list of the behavioral cues[2] of each of the dimensions of the model:

Affiliation/support:

1. Eye behavior (Argyle, 1969; Exline, 1971; Mehrabian & Ksionzky, 1972; Wiemann 1974).
2. The alternation and co-occurrence of specific speech choices which mark the status and affiliative relationships of the interactants, e.g., honorifics—"Professor," "Your Honor"—pet names, or multiple names as markers of a relationship (Brown & Gilman, 1960; Ervin-Tripp, 1964, 1972; Wiener & Mehrabian, 1968; Argyle, 1969).
3. Head nods (Mehrabian, 1972).
4. Duration of speaking time and number of statements per minute (Mehrabian, 1972).
5. Pleasantness of facial expression—smiling (Mehrabian, 1972; Rosenfeld, 1972).
6. Statements indicating "owning" of one's perceptions about another (Bochner & Kelly, 1974).
7. Physical proximity chosen during interaction (Argyle & Dean, 1965; Hall, 1966).

Social relaxation:

1. General postural relaxation cues, including rocking movements, leg and foot movements, and body lean (Mehrabian, 1971, 1972; Mehrabian & Ksionzky, 1972).
2. Rate of speech (Argyle, 1969).
3. Speech disturbances, hesitations, and nonfluencies (Kasl & Mahl, 1965).
4. Object manipulations (Mehrabian & Ksionzky, 1972).

Empathy:

1. Reciprocity of affect displays, e.g., smiling and other immediacy cues (Argyle & Dean, 1965; Mehrabian, 1972).
2. Verbal responses indicating understanding of and feeling for the other's situation, e.g., "I know how you feel."
3. Perceived active listening as indicated by head nods and verbal listener responses or reinforcers (Dittman, 1972; Wiemann & Knapp, 1975).

Behavioral flexibility: The adaptations one makes within a situation and from situation to situation, including:

1. Verbal immediacy cues (Wiener & Mehrabian, 1968).
2. The alternation and co-occurrence of specific speech choices which mark the status and affiliative relationships of interactants (Brown & Gilman, 1960; Ervin-Tripp, 1964, 1972; Argyle, 1969; Robinson, 1972).

Interaction management: Argyle (1969) lists two general interaction management skills that are critical to competence: (1) "the ability to establish and sustain a smooth and easy pattern of interaction" (pp. 327–328) and (2) the ability to maintain control of the interaction without dominating—"responding in accordance with an internal plan, rather than simply reacting to the other's behaviour" (p. 328).

The first of these skills is dependent on the rule-governed nature of face-to-face encounters. It is the adherence or nonadherence to these culturally sanctioned rules which behaviorally define this dimension of communicative competence. Of the many rules applicable to face-to-face encounters, those most pertinent to communicative competence are:

1. Interruptions of the speaker are not permitted (Goffman, 1967; Duncan, 1973; Speier, 1973; Wiemann & Knapp, 1975).
2. One person talks at a time (Duncan, 1973; Speier, 1973; Sacks et al., 1974; Wiemann & Knapp, 1975).
3. Speaker turns must interchange (Speier, 1973; Sacks et al., 1974; however, this rule is subject to different interpretations, cf. Schegloff, 1972; Scheidel, 1974).
4. Frequent and lengthy pauses should be avoided (Jaffee & Feldstein, 1970).
5. An interactant must be perceived as devoting full attention to the encounter (Goffman, 1967).

The second of the above-mentioned interaction management skills—responding according to plan—can be described behaviorally as the topic control exercised by an interactant....

Before proceeding, a note about the importance of interaction management is in order. Interaction management is concerned with the "procedural" aspects that structure and maintain an interaction. These include initiation and termination of the encounter, the allocation of speaking turns, and control of topics discussed. Skillful interaction management is defined as the ability to handle these procedural matters in a manner that is mutually satisfactory to all participants. There is more evidence relating interaction management skills to communicative competence than is available for any of the previously discussed components of the model. It is the mastery of these skills which permits a person to implement (or conform to) the interaction rules of his culture. Speier (1972) states this position strongly:

> Competence in using conversational procedures in social interaction not only displays adequate social membership among participants in the culture, but more deeply, it *provides a procedural basis for the ongoing organization of that culture* when members confront and deal with one another daily. (p. 398, emphasis in original)

Based on the available evidence, it seems that interaction management is the *sine qua non* of competence.

Some consideration of the "quantity" of competent behaviors is also in order. As presented to this point, the CC model implies that "more is better." Both intuition and empirical evidence (though inconclusive) argue against this position. Intuitively, the interactant who is too smooth, too practiced, is suspect. His "commitment" to his message seems out of proportion to the spontaneity common to conversational encounters (cf. Hart & Burks, 1972, for a discussion of "appropriate commitment" in social interaction). Additionally, evidence reported by Exline (1971), Mehrabian (1972), Wiemann (1974), and others indicates that a moderate amount of any given behavior is more highly valued by interactants than either extremely high or low amounts. Consequently, it seems that there is an inverted parabolic relationship between the performance of behaviors indicative of CC and judgments of actual competence.

Hypotheses

Because of its apparent centrality to communicative competence, interaction management skill was the independent variable used to partially test the model. Subjects' evaluations of the competence of a person was the dependent variable of primary interest. Subjects viewing an encounter (as third-party observers) made judgments of the competence of a person in an ongoing interaction. Since the model indicates that a "moderate" or "medium" level of exhibited management skill is *optimal*—too little or too much management will be dysfunctional—Hypothesis 1 can be stated:

> H1: The level of interaction management skill displayed by an interactant is nonlinearly related to observers' perceptions of that interactant's communicative competence. Specifically, it is an inverted parabolic relationship.

If the model is valid, the other four components of CC should be correlated with the level of interaction management, and all components should be related to a general measure of communicative competence as is interaction management. In any given situation, a person evaluated as highly competent, because of the management skills displayed, should also be judged high on affiliation/support, empathy, behavioral flexibility, and social relaxation.

Stated differently, the components of the model *do not appear to be independent;* each component defines—partially, at least—relatively the same domain of experience (i.e., communicative competence). For example, some behaviors that convey empathy can also serve to manage the interaction. These components are distinguishable from each other to the extent that *not all* empathic behavior for example, serves as interaction management.

Thus, it was further hypothesized that:

> H2: An interactant's interaction management skill as perceived by observers is positively and linearly related to perceptions of that interactant's: (a) behavioral flexibility, (b) empathy, (c) affiliativeness/supportiveness, and, (d) social relaxation.

A corollary of this hypotheses is that the relationship of these four dependent variables with perceived competence can also be described as an inverted parabola....

DISCUSSION

Taken together, the data present a picture of communicative competence which is in general agreement with the model developed here. The agreement can only be characterized as "general" because three facets of the results are at odds with the model. The results (1) did not reflect the predicted inverted parabolic relationship between displayed interaction management and perceptions of communicative competence, (2) revealed a relatively weak (though statistically significant) relationship between social relaxation and interaction management, and (3) yielded a one-factor solution where the model implied a five-factor solution. Each of these facets will be briefly discussed.

The Competence-Management Relationship

Prediction of a nonlinear relationship between interaction management and communicative competence was based primarily on the assumption that too much other-directedness would be dysfunctional. It seemed reasonable that a person displaying "too smooth" a presentation might be seen as trying to appear interested in his audience when, in fact, his interest was really in his message. The appearance of commitment to audience is a facade—an inappropriate claim on the relationship. The prototype of this communicator is the previously mentioned used car salesman who tries to demonstrate interest in his customer's welfare, but is actually interested only in a sale, no matter what must be said or done to achieve his goal.

Why was no nonlinear relationship between interaction management and communicative competence observed in this research? Several explanations are possible. First, the primary assumption—that an overly smooth presentation will be suspect—could be wrong. Perhaps people do not penalize others for being extremely good interactants, since the smoother the management of the interaction, the easier it is for *all* participants to accomplish their objectives.

Second, many of the studies which support the primary assumption tend to be rather artificial. For example, Exline's (1971) research required subjects to *imagine* how they would feel in a particular situation. Mehrabian (1972) also relied on noninteractive situations; his subjects listened to single words or pretended a coat rack was their fellow interactant. In the cases mentioned here, only one component of the interaction was studied at a time, and there was not even a semblance of normal interaction. The generally nonlinear relationships found in these studies could thus be an artifact of the artificially-contrived situations in which the subjects found themselves. The more extreme the treatment, the more unnatural it became, and thus the lower the subjects evaluated it. In the more interactive situation of this study, subjects were able to observe the whole spectrum of behavior. Behavioral extremes of one kind may have been offset by moderation in others, thus affecting the overall perceptions of competence. In spite of the weaknesses of these studies, the nonlinear trends they report are not unlike the commonsense perception that too-practiced a presentation is somehow less valued than a spontaneous one in everyday conversational encounters.

A third possibility for the lack of a nonlinear relationship between management and competence involves the nature of the situation itself. It is possible that in an initial interaction, people are more tolerant of others. They lack information about the other interactant, and consequently, do not judge him too severely. Similarly, in an initial interaction, a person may not spend enough time with the other for his evaluation to crystalize. That is, a nonlinear relationship develops only after some period of time; initially, the smoothness of presentation is acceptable because it is anticipated—everyone is expected to make a good impression, and we do not take offense at even the most practiced attempts. After a time, however, the smoothness is seen as insincerity, phoniness, or shallowness.

Each of these three explanations probably accounts in part for the failure of the nonlinear relationship to emerge in this study—the first to a lesser extent than the latter two. The third explanation, however, seems to be most viable. What these results indicate is that at initial meetings a certain smoothness in presentation is considered communicatively competent; the smoother the initial meeting goes, the more competent the communicator is perceived to be.

The Management-Social Relaxation Relationship

The interaction management-social relaxation relationship is less clear than are the relationships of management with the other components of the model. Only in the Hi treatment condition was social relaxation evaluated in the same way as the other components. In the other treatments, the strength of the relationship either broke down or social relaxation became less salient. The relaxation-competence relationship is similar to the relaxation-management relationship (r's by treatment are: Hi, .81; Me, .15; Lo, .58; Ru, .35; and combined treatments, .63; Hi, Lo, and combined r's are statistically significant at the .001 level; Ru r, at the .003 level; the Me r is not significant). Since the question of primary interest here is one of the appropriateness of including social relaxation in the communicative competence model, this discussion is couched in terms of the competence-relaxation relationship.

Several explanations of this finding present themselves. First, social relaxation may not be a major component of communicative competence. This possibility can be rejected out of hand because of the strong positive correlation between both management and competence and management and social relaxation in the Hi treatment. This treatment was communicative competence in its purest form, the form in which its components should be most easily identifiable. (In fact, Habermas, 1970, argues that competence can only be identified with any certainty in its "ideal" form.)

Another explanation lies in the behaviors used to communicate social relaxation. Such things as body lean and postural shifts may be too subtle to be monitored when there is considerable activity among the other competence components. Thus, the level of social relaxation would be less important or play less of a role in perceptions of communicative competence in any situation except one in which other aspects of the performance were "under control."

This explanation seems to fit these data. In the Hi treatment, social relaxation is clearly evaluated as part of general communicative competence. In the Me treatment—probably the most confusing in terms of what the confederate is doing, i.e., trying but not quite succeeding at being a "good" interactant—relaxation drops out completely. The tie appears again, although relatively weakly, in the Lo and Ru treatments, where clear patterns of behavior are established by the confederates. When all data are considered, however, the relaxation-competence relationship must be considered tentative, at best.

Factor Analysis Results

The results of the factor analysis indicate that subjects saw communicative competence as composed of a single factor. Is this to say that communicative competence should be described as a unitary set of behaviors? For this sample, such a unitary description seems to be in order. Yet, both intuition and empirical data (unfortunately, not these data) argue that different components of communicative competence can and should be differentiated.

The research cited earlier clearly demonstrates that empathy, behavioral flexibility, interaction management, social relaxation, and affiliation/support can be differentiated from each other behaviorally and conceptually. Heuristically, the five-component (or an n-component) model is valuable because it directs us to the types of behaviors which might make a difference in perceptions of competence. The empirical evidence of this one study notwithstanding, the "component" conceptualization of competence should not be abandoned.

While it is often unproductive to let statistical analysis guide one's thinking (cf. Blommers & Lindquist, 1960), the empirical evidence of this study cannot be ignored. These subjects did not distinguish between general competence and specific components (especially behavioral flexibility, empathy, affiliation/support). This could be due to a rating "halo" effect. It seems probable that subjects could not or did not attend to all of the cues available. They made judgments based on the cues to which they attended and then generalized these judgments to include all cues. Another explanation, of course, is that pragmatically, competence is a unitary set of behaviors in that the person who is high on one of the dimensions proposed here will also be high on all of the others.

Communicative Competence: Some Conclusions

In arriving at conclusions, these data leave little room for interpretation; they are sufficiently straightforward that rival interpretations are not parsimonious. Interaction management, affiliation/support, empathy, behavioral flexibility, and social relaxation are interdependent components of communicative competence. It is by definition that competence is the construct that encompasses the five components; it is a more inclusive, abstract construct than interaction management, empathy, or the other components of the model.

In this study the goal of each interactant (the confederates) was to get acquainted with the other. To accomplish this, each was responsible for both giving information about herself and receiving information about the other. Communicative competence was demonstrated when the on-camera confederate facilitated the other's giving of information and reciprocated in kind with her own information. In all but the Hi treatment, this mutuality of exchange was less than ideal, and the subjects evaluated the confederate lower accordingly. (It is interesting to note, in line with the dyadic conceptualization of competence, that each interactant's goal must be met simultaneously in this type of situation. One interactant must allow the other to give if she is to receive.)

These data also bear out the centrality of interaction management in the communicative competence model. *Even relatively small changes in management behavior resulted in large variations in evaluations of communicative competence.* As interaction management behavior was varied, perceptions of all of the other components of competence and general competence itself varied linearly with it. It remains to be seen whether variations in any of the other components of CC will similarly affect perceptions of interaction management.

These results support the theoretical formulations of competence put forth by Argyle (1969; Argyle & Kendon, 1967) and Bochner and Kelly (1974), as reviewed earlier in this report. Similarly, Goffman's (1959, 1961, 1963, 1967) observations concerning competent self-presentation have withstood this experimental test. The confederate was evaluated as less competent when she did not give complete attention to the interaction, when she showed disrespect of her fellow interactant, and when she did not fully contribute to the maintenance of a smooth and continuous flow of talk. Furthermore, the more negligent she was in these areas, the lower she was evaluated.

In spite of the straightforwardness of the data, the generalizability of this study is limited by two factors: (1) the stimulus situation, and (2) the role the subjects played in the study.

The stimulus situation used here, although pervasive and important, is comparatively unique. Each relationship has only one initial interaction. As has already been suggested, criteria used to evaluate others probably change over time; people may be more tolerant of some types of behavior in initial interactions because they *are* initial interactions. While the basic components of communicative competence as outlined here remain the basis of evaluation, other idiosyncratic components are probably added as the relationship develops. For example, Suttles (1970) states that one indicator of friendship is development of norms between the friends which often are at odds with general cultural norms concerning polite behavior. It is the implicit agreement to break the cultural norms that is a marker of the friendship. The way idiosyncratic behaviors might modify the basic components of competence is an empirical question.

The second limitation of this study is the role the subjects played—the role of observers. It seems likely that a person's perceptions and evaluations of another interactant are based, in part at least, on the type of communicative relationship the two have at any given time. It would be expected then that a person could perceive another from one perspective when they are interacting with each other and differently when watching the other interact with a third party.

In sum, the competent communicator is one who is other-oriented, while at the same time maintaining the ability to accomplish his own interpersonal goals. This other-orientation is demonstrated by the communicator being empathic, affiliative and supportive, and relaxed while interacting with others. Moreover, the competent communicator is capable of adapting his behavior as the situation within an encounter changes and/or as he moves from encounter to encounter. The way the communicator manages an interaction contributes, in part at least, to his fellow interactants' perceptions of his competence. It is this communicative competence which enables a person, in a very real and practical way, to establish a social identity.

NOTES

[1] Communicative competence in the sense used here is not to be confused with linguistic competence. Communicative competence is a performance-based concept (Weinstein, 1966), whereas linguistic competence is a "set of principles" necessary for a person to be a speaker of a language (Dale, 1972). Hymes (1974) argues the necessity for emphasis on the performance aspects of language. Hymes' argument can be extended to all aspects of socially communicative behavior. A knowledge of appropriate behavior is of little use to an interactant if he cannot implement that knowledge when called upon to do so. Therefore, it seems unwise to make the competence-performance distinction for social behavior.

[2] These cues can be reliably identified only for middle-class English speakers. The cues for each of the dimensions of competence may vary among cultures, but the salience of the dimensions is probably transcultural.

REFERENCES

Altman, I., & Taylor, D.A. *Social penetration.* New York: Holt, Rinehart & Winston, 1973.

Argyle, M. *Social interaction.* Chicago: Aldine Atherton, 1969.

Argyle, M., & Dean, J. Eye contact, distance and affiliation. *Sociometry,* 1965, 28, 289–304.

Argyle, M., & Kendon, A. The experimental analysis of social performance. In L. Berkowitz (Ed.), *Advances in experimental social psychology,* Vol. 3. New York: Academic Press, 1967, 55–98.

Argyris, C. *Interpersonal competence and organizational effectiveness.* Homewood, Ill.: Irwin-Dorsey, 1962.

Argyris, C. Explorations in interpersonal competence—I. *Journal of Applied Behavioral Science,* 1965, 1, 58–83.

Blommers, P., & Lindquist, E.F. *Elementary statistical methods.* Boston: Houghton Mifflin, 1960.

Bochner, A.P., & Kelly, C.W. Interpersonal competence: Rationale, philosophy, and implementation of a conceptual framework. *Speech Teacher,* 1974, 23, 279–301.

Brown, R., & Gilman, A. The pronouns of power and solidarity. In T.A. Sebeok (Ed.), *Style in language.* Cambridge: MIT Press, 1960, 253–276.

Dale, P.S. *Language development.* Hinsdale, Ill.: Dryden Press, 1972.

Dittman, A.T. Developmental factors in conversation behavior. *Journal of Communication,* 1972, 22, 404–423.

Duncan, S. Toward a grammar for dyadic conversation. *Semiotica,* 1973, 9, 29–46.

Ervin-Tripp, S. An analysis of the interaction of language, topic and listener. *American Anthropologist,* 1964, 66, 86–94.

Ervin-Tripp, S. On sociolinguistic rules: Alternation and co-occurrence. In J. J. Gumperz and D. Hymes (Eds.), *Directions in sociolinguistics.* New York: Holt, Rinehart & Winston, 1972, 213–250.

Exline, R. V. Visual interaction: The glances of power and preference. In J. K. Cole (Ed.), *Nebraska symposium on motivation.* Lincoln: University of Nebraska Press, 1971, 163–206.

Garfinkel, H. Studies of the routine grounds of everyday activities. In D. Sudnow (Ed.), *Studies in social interaction.* New York: Free Press, 1972, 1–30.

Goffman, E. *The presentation of self in everyday life.* Garden City, N.Y.: Doubleday Anchor, 1959.

Goffman, E. *Encounters.* Indianapolis: Bobbs-Merrill, 1961.

Goffman, E. *Behavior in public places.* New York: Free Press, 1963.

Goffman, E. *Interaction ritual.* Garden City, N.Y.: Anchor, 1967.

Habermas, J. Toward a theory of communicative competence. In H.P. Dreitzel (Ed.), *Recent sociology* (No. 2). New York: Macmillan, 1970, 114–148.

Hall, E.T. *The hidden dimension.* Garden City, N.Y.: Doubleday, 1966.

Hart, R.P., & Burks, D.M. Rhetorical sensitivity and social interaction. *Speech Monographs,* 1972, 39, 75–91.

Holland, J.L., & Baird, L.L. An interpersonal competency scale. *Educational and Psychological Measurement,* 1968, 28, 503–510.

Hymes, D. *Foundations in sociolinguistics.* Philadelphia: University of Pennsylvania Press, 1974.

Jaffe, J., & Feldstein, S. *Rhythms of dialogue.* New York: Academic Press, 1970.

Kasl, S.V., & Mahl, G.F. The relationship of disturbances and hesitations in spontaneous speech to anxiety. *Journal of Personality and Social Psychology,* 1965, 1, 425–433.

McCall, G.J., & Simmons, J.L. *Identities and interactions.* New York: Free Press, 1966.

Mehrabian, A. Nonverbal betrayal of feeling. *Journal of Experimental Research in Personality,* 1971, 5, 64–73.

Mehrabian, A. *Nonverbal communication.* Chicago: Aldine Atherton, 1972.

Mehrabian, A., & Ksionzky, S. Some determinants of social interaction. *Sociometry,* 1972, 35, 588–609.

Robinson, W.P. *Language and social behaviour.* Baltimore: Penguin, 1972.

Rodnick, R., & Wood, B. The communication strategies of children. *Speech Teacher,* 1973, 22, 114–124.

Rosenfeld, H.M. The experimental analysis of interpersonal influence processes. *Journal of Communication,* 1972, 22, 424–442.

Sacks, H., Schegloff, E.A., & Jefferson, G. A simplest systematics for the organization of turn-taking for conversation, *Language,* 1974, 50, 696–735.

Scheidel, T.M. A systems analysis of two person conversations. Paper presented at the Doctoral Honors Seminar on Modern Systems Theory in Human Communication, University of Utah, 1974.

Schegloff, E.A. Sequencing in conversational openings. In J. J. Gumperz and D. Hymes (Eds.), *Directions in sociolinguistics.* New York: Holt, Rinehart & Winston, 1972, 346–380.

Snyder, M. The self-monitoring of expressive behavior. *Journal of Personality and Social Psychology,* 1974, 30, 526–537.

Speier, M. Some conversational problems for interaction analysis. In D. Sudnow (Ed.), *Studies in social interaction.* New York: Free Press, 1972, 397–427.

Speier, M. *How to observe face-to-face communication: A sociological introduction.* Pacific Palisades, Calif.: Goodyear, 1973.

Suttles, G.D. Friendship as a social institution. In G.J. McCall, M.M. McCall, N.K. Denzin, G.D. Suttles, and S.B. Kurth, *Social relationships.* Chicago: Aldine, 1970, 95–135.

Weinstein, E.A. Toward a theory of interpersonal tactics. In C.W. Backman and P.F. Secord (Eds.), *Problems in social psychology.* New York: McGraw-Hill, 1966, 394–398.

Wiemann, J.M. An experimental study of visual attention in dyads: The effect of four gaze conditions on evaluations of applicants in employment interviews. Paper presented at the annual convention of the Speech Communication Association, Chicago, December 1974.

Wiemann, J.M. An exploration of communicative competence in initial interactions: An experimental study. Unpublished doctoral dissertation, Purdue University, 1975.

Wiemann, J.M., & Knapp, M.L. Turn-taking in conversations. *Journal of Communication,* 1975, 25, 75–92.

Wiener, M., & Mehrabian, A. *Language within language.* New York: Appleton-Century-Croft, 1968.

Mark L. Knapp and Anita L. Vangelisti

Stages of Coming Together and Coming Apart

> *Mark Knapp and Anita Vangelisti are two of the top names in interpersonal communication research, and they are particularly well respected for their popular theory of relationship stages. The idea that relationships build and then deteriorate through a cycle of discernible stages gained acceptance with Irwin Altman and Dalmas Taylor's (1973/1983) Social Penetration Theory. There are now many stage theories available for instruction (DeVito 2004; Knapp & Vangelisti, 2005; Phillips & Wood, 1983), but all are premised on the idea that dyads are not necessarily random progressions; rather, dyads use communication to carry us forward in predictable stages of maturity and deterioration (Duck, 1982). Knapp and Vangelisti posit ten stages to the building and deterioration of relationships. Five constitute "coming together" and five more comprise "coming apart." Each stage is characterized by a typical kind of communication; for example, during the first stage, initiating, the dyad uses phatic or social communication to come across as pleasant and to attract someone in order to get a relationship started. Reading about relationship stages is essential because this concept is so much a part of our belief in human growth and development.*
>
> *The following is an excerpt from a chapter called "Stages of Coming Together and Coming Apart," in the second edition of Knapp and Vangelisti's text* Interpersonal Communication and Human Relationships *(1992). I specifically chose this version because the format of the material is easier to read; however the newest version of their developmental theory is available in the fifth edition of the text published in 2005. In this excerpt, I have edited out the discussion about "movement in, out, and around the stages" so the reader can grasp the essential description of the stages. My students write relationship analyses in which they discuss the stages of their relationship, and they have found the concept of stages to be highly useful and applicable to all types of dyads.*

A MODEL OF INTERACTION STAGES IN RELATIONSHIPS

Scientists are forever seeking to bring order to a seemingly chaotic world of overlapping, interdependent, dynamic, and intricate processes. Frequently, the process of systematizing our life and environment is discussed in terms of stages of growth, stages of deterioration, and the forces that shape and act on this movement through stages. For instance, developmental psychologists recount regularized patterns of behavior accompanying stages of infancy, childhood, adolescence, maturity, and old age. Anthropologists and geologists plot the evolutionary stages of human beings and human environments. Biologists note similarities in the life processes of such seemingly diverse

149

organisms as trees and fish. Physical and social scientists talk about affinity and attraction, weak and strong interactions, friction, repulsion, and splitting-up as basic forces acting on matter and people. Rhetorical critics often dissect spoken messages by noting patterns regularly occurring during the introduction, development toward the main points, transitions, and conclusion.

The idea that there are stages in the development of relationships that are characterized by certain patterns of communication is not new.[6] We tried to synthesize as well as expand on this previous work in the development of the model presented in Table 4.1.

TABLE 4.1. A Model of Interaction Stages

Process	Stage	Representative Dialogue
	Initiating	"Hi, how ya doin'?" "Fine. You?"
	Experimenting	"Oh, so you like to ski…so do I." "You do?! Great. Where do you go?"
Coming Together	Intensifying	"I…I think I love you." "I love you too."
	Integrating	"I feel so much a part of you." "Yeah, we are like one person. What happens to you happens to me."
	Bonding	"I want to be with you always." "Let's get married."
	Differentiating	"I just don't like big social gatherings." "Sometimes I don't understand you. This is one area where I'm certainly not like you at all."
	Circumscribing	"Did you have a good time on your trip?" "What time will dinner be ready?"
Coming Apart	Stagnating	"What's there to talk about?" "Right. I know what you're going to say and you know what I'm going to say."
	Avoiding	"I'm so busy, I just don't know when I'll be able to see you." "If I'm not around when you try, you'll understand."
	Terminating	"I'm leaving you…and don't bother trying to contact me." "Don't worry."

Before each stage is described in greater detail, several preliminary remarks about the model are in order. First, we should resist the normal temptation to perceive the stages of coming together as "good" and those of coming apart as "bad." It is not "bad" to terminate relationships nor is it necessarily "good" to become more intimate with someone. The model is descriptive of what seems to happen—not what should happen.

We should also remember that in the interest of clarity the model simplifies a complex process. For instance, the model shows each stage adjacent to the next—as if it was clear when a communicating couple left one stage and entered another. To the contrary. Each stage contains some behavior from other stages. So stage identification becomes a matter of emphasis. Stages are identified by the proportion of one type of communication behavior to another. This proportion may be the frequency with which certain communication acts occur or proportion may be determined by the relative weight given to certain acts by the participants. For example, a couple at the Intensifying Stage may exhibit behaviors that occur at any of the other stages, but their arrival at the Intensifying Stage is because: (1) the most frequent communication exchanges are typical of the Intensifying Stage and/or (2) the exchanges that are crucial in defining the couple's relationship are statements of an intensifying nature. The act of sexual intercourse is commonly associated with male–female romantic couples at the Intensifying or Integrating Stages, but it may occur as an isolated act for couples at the Experimenting Stage. Or it may occur regularly for a couple at the Experimenting Stage, but remain relatively unimportant for the couple in defining the closeness of their relationship. Thus, interaction stages involve both overt behavior and the perceptions of behavior in the minds of the parties involved. During the formation of a romantic relationship, the couple's overt behavior (to each other and in front of others) may be a good marker of their developmental stage. During periods of attempted rejuvenation of a relationship we may find that the overt behavior is an effective marker of the stage *desired*. However, in stable or long-established relationships, overt behavior may not be a very accurate indicator of closeness. Instead it is the occasional behavior or memories of past behaviors that are perceived by the couple as crucial in defining their relationship. For example, the married couple of fifteen years may spend much of their interaction time engaging in small talk—a behavior typical of an early developmental stage. And even though the small talk does play an important role in maintaining the relationship, it is the less frequent but more heavily weighted behavior that the couple uses to define their relationship, as at the Integrating Stage. Similarly, close friends may not engage in a lot of talk that outside observers would associate with closeness. In some cases, friends are separated for long periods of time and make very little contact with one another. But through specific occasional acts and the memory of past acts, the intimacy of the friendship is maintained.

The dialogue in the model is heavily oriented toward mixed-gender pairs. This does not mean the model is irrelevant for same-gender pairs. Lovers and tennis buddies go down the same road, but lovers go further; business partners and sorority sisters find different topics, but both engage in a lot of small talk.

Even at the highest level of commitment, the model may apply to same-gender pairs. The bonding ceremony, for instance, need not be marriage. It could be an act of becoming "blood brothers" by placing open wounds on each other to achieve oneness. Granted, American cultural sanctions against the direct expression of high-level intimacy between same-sexed pairs often serve to inhibit, slow down, or stop the growth of relationships between same-sexed pairs. But when such relationships do develop, similar patterns are reported.[7]

The model...also focuses primarily on relationships where people voluntarily seek contact with, or disengagement from, one another. But the model is not limited to such relationships. All people drawn into, or pulled out of, relationships by forces seemingly outside their control will like or not like such an event and communicate accordingly. For instance, a child's relationship with his or her parent (involuntary) may, at some point, be very close and loving, at another time be cold and distant, and at another time be similar to relationships with other friends....

INTERACTION STAGES

Initiating

This stage incorporates all those processes enacted when we first come together with other people. It may be at a cocktail party or at the beach; it may be with a stranger or with a friend. As we scan the other person we consider our own stereotypes, any prior knowledge of the other's reputation, previous interactions with this person, expectations for this situation, and so on. We are asking ourselves whether this person is "attractive" or "unattractive" and whether we should initiate communication. Next, we try to determine whether the other person is cleared for an encounter—is he or she busy, in a hurry, surrounded by others? Finally, we search for an appropriate opening line to engage the other's attention.

Typically, communicators at this stage are simply trying to display themselves as a person who is pleasant, likable, understanding, and socially adept. In essence, we are saying: "I see you. I am friendly, and I want to open channels for communication to take place." In addition, we are carefully observing the other to reduce any uncertainty we might have—hoping to gain clarification of mood, interest, orientation toward us, and aspects of the other's public personality. Our conscious awareness of these processes is sometimes very low. "Morning, Bob. How ya doin'?" "Morning, Clayton. Go to hell." "Fine, thanks."

Obviously, specific methods and messages used to initiate communication vary with:

1. The kind of relationship and whether the participants have been through this stage before. *Stranger:* "Hello. Nice to meet you." *Friend:* "Hi dude. What's up?"
2. The time allowed for interaction—passing each other on the street versus a formal appointment.

3. The time since last greeting—re-greeting a person you saw just five minutes before versus greeting a relative at the airport who visits once a year.
4. The situational or normative constraints—meeting in the library versus meeting at a rock concert.
5. The special codes of particular groups—fraternity handshake.

In spite of the possibility for considerable variance of initiating behaviors, people generally exercise a good deal of caution and communicate according to conventional formulas.

Experimenting

Once communication has been initiated, we begin the process of experimenting—trying to discover the unknown. Strangers trying to become acquaintances will be primarily interested in name, rank, and serial number—something akin to the sniffing ritual in animals. The exchange of demographic information is frequent and often seems controlled by a norm that says: "If you tell me your hometown, I'll tell you mine." Strangers at this stage are diligently searching for an integrating topic, an area of common interest or experience. Sometimes the strain of this search approaches the absurd: "Oh, you're from Oklahoma. Do you know...?" Obviously, the degree to which a person assists another in finding this integrating topic shows the degree of interest in continuing the interaction and the willingness to pursue a relationship.

Miller and his colleagues have pointed out that we use three bases for predictions in interpersonal encounters.[8] With strangers we may have to rely primarily on *cultural information.* If one's partner is from this culture, they probably share some predictable ways of behaving and thinking. You assume they have knowledge of certain cultural happenings. It is a place to begin, but the potential sources of error are many.

As we gain information about another person, we may begin to use *sociological information* as a basis for conversational strategies and adaptations. This knowledge of a person's reference and membership groups is frequently used in casual social gatherings. When we hear that a person is a feminist, a physician, or a Southern Baptist, we immediately begin scanning associations with these labels that may be useful to us in our conversational pursuits.

The third basis for predictions involves *psychological information.* This information recognizes the individual differences associated with one's conversational partner. It is more likely to occur with conversational partners who are better known to you. These sources of information are important because they will mark differences in the small talk of strangers, people from very different cultures, people who have a close relationship, and people whose relationship is close in name only.

It should be noted that people in established close relationships do spend a lot of time experimenting. It may be an effort to seek greater breadth, to pass the time, or to avoid some uncomfortable vibrations obtained at a more intense level of dialogue. Both strangers and friends are searching for possible similarities;

both are trying to present a desirable "come-on self" ("If you like the label, you might like what's in the container"); both are concerned about setting up the next encounter where consistency of behavior can be examined.

Small talk is the sine qua non of experimenting. It is like Listerine; we may hate it, but we may also take large quantities of it every day. If we hate it, why do we do it? Probably because we are vaguely aware of several important functions served by small talk: (1) It is a useful process for uncovering integrating topics and openings for more penetrating conversation. (2) It can be an audition for a future friendship or a way of increasing the scope of a current relationship. (3) It provides a safe procedure for indicating who we are and how another can come to know us better (reduction of uncertainty). (4) It allows us to maintain a sense of community with our fellow human beings.

Relationships at this stage are generally pleasant, relaxed, overtly uncritical, and casual. Commitments are limited. And, like it or not, most of our relationships probably don't progress very far beyond this stage.

Intensifying

When people achieve a relationship known as "close friends," indicators of the relationships are intensified. Active participation and greater awareness of the process typify this stage when it begins. Initial probes toward intensification of intimacy are often exercised with caution, awaiting confirmation before proceeding. Sitting close, for instance, may precede hugging; holding hands will generally precede holding genitals. Requests for physical or psychological favors are sometimes used to validate the existence of intensity in a relationship....

The amount of personal disclosure increases at this stage and we begin to get a glimpse of some previously withheld secrets—that my father was an alcoholic, that I masturbate, that I pretend I'm a rhino when I'm drunk, and other fears, frustrations, failures, imperfections, and prejudices. Disclosures may be related to any topic area, but those dealing most directly with the development of the relationship are crucial. These disclosures make the speaker vulnerable—almost like an animal baring its neck to an attacker.

Verbally, a lot of things may be happening in the intensifying stage:

1. Forms of address become more informal—first name, nickname, or some term of endearment.
2. Use of the first personal plural becomes more common—"*We* should do this" or "*Let's* do this," One study of married couples found that the use of "we" was more likely to be associated with a relationship orientation while the use of "I" was more likely to be associated with a task orientation or the functional requirements and accomplishments of marriage.[9]
3. Private symbols begin to develop, sometimes in the form of a special slang or jargon, sometimes using conventional language forms that have understood, private meanings. Places they've been together; events and times they've shared; and physical objects they've purchased or exchanged; all become important symbols in defining the nature of

developing closeness.[10] Such items or memories may be especially devastating and repulsive reminders if the relationship begins to come apart unless the symbols are reinterpreted ("I like this diamond ring because it is beautiful, not because he gave it to me") or put in a different perspective ("It really was fun when we did——, but in so many other ways he was a jerk").

4. Verbal shortcuts built on a backlog of accumulated and shared assumptions, expectations, interests, knowledge, interactions, and experiences appear more often; one may request a newspaper be passed by simply saying, "paper."
5. More direct expressions of commitment may appear—"We really have a good thing going" or "I don't know who I'd talk to if you weren't around." Sometimes such expressions receive an echo—"I really like you a lot." "I really like you, too, Elmer."
6. Increasingly, one's partner will act as a helper in the daily process of understanding what you're all about—"In other words, you mean you're…" or "But yesterday, you said you were…"

Sophistication in nonverbal message transmission also increases. A long verbalization may be replaced by a single touch; postural congruence may be seen; clothing styles may become more coordinated; possessions and personal space may be more permeable.

As the relationship intensifies, each person is unfolding his or her uniqueness while simultaneously blending his or her personality with the other's.

Integrating

The relationship has now reached a point where the two individual personalities almost seem to fuse or coalesce, certainly more than at any previous stage. Davis discusses this concept, which he calls *coupling:*

> The extent to which each intimate tries to give the other his own self-symbols or to collect the other's self-symbols measure the degree to which he wants to increase their communion.[*]

The experience of Florida State Senator Bruce Smathers and his fiancée provides one example of movement toward this interpersonal fusion. He switched from Methodist to Presbyterian; she switched from Republican to Democrat. The wire service report indicated this was "a compromise they say will help pave the way for their wedding."

Verbal and nonverbal manifestations of integrating may take many forms: (1) Attitudes, opinions, interests, and tastes that clearly distinguish the pair from others are vigorously cultivated—"We have something special; we are unique." (2) Social circles merge and others begin to treat the two individuals as a common package—one present, one letter, one invitation. (3) Intimacy "trophies" are exchanged so each can "wear" the other's identity—pictures, pins, rings.

---

* Reprinted with permission of Macmillan Publishing Co., Inc. from *Intimate Relations* by Murray S. Davis. Copyright © 1973 by Murray S. Davis.

(4) Similarities in manner, dress, and verbal behavior may also accentuate the oneness. (5) Actual physical penetration of various body parts contributes to the perceived unification. (6) Sometimes common property is designated—"our song," a joint bank account, or a coauthored book. (7) Empathic processes seem to peak so that explanation and prediction of behavior are much easier. (8) Body rhythms and routines achieve heightened synchrony. (9) Sometimes the love of a third person or object will serve as glue for the relationship—"Love me, love my rhinos."

Obviously, integration does not mean complete togetherness or complete loss of individuality. Maintenance of some separate and distinct selves is critical, and possible, due to the strength of the binding elements. One married woman of ten years told us: "I still hold some of myself back from John because it's the only part of me I don't share, and it's important to have something that is uniquely mine."

Thus, we can see that as we participate in the integration process we are intensifying and minimizing various aspects of our total person. As a result, we may not be fully conscious of the idea but when we commit ourselves to integrating with another, we also agree to become another individual.

Bonding

Bonding is a public ritual that announces to the world that commitments have been formally contracted. It is the institutionalization of the relationship. There are many kinds of bonding rituals and they characterize several stages of the mixed-sex relationship—going steady, engagement, and ultimately marriage. American society has not sanctioned similar rituals for same-sexed romantic pairs, although some exist in certain sub-cultural groups.

Since bonding is simply the contract for the union of the pair at any given stage of the relationship, one might question why it has been designated as a separate stage. It is because the act of bonding itself may be a powerful force in changing the nature of the relationship "for better or for worse." The institutionalization of the relationship hardens it, makes it more difficult to break out of, and probably changes the rhetoric that takes place without a contract. The contract becomes, either explicitly or implicitly, a frequent topic of conversation. Communication strategies can now be based on interpretation and execution of the commitments contained in the contract. In short, the normal ebb and flow of the informal relationship can be, and often is, viewed differently.

When bonding is an extension of integrating, it is probably seen as a way to help stabilize one's newly formed individuality and integrated selves. It is a commitment to a common future:

> One's future in Western society at least, is one's most prized possession (or particularization). To commit it to another is the most important gift one can give.*

Bonding is a way of gaining social or institutional support for the relationship. It enables the couple to rely on law or policy or precedent. Bonding also provides guidance for the relationship through specified rules and regulations.

Differentiating

Literally, to differentiate means to become distinct or different in character. Just as integrating is mainly a process of fusion, differentiating is mainly a process of disengaging or uncoupling. While individual differences are of some concern at any stage in the developing relationship, they are now the major focus and serve as a prelude to increased interpersonal distance. A great deal of time and energy are spent talking and thinking about "how different we really are."

Joint endeavors formerly described by "we" or "our" now assume a more "I" or "my" orientation—a sort of "Please mother, I'd rather do it myself" approach. Previously designated joint possessions often become more individualized—"my friends," "my daughter," or "my bathroom." Communication is generally characterized by what distinguishes the two persons, or how little they have in common. Differences may be related to attitudes, interests, personality, relatives, friends, or to a specific behavior such as sexual needs or picking one's nose. Individuals who persist in interaction at this stage perceive these differences as strongly linked to basic or core values. Hence, we would expect to see less conversation about certain central areas of personality that may reflect these basic values. Persons who move in and out of this stage develop a history of expectations for the manner in which such difficulties will be settled, even if it is simply an agreement to seal off the areas of potential conflict.

When an unusually intense siege of differentiating takes place following bonding, it may be because bonding took place before the relationship achieved sufficient breadth and depth. It may also be due to some unplanned individual or social changes that altered the data upon which the original commitment was made. Advocates of renewable-term marriage argue that couples would be more likely to face, discuss, and work out unexpected changes in their lives if the marriage bond was not a lifelong commitment—if "till death do us part" meant the death of the relationship rather than the death of the participants.

The most visible communication form of differentiating, or affirming individuality, is fighting or conflict, although it is possible to differentiate without conflict.... Often conflict is a matter of one person simply testing the toleration of the other for something that threatens the relationship; it ultimately ends up with an explicit or implicit "love me (as I am) or leave me."

Circumscribing

At almost any stage of a relationship we can see some evidence of communication being constricted or circumscribed. In decaying relationships, however, information exchange qualitatively and quantitatively decreases. The main message strategy is to carefully control the areas of discussion, restricting communication to safe areas. Thus, we find less total communication in number of interactions as well as depth of subjects discussed, and communications of shorter duration.

Communication restraint applies to both breadth and depth. As the number of touchy topics increases, almost any topic becomes dangerous because it is not clear whether the new topic may in some way be wired to a previous area of static. When communication does take place, superficiality and public aspects are increasingly the norm. Communications related to one's basic values and hidden secrets may have a history of unpleasantness surrounding them; hence, we see a lot less information exchanged about "who I am and what our relationship is like." A corresponding decrease in expressions of commitment may be seen. When one person ventures such an expression, the echo response may not be so prevalent. "In spite of our differences, I still like you a lot." (Silence)

Familiar phrases typical of this stage include: "Don't ask me about that"; "Let's not talk about that anymore"; "It's none of your business"; "Just stick to the kind of work I'm doing and leave my religion out of it"; "You don't own me and you can't tell me what to think"; or "Can't we just be friends?" The last example is a suggestion that prescribes a whole new set of ground rules for permissible topics in the interaction.

When circumscribing characterizes the relationship, it may also have an impact on public social performances. Sometimes mutual social circles are also circumscribed, sometimes the presence of others is the only time when communication seems to increase—an effort to avoid being seen as not getting along. The following routine is not at all uncommon for some couples: Driving to a party, the two people exhibit mutual silence, empty gazes, and a general feeling of exhaustion. While playing out their party roles we see smiling, witticisms, and an orientation for being the life of the party. The trip home becomes a replay of the pre-party behavior.

Stagnating

To stagnate is to remain motionless or inactive. Rather than orally communicate, participants often find themselves conducting covert dialogues and concluding that since they "know" how the interaction will go, it is not necessary to say anything. At this stage, so many areas are closed off, efforts to communicate effectively are at a standstill. Even superficial areas have become so infected by previous communicative poison that they are generally left untried. In a sense, the participants are just marking time.

Some of the messages that are sent reflect unpleasant feeling states through the medium of nonverbal behavior. Other messages are very carefully chosen and well thought out. Language choices and message strategies seem to come even closer to those used with strangers, and the subject of the relationship is nearly taboo....

Extended stagnating can be seen in many relationships: between parents and children, just prior to divorce, just prior to the termination of a courtship, following unproductive small talk. The main theme characterizing this stage is "There is little sense bringing anything up because I know what will happen, and it won't be particularly pleasant." Experimentation is minimal because the unknown is thought to be known. It is during this time that each partner may engage in "imagined interactions."[11] These imagined dialogues will either take the form of narrative (e.g., "I'll say this and then she'll say this, and then ...") or actual dialogues (e.g., "I'll do it." "You don't have to." "Ok." "Ok, what?" "Ok, I won't." "Your typical attitude." "And *Your Typical Attitude!*"...).

You might legitimately question why people would linger at this stage with so many apparent costs accumulating. Most don't. But when persons continue interacting at this stage they may be getting some rewards outside of the primary relationship, through increased attention to their work or in developing another relationship. They also avoid the pain of terminating the relationship, which they may anticipate will be stronger than the current pain. Others may have hope that they can still revive the relationship. Still others may spend time at this stage because of some perverse pleasures obtained in punishing the other person.

Avoiding

While stagnating, the participants are usually in the same physical environment. Avoiding attempts to eliminate that condition. The rhetoric of avoidance is the antithesis of the rhetoric of initiation. Here, communication is specifically designed to avoid the possibility of face-to-face or voice-to-voice interaction. The overriding message seems to be: "I am not interested in seeing you; I am not interested in building a relationship; and I would like to close the communication channels between us." In this sense, then, avoiding suggests a much more permanent state of separation than that communicated by most people in their everyday leavetaking.

When the need to communicate avoidance results from an intimate relationship gone sour, the particular messages may contain overtones of antagonism or unfriendliness. They are more likely to be direct and to the point. "Please don't call me anymore. I just don't want to see or talk to you." This bluntness may naturally evolve from other conditions as well, such as when one person wants to pursue the relationship and ignores the more subtle avoidance cues. These subtle or indirect cues may take the form of being consistently late for appointments or preceding each encounter with "I can't stay long." Here the avoiding tactics are not motivated so much by dislike of the other as a lack of desire to expend time and energy pursuing a relationship. Sometimes an inordinate number of conflicting engagements can make the point: "I'm so busy I don't know when I'll be able to see you. Friday? I'm going home for the weekend. Monday? I have a sorority meeting. Tuesday? I have to study for a test," etc., etc.

In certain situations physical separation simply cannot be achieved, so a form of avoiding takes place in the presence of the other—it's as if the other person didn't exist. Not surprisingly under such conditions we find the receiver participating less in what interaction is available, not evaluating the other highly, and being less inclined to provide a reward to the other when an opportunity arises. The less obvious result of being ignored is the possibility of a lowered self-concept.[12]

Terminating

Relationships can terminate immediately after a greeting or after twenty years of intimacy. Sometimes they die slowly over a long period of time. The bonds that held the pair together wear thin and finally pull apart. The reasons behind such deterioration may be something obvious like living in parts of the country separated by great distance; or termination may just be the end result of two people growing socially and psychologically at different rates and in different directions. At other times, the threads holding two people together may be abruptly cut. It may be the death of one partner, radically changed circumstances, or an effort by one person to spare both of them the anticipated agony of a prolonged termination period.

Naturally, the nature of the termination dialogue is dependent on many factors: the relative status held or perceived between the two communicators; the kind of relationship already established or desired in the future; the amount of time allowed; whether the dialogue is conducted via the telephone, through a letter, or face to face; and many other individual and environmental factors.

Generally, however, we would predict termination dialogue to be characterized by messages of distance and disassociation. *Distance* refers to an attempt to put psychological and physical barriers between the two communicators. This might take the form of actual physical separation, or it may be imbedded in other nonverbal and verbal messages. *Disassociation* is found in messages that are essentially preparing one or both individuals for their continued life without the other—increasing concern for one's own self-interests, emphasizing differences. Obviously, the amount of distancing and disassociation will vary with the kind of relationship being dissolved, time available, and so on.

We would also predict that the general dimensions of communicative behavior reviewed earlier in this chapter would polarize more than ever around narrow, stylized, difficult, rigid, awkward, public, hesitant, and suspended judgments.

Finally, we would like to take a finding derived from the study of conversations and apply it to relationships. Thus, we would predict that termination dialogue would regularly manifest: (1) a summary statement; (2) behaviors signaling the impending termination or decreased access; and (3) messages that indicate what the future relationship (if any) will be like.[13] A summary statement reviews the relationship's history and provides the rationale for the imminent termination. Decreased-access messages clarify what is happening. Addressing the future avoids awkward interactions after parting. Even when dissolving a long-term relationship, the subject of being future friends or enemies must be addressed. "I'll always respect you, but I don't love you anymore," or "I don't ever want to see you again!" Saying goodbye to a long-term relationship may take longer, especially if one party does not want to end it and seeks to delay the final parting....

ENDNOTES

[6]Representative works include: R. Lacoursiere, *The Life Cycle of Groups* (New York: Human Sciences Press, 1980); R. Thornton and P. M. Nardi, "The Dynamics of Role Acquisition," *American Journal of*

Sociology 80 (1975): 870–885; I. Altman and D. A. Taylor, *Social Penetration: The Development of Interpersonal Relationships* (New York: Holt, Rinehart & Winston, 1973); B. W. Tuckman, "Developmental Sequence in Small Groups," *Psychological Bulletin* 63 (1965): 384–399; S. W. Duck, *Personal Relationships and Personal Constructs: A Study of Friendship Formation* (New York: John Wiley & Sons, 1973); M. S. Davis, *Intimate Relations* (New York: Free Press, 1973); T. M. Newcomb, *The Acquaintance Process* (New York: Holt, Rinehart & Winston, 1961); C. B. Broderick, "Predicting Friendship Behavior: A Study of the Determinants of Friendship Selection and Maintenance in a College Population" (Doctoral diss. Cornell University, 1956); G. M. Phillips and N. J. Metzger, *Intimate Communication* (Boston: Allyn & Bacon, 1976), pp. 401–403; C. R. Berger and R. J. Calabrese, "Some Explorations in Initial Interaction and Beyond: Toward a Developmental Theory of Interpersonal Communication," *Human Communication Research* 1 (1975): 99–112; C. R. Rogers, "A Process Conception of Psychotherapy," *American Psychologist* 13 (1958): 142–149; G. Simmel, *The Sociology of George Simmel,* trans. K. Wolff (New York: Free Press of Glencoe, 1950); K. Lewin, "Some Social Psychological Differences Between the United States and Germany," *Character and Personality* 4 (1936): 265–293; J. T. Wood, "Communication and Relational Culture: Bases for the Study of Human Relationships," *Communication Quarterly* 30 (1982): 75–83; D. P. McWhirter, and A. M. Mattison, *The Male Couple* (Englewood Cliffs, NJ: Prentice-Hall, 1984); W. J. Dickens and D. Perlman, "Friendship over the Life-Cycle." In S. Duck and R. Gilmour, eds. *Personal Relationships: 2. Developing Personal Relationships.* New York: Academic Press, 1981; C. A. VanLear, Jr. and N. Trujillo, "On Becoming Acquainted: A Longitudinal Study of Social Judgment Processes," *Journal of Social and Personal Relationships* 3 (1986): 375–392; and J. M. Honeycutt, J. G. Cantrill, and R. W. Greene, "Memory Structures for Relational Escalation: A Cognitive Test of the Sequencing of Relational Actions and Stages. *Human Communication Research* 16 (1989): 62–90.

[7] McWhirter and Mattison, *The Male Couple.*

[8] G. R. Miller and M. Steinberg, *Between People: A New Analysis of Interpersonal Communication.* Chicago: Science Research Associates, 1975; G. R. Miller and M. J. Sunnafrank, "All Is for One But One Is Not for All: A Conceptual Perspective of Interpersonal Communication." In F. E. X. Dance, ed., *Human Communication Theory.* New York: Harper & Row, 1982.

[9] H. L. Rausch, K. A. Marshall, and J. M. Featherman., "Relations at Three Early Stages of Marriage as Reflected by the Use of Personal Pronouns." *Family Process* 9 (1970): 69–82.

[10] L. A. Baxter, "Symbols of Relationship Identity in Relationship Cultures." *Journal of Social and Personal Relationships* 4 (1987): 261–280.

[11] Imagined interactions may occur at other points in the relationship as well—and for different purposes. For example, a person may construct an imagined dialogue relative to a forthcoming date or marriage proposal. See J. M. Honeycutt, K. S. Zagacki, and R. Edwards, "Intrapersonal Communication, Social Cognition, and Imagined Interactions." In C. Roberts and K. Watson, eds., *Readings in Intrapersonal Communication.* Birmingham, AL: Gorsuch Scarisbrick, 1989.

[12] D. M. Geller, L. Goodstein, M. Silver, and W. C. Sternberg, "On Being Ignored: The Effects of the Violation of Implicit Rules of Social Interaction." *Sociometry* 37 (1974): 541–556.

[13] M. L. Knapp, R. P. Hart, G. W. Friedrich, and G. M. Shulman, "The Rhetoric of Goodbye: Verbal and Nonverbal Correlates of Human Leave-Taking." *Speech Monographs* 40 (1973): 182–198.

Leslie A. Baxter and Barbara M. Montgomery

Rethinking Communication in Personal Relationships from a Dialectical Perspective

Leslie Baxter is best known for her work in relational dialectics. Baxter first described her ideas in a 1988 article in the Handbook of Personal Relationships. *After a decade of work, she teamed with Barbara Montgomery, and the two published their comprehensive work on the subject,* Relating: Dialogues & Dialectics *(1996). A more recent reflection on their work appears in* Communication and Personal Relationships *(Baxter & Montgomery, 2000), which is the excerpt presented here. Note that this reading does not so much emphasize the research of Baxter and Montgomery as it does to provide an overall essential framework for understanding dialectics from a theoretical point of view. If you want to see dialectics in action, I recommend Baxter's 1990 article in the* Journal of Social and Personal Relationships. *That empirical study describes the three sets of dialectical tensions common to dyads and the six management strategies that dyads use to deal with tension during the life of a relationship.*

Reading about dialectics is essential because it augments stage theory and is considered one of the most realistic explanations for the general process of interpersonal communication. A dialectical perspective posits that relationships are actually messy and that partners constantly feel and negotiate contradictions that characterize all dyads. This perspective has been around since Taoism divided the world into yin and yang, and thus has a long and historic appeal. Knowledge of a dialectical perspective helped me to see that the linear idea of stage theory is complemented by nonlinear processes. Dialectics can be considered an interior look at what happens within general stages of relational growth and maintenance. My own students see relational dialectics as a practical explanation of relational life and appreciate knowing how to label such tensions so that they can think about the kinds of communication that will help them manage the messiness of wanting "both/and" in a given relationship: "I want both autonomy and connection with my partner."

I have selected this excerpt because it is the most succinct piece by Baxter and Montgomery. It shows that dialectics is a big concept that a number of theorists have explored and contains the essential theoretical assumptions of a dialectical perspective and the people who have theorized about dialectics. The third section of the chapter, on directions for future research, has not been reprinted here so that we may concentrate on information relevant to teaching. Please note that the full information for the references in this article can be found in Communications and Personal Relationships *(Baxter & Montgomery, 2000)*

A dialectical perspective on communication in personal relationships was presented in the 1988 edition of the *Handbook of Personal Relationships* (Baxter, 1988). Since then, substantial empirical and theoretical work has appeared in which the term "dialectical" has been invoked. Rather than simply updating the 1988 chapter, we think it is more useful to offer a fresh articulation of this perspective, organized around three themes: (1) the commonly shared assumptions of a dialectical perspective; (2) major scholarly research programs emanating from a dialectical perspective; and (3) directions for future research. Our motive for addressing "shared assumptions" is to advance criteria by which a perspective can rightfully be described as dialectical; our observation is that the term "dialectical" has been invoked too loosely by some to describe work that is not fully dialectical in nature. Our motives for summarizing the major scholarly research programs are twofold: first, we want to give the reader bibliographic guidance to the major programmatic approaches that adopt a dialectical perspective; and second, we want to emphasize that each of the major dialectical scholars contributes something unique to the study of communication in personal relationships. Several excellent pieces of dialectically-oriented research have been conducted outside the framework of the research programs which we will be summarizing, and we refer the reader elsewhere for more comprehensive reviews of this work (Baxter & Montgomery, 1996; Montgomery & Baxter, 1998; Werner & Baxter, 1994). We reserve the bulk of the chapter to a discussion of directions for future research based on our reading of the dialogic perspective articulated by the Russian scholar Mikhail Bakhtin.

SHARED ASSUMPTIONS OF A DIALECTICAL PERSPECTIVE

Dialectics is not a theory in the traditional sense. It lacks the structural intricacies of formal theories of prediction and explanation; it offers no extensive hierarchical array of axiomatic or propositional arguments. It does not represent a single, unitary statement of generalizable predictions. Dialectics describes, instead, a family of theoretical perspectives with a shared set of conceptual assumptions (Baxter & Montgomery, 1998). Those assumptions, which revolve around the notions of contradiction, change, praxis and totality, constitute what is better thought of as a metatheoretical perspective (Benson, 1977; Buss, 1979; Cornforth, 1968, Murphy, 1971; Rawlins, 1989; Rychlak, 1976).

Contradiction

From a dialectical perspective, contradictions are inherent in social life and are the basic "drivers" of change and vitality in any social system. The term "contradiction" holds a technical meaning to dialectical theorists and refers to "the dynamic interplay between unified opposites."

In general terms, tendencies or features of a phenomenon are "opposites" if they are incompatible and mutually negate one another. Not all oppositions are alike, however. A logically defined, or "negative," opposition takes the form

"X and not X". That is, an opposition consists of some feature and its absence; for instance, stable vs. not stable, autonomous vs. not autonomous, and loving vs. not loving are logically defined contradictions in personal relationships. By contrast, functionally-defined, or "positive", oppositions take the form "X and Y", where both "X" and "Y" are distinct features that function in incompatible ways, such that each negates the other. Examples include stable vs. fluid, autonomous vs. connected, and loving vs. hateful. In practice, functionally defined oppositions are easier to study than logically defined contradictions, simply because both oppositional poles are more explicitly referenced phenomena (Adler, 1927, 1952; Altman, Vinsel & Brown, 1981; Georgoudi, 1983; Israel, 1979).

But functionally defined oppositions have their own complications. First, because the researcher does not have the luxury of logical negation (i.e., "X" and "not X") as the basis of defining an opposition, he/she bears the burden of demonstrating that "X" and "Y" are functionally opposite, that is, that the totality of one precludes the other. What constitutes a functional opposition in one context, culture, or time period might not generalize to another.

A second complication of functionally defined oppositions is that they are likely to be more complicated than a simple binary pair; that is, many oppositions, not just one, are likely to exist in relation to a given feature. For example, the researcher interested in examining the feature of "certainty" from a dialectical perspective might identify several dialectical oppositions that could co-exist: certainty-unpredictability, certainty-novelty, certainty-mystery, certainty-excitement, etc. The complete dialectical understanding of "certainty" rests on the researcher's ability to understand the complexity of multiple oppositions of which "certainty" is an element.

Opposition is a necessary but not sufficient condition for contradiction. In addition, the opposites must simultaneously be unified or interdependent with one another, a concept often referred to as "the unity of opposites". Dialectical unity can occur in two basic ways (Altman, Vinsel & Brown, 1981). First, each oppositional tendency presupposes the existence of the other for its very meaning; this is a unity of identity. The concept of "certainty", for example, is meaningful only because we have an understanding of its logical and/or functional opposites; without knowledge of "uncertainty", "chaos", "unpredictability" and so forth, the concept of "certainty" would be meaningless.

Second, the oppositional tendencies are unified as interdependent parts of a larger whole; this is interdependent unity. For example, in the context of personal relationships, individual autonomy and relational connection are unified opposites. The two tendencies form a functional opposition in that the total autonomy of parties precludes their relational connection, just as total connection between parties precludes their individual autonomy. However, individual autonomy and relational connection form an interdependent unity, as well. Connection with others is necessary in the construction of a person's identity as an autonomous individual (e.g., Askham, 1976; Mead, 1934; Zicklin, 1969), just as the ever-changing nature of a relational connection is predicated on the existence of the parties' unique identities (e.g., Askham, 1976; Karpel,

1976; Kernberg, 1974; L'Abate & L'Abate, 1979; Ryder & Bartle, 1991). Thus, in a contradiction, opposites negate one another. Unity is the basis of the "both/and" quality of contradictions.

Third, a requisite condition for a contradiction is dynamic interplay or tension between the unified opposites. Within the dialectical perspective, the concept of tension carries no negative connotations; instead, the term simply refers to the ongoing, ever-changing interaction between unified oppositions. This interplay is what distinguishes a dialectical perspective from a dualistic one. It is easy to confuse dialectics with dualism, because both perspectives emphasize the presence of opposites. In dualism, however, opposites are conceived as more or less static and isolated phenomena that coexist in parallel fashion. For example, research exists on self-disclosure and on its binary opposite, privacy regulation. However, this research is dualistic so long as each phenomenon is conceived to be definitionally, developmentally, and practically independent. By contrast, a dialectical perspective emphasizes how parties manage the simultaneous but ever-changing exigence for both disclosure and privacy in their relationships and, especially, how the "both/and"-ness of disclosure and privacy is patterned through their mutual influence across the developmental course of a relationship. In short, dualism emphasizes opposites in parallel, whereas dialectics emphasizes the interplay of opposites.

Dialectical Change

The interplay of unified opposites means that all social systems experience the dynamic tension between stability and change. Although all dialectical approaches presume that change is an inherent feature of dialectical contradiction, differences of emphasis can be identified with respect to two underlying issues related to change: (1) the position taken with respect to causation, that is, the relative weighting given to Aristotle's "efficient cause" and "formal cause"; and (2) whether change is regarded as fundamentally indeterminate or teleological.

Aristotle's "efficient cause" refers to linear antecedent–consequent relations, that is, the familiar cause–effect relation, whether this relation is one-way (X is a cause of Y) or reciprocal (X and Y cause and are caused by one another) (Rychlak, 1988). By contrast, Aristotle's "formal cause" refers to the patterned relations among phenomena, that is, the "pattern, shape, outline, or recognizable organization in the flow of events or in the way that objects are constituted" (Rychlak, 1988, pp. 5–6). Unlike an emphasis on one-way or reciprocal cause–effect relations, formal cause focuses on how phenomena mutually define one another in patterned ways, how events flow and unfold over time, and how patterns shift and change; from the perspective of formal cause, none of the component phenomena is "caused" by any prior occurrence of another phenomena. Dialectical theorists differ in their emphasis on efficient causation and formal causation, as we illustrate later in the chapter.

A second issue around which dialectical theorists differ is whether the change process is presumed to be fundamentally indeterminate or teleological in nature. A teleological approach to change presumes that change is the servant of ideal endstates or goals; phenomena are more or less "pulled" toward an ideal outcome. By contrast, indeterminacy presumes that change is not directed toward some necessary or ideal end-state; rather, change involves ongoing quantitative and qualitative shifts that simply move a system to a different place. Some dialectical theorists endorse a teleological view of change, in which contradictions are transcended in a thesis–antithesis–synthesis dynamic. At a given point in time, one pole or aspect of a given contradiction is dominant (the so-called "thesis"), which in turn sets in motion a qualitative change that leads to the salience at a second point in time of the opposing aspect or pole (the so-called "antithesis"), after which a transformative change occurs in which the original opposition of poles is somehow transcended, such that the contradiction no longer exists (the so-called "synthesis").

Other dialectical theorists reject the teleological goal of transcendent change or synthesis, endorsing instead a model of indeterminacy in which two opposing tendencies simply continue their ongoing interplay (Rychlak, 1976). This indeterminate interplay of opposites can involve both cyclical change and linear change. That is, change can be characterized by a repeating patter (cyclical) and/or a series of changes representing progression from one state to another (linear). Cyclical change occurs when the interplay of oppositions takes on a back-and-forth flavor, with relationship parties emphasizing first one oppositional tendency and then the other in an ongoing ebb-and-flow pattern. Visually and theoretically, such an ebb-and-flow pattern would look like repeating sine waves; in actuality, the cycles are characterized by varying amplitudes and rhythms through time, rather than by the uniformity and regularity of sine waves (Altman, Vinsel & Brown, 1981). In contrast, linear change involves a series of non-repeating changes in which the system never returns to a previous state. Further, these two types of change can be combined into linear, cyclic change, or what Werner and Baxter (1994) refer to as "spiraling change". Strictly speaking, cyclicity assumes that phenomena recur in identical form. A spiral, by contrast, involves recurrence but recognizes that phenomena never repeat in identical form; a spiral thus combines elements of both cyclical change (recurrence) and linear change (the absence of identical repetition). Because cyclicity in its strict sense is counter to most conceptualizations of social interaction, spiraling change is probably a more accurate characterization of indeterminate change.

The ebb-and-flow nature of indeterminate, spiraling change often leads people mistakenly to conclude that the teleological goal of homeostasis or equilibrium "drives" this form of dialectical change (e.g., Stafford, 1994). Just the opposite is the case. What propels a spiral to shift toward the other pole(s) is not homeostasis but neglect of that pole. As Bopp and Weeks (1984) observed, the concept of homeostatic equilibrium privileges permanence and stability, thereby ignoring the pervasive dialectic tension between stability and change. Attempts to categorize dialectics as an equilibrium theory fail to recognize its core presumption that spiraling is "driven" by the nature of contradiction, which assumes that some aspect of the opposition is *always* left wanting.

Praxis

The third tenet of dialectics is that people are at once both actors and objects of their own actions, a quality dialectical theorists have termed "praxis" (e.g., Benson, 1977; Israel, 1979; Rawlins, 1989). People function proactively by making communicative choices. Simultaneously, however, they are reactive, because their actions become reified in a variety of normative and institutionalized practices that establish the boundaries of subsequent communicative choices. People are actors in giving communicative life to the contradictions that organize their social life, but these contradictions, in turn, affect their subsequent communicative actions. Every interaction event is a unique moment at the same time that each is informed by the history of prior interaction events and informs future events.

Praxis is an abstract and empty construct without consideration of the concrete practices by which social actors produce the future out of the past in their everyday lives. Dialectical theorists situate praxis in various domains of social life, depending on their particular interests. Marxist dialectical materialists, for example, center their study of contradiction in the material resources of production and consumption by the proletariat and bourgeoisie classes in capitalist societies. By contrast, dialectical theorists who study communication in relationships situate the interplay of opposing tendencies in the symbolic, not material, practices of relationship parties. They emphasize communication as a symbolic resource through which meanings are produced and reproduced. Through their jointly enacted communicative choices, relationship parties react to dialectical exigencies that have been produced from their past interactional history together. At the same time, the communicative choices of the moment alter the dialectical circumstances that the pair will face in future interactions together. Many possible patterns of dialectical change result from a pair's communicative choices (Baxter, 1988; Baxter & Montgomery, 1996), and we will return to this point later.

Totality

The fourth and final core concept of dialectics is "totality"; that is, the assumption that phenomena can be understood only in relation to other phenomena (Benson, 1977; Israel, 1979; Mirkovic, 1980; Rawlins, 1989). From a dialectical perspective, the notion of totality does not mean "completeness" in the sense of producing a total portrait of a phenomenon; the world is an unfinalizable process in which we can point, at best, to fleeting and fluid patterns of the moment. Totality, from a dialectical perspective, is a way to think about the world as a process of relations or interdependencies. On its face, the concept of totality appears to be the same as any number of other theoretical orientations that emphasize such holistic notions as contextuality or relatedness. Put simply, dialectics is one form of holism but not all holistic theories are dialectical; the criterion that distinguishes dialectical holism from other holistic perspectives is the focus on contradictions as the unit of analysis. Dialectical totality, in turn, implicates three issues: where contradictions are located, interdependencies among contradictions, and contextualization of contradictory interplay.

The Location of Contradictions. The first important implication of the dialectical emphasis on the whole is that the tension of opposing dialectical forces is conceptually located *within* the interpersonal relationship, not necessarily as antagonisms *between* individual partners. That is, dialectical attention is directed away from the individual as the unit of analysis and toward the dilemmas and tensions that inhere in relating. Dialectical tensions are played out, relational force against relational force rather than relational partner against relational partner (Montgomery, 1993). As people come together in any social union, they create a host of dialectical forces. Although partners are aware of many of the dialectical dilemmas they face (e.g., Baxter, 1990), a dialectical tension does not need to be consciously felt or expressed. Dialectical interplay may work "backstage" beyond partners' mindful awareness, nonetheless contributing to relational change.

Dialectical tension is thus jointly "owned" by the relationship parties by the very fact of their partnership. But joint ownership does not translate to perfect synchrony in the parties' perceptions; often there is little commonality in partners' experiences of relational contradictions. As Giddens (1979) has noted, dialectical interplay may surface as interpersonal conflict between parties if they are "out of sync" in their momentary experience of a contradiction, such that one person aligns his/her interests with one pole and the other person aligns his/her interests with the other pole. For example, one relationship party may want greater independence between the two of the partners, while the other may want less independence. Mao (1965, p. 48) refers to this asynchrony as antagonistic struggle. Thus, interpersonal conflict is not the equivalent of dialectical tension although, under special circumstances, dialectical tension may be manifested in interpersonal conflict between the parties.

Interdependencies among Contradictions. A system usually contains not one but many contradictions; Cornforth (1968, p. 111) describes this as the "knot of contradictions" that coexist and change in relation to one another over time. In analytically disentangling this dialectical "knot", dialectical theorists have introduced two basic distinctions in types of contradictions. The first, between principal and secondary contradictions, hierarchically organizes contradictions with respect to their impact on or centrality to the dialectical knot. Primary contradictions are those which are more central or salient to a dialectical system at a given point in time. For example, the interplay between autonomy and interdependence has often been identified by dialectical theorists as the most central of all relational contradictions, organizing the pattern of interdependencies among such secondary contradictions as openness and closedness (e.g., Baxter, 1988).

The second distinction is between internal contradictions and external contradictions (Ball, 1979; Cornforth, 1968; Israel, 1979; Mao, 1965; Riegel, 1976). As the term "internal" might suggest, an internal contradiction is constituted within the boundaries of the system under study, whereas an external contradiction is constituted at the nexus of the system with the larger system in which it is embedded. Within the context of personal relationships, internal contradictions are those oppositional forces that function within the boundaries of the dyad and which are inherent to dyadic relating; for example, how the partners can be open and expressive at the same time that they sustain privacy and protectiveness. By contrast, external contradictions are those inherent oppositional forces that operate at the nexus of the dyad and its external environment; for instance, how partners can both conform to society's conventions for relating at the same time that they construct a unique relational bond. External contradictions underscore that relationships are inherently social entities. That is, couples and society sustain a relationship, and in so doing they engage inherent contradictions of such relationships. From a dialectical perspective, internal and external contradictions are presumed to interrelate in dynamic ways. For example, society's conventions for self-disclosure in relationships no doubt are associated with a given couple's experience of their internal dilemma between openness and closedness.

Contextualization of Contradictory Interplay.   As Mao (1965) observed, the fact of contradiction is universal but the particulars of the contradicting process vary from one context to another. Dialectical scholars are thus obliged to study contradictions in situ at both universal and particular levels, in contrast to efforts which might seek to reduce contradictions to abstractions stripped of their localized particularities. Social phenomena encompass concrete environmental, situational and interpersonal factors which are integrally related with issues of praxis and the nature of dialectical change.

MAJOR DIALECTICAL RESEARCH PROGRAMS IN THE STUDY OF COMMUNICATION IN PERSONAL RELATIONSHIPS

A number of perspectives on communication in personal relationships echo with dialectical reverberations, some quite strongly (e.g., Altman, 1993; Conville, 1991; Rawlins, 1992), and others more faintly (e.g., Billig, 1987; Shotter, 1993). We cannot provide an exhaustive summary of this work here (see Baxter & Montgomery, 1996), but we hope to give a flavor of the contributions currently being made to a dialectical understanding of communication in personal relationships.

Bochner's Work on the Dialectics of Family Systems

Bochner (1984) articulated an early dialectical framework for understanding communication in personal relationships, which has been developed more recently in studies of family systems (Bochner & Eisenberg, 1987; Cissna, Cox, & Bochner, 1990; Ellis & Bochner, 1992; Yerby, Buerkel-Rothfuss, & Bochner, 1995). Bochner and his colleagues emphasize three particular functional contradictions in social interaction: (1) how partners are both expressive, revealing, and vulnerable (open) and, simultaneously, discrete, concealing, and protective (closed) with each other; (2) how family members sustain unique individual identities and behave independently (differentiation), while at the same time sharing a family identity and behaving in interdependent ways (integration); and (3) how the family system manages to be both stable (stability) yet adaptive to fluctuating demands placed on it (change).

Bochner is interested in formal cause, not efficient cause, and he argues that scholars should not "confuse predictive efficiency with an understanding of developmental processes" (Bochner, 1984, p. 580). He suggests that the contradictions that organize social life are ongoing throughout a relationship's life cycle, a position that implies indeterminate change rather than teleological change. He also calls for developing a research language of process and change that would recognize incremental variations but also temporally complex "turning points" and momentum reversions. In this recent work (e.g., Ellis & Bochner, 1992), Bochner has emphasized the "lived experience" of contradictory dilemmas as they are concretely and subjectively felt by relationship parties. Bochner's empirically-oriented work is interpretive and particularly emphasizes the study of narratives (Bochner, 1994).

The work of Bochner and his colleagues builds productively on a tradition of dialectical approaches to family systems that goes back as much as three decades. Family therapists, for example, have long been intrigued by contradictions, paradox, disequilibrium and inconsistencies (e.g., Haley, 1963; Selvini-Palazzoli et al., 1978; Watzlawick, Weakland, & Fisch, 1974). In addition, the conceptual ground in family studies was fertile for nurturing the seeds of dialectics in the 1970s and 1980s, and many dialectical perspectives were produced (e.g., Bopp & Weeks, 1984; Hoffman, 1981; Kempler, 1981; Minuchin, 1974; Wynne, 1984).

Altman's Transactional World View

Over the past 20 years, Irwin Altman and his colleagues have contributed significantly to scholarly discourse about such topics as relationship development (Altman & Taylor, 1973, Altman, Vinsel & Brown, 1981), privacy regulation (Altman, 1977), cross-cultural relationship rituals and practices (Altman et al., 1992; Werner et al., 1993), and social psychological implications of the home environment (Altman & Gauvain, 1981). This body of work stems from a particular theoretical perspective, which Altman (1990, 1993) refers to as "a transactional world view". Altman uniquely couples transactionalism with dialectics to explore phenomena particularly salient to personal relationships. The mainstay of this work is a holistic integration of interpersonal processes (e.g., intimacy, self-disclosure), physical and social environments (e.g., the home, the culture) and temporal qualities (e.g., pace and rhythm of change) to understand social phenomena. Transactional dialectics thus gives particular emphasis to dialectical totality. Phenomena are not viewed in antecedent-consequent relations, but instead are seen as embedded in a continuing and dynamic process of patterned interplay. Altman and his colleagues contend that these coherent patterns of change and fluidity (i.e., formal causation) maintain a "transactional unity" among the elements of processes, environments and time.

Altman and his colleagues view dialectical contradiction as an intrinsic aspect of social existence. They have focused especially on the functional oppo-sitions of openness and closedness, stability and change (Altman, Vinsel & Brown, 1981), and individuality and communality (Altman & Gauvain, 1981) as specific manifestations of social dialectics. Some of their work examines these basic contradictions with the individual as the unit of analysis; for example, how individuals both open themselves up to interaction with others yet maintain a boundary of privacy (e.g., Altman, Vinsel & Brown, 1981). Other work examines larger social units, including couples, families, neighborhoods, and cultures; for example, how couples within different cultures are integrated into the social networks of their families and friends while, at the same time, are differentiated as separate social entities (e.g., Altman & Ginat, 1996).

Temporally-oriented descriptions of change are paramount in Altman's work. He and his colleagues view the focus on change "as a necessary antidote to the proliferation of social psychological approaches that emphasized stabil-ity, consistency, or homeostasis as relational goals to the exclusion of needs for change, growth, and movement" (Brown, Altman, & Werner, 1992, p. 510). Col-laborations with Werner and others (Werner, Altman, & Oxley, 1985; Werner et al., 1987, 1988) have produced a conceptual framework of temporal qualities like pace, rhythm and duration, which have been used to describe the changing qualities of relationships, home environments and cultural practices.

One of the strongest themes in the Altman et al. work is its multi-method orientation. Multiple sources of data (e.g., interviews, observations, archival data) are emphasized in order to represent different perspectives on events. "Methodological eclecticism" is valued with respect to research designs, proce-dures and measures (Brown, Werner & Altman, 1998).

Rawlins' View of Friendship over the Life Course

Like Altman, Rawlins (1983a, 1983b, 1989, 1992, 1994a, 1998; Rawlins & Holl, 1987, 1988) stresses totality by incorporating dialectics into what could be called a transactional view, although Rawlins limits his study to platonic friendships. To Rawlins (1992, p. 273), "A dialectical perspective calls for inves-tigating and situating enactment of friendships in their concrete social condi-tions over time". The concrete social conditions of friendships which are most salient in Rawlins' studies are work, marriage, family, retirement and personal crisis. Time, for Rawlins, is defined predominantly by the life stages of child-hood, adolescence, young adulthood, adulthood and later adulthood.

Rawlins has relied on the interpretive analysis of interviews with people of all ages to gain a dialectical perspective on a number of functionally defined contradictions, which he calls the "pulse" of friendships. He identifies two fun-damental types. "Contextual dialectics" represent contradictions in culture-based notions, norms and expectations that frame the way any particular friendship is experienced or enacted. These include the tension between public and private enactments of friendship and the tension between abstract ideals and actual realities of friendship. "Interactional dialectics" represent the contradictions involved as friends manage and sustain their relationship on an ongoing, everyday basis. These "communicative predicaments of friendships" include the dialectics of exercising the freedoms to be independent and dependent, caring for a friend as a means-to-an-end (instrumentality) and as an end-in-itself (affection), offering evaluative judgements and offering unconditional acceptance, and, finally, being open and expressive and also being strategic and protective. While Rawlins focuses most on these six contextual and interactional contradictions, he has introduced others through his analyses, like the tension between historical perspectives and present experiences, a dialectic found to be particularly evident in adolescents' interactions with parents and friends (e.g., Rawlins & Holl, 1988).

Rawlins implicates both efficient cause and formal cause in his elucidation of dialectical change. Much of his empirical work seeks to describe the complex, patterned interplay among contradictions indicative of formal causation. However, in total, his extensive analyses construct an argument for efficient cause in that variations in the manifestations of dialectical tensions are due to types and degrees of friendship, cultural constraints, and individual characteristics, especially age and gender. Indeed, change and flux are represented most strongly in the transitions between life stages and not in day-to-day interaction. Rawlins appears to suggest that an individual's age is the antecedent causal variable that results in particular manifestations of given contradictions. Thus, both adolescents and older persons experience the dialectical interplay of independence and interdependence, but these two developmental stages lead people to experience this interplay differently.

Rawlins recognizes both teleological change and indeterminate change. Teleological change, or what Rawlins (1989) calls the "dialectic of transcendence", occurs when friends resolve contradictions and, in so doing, create new ones through the process of thesis–antithesis–synthesis. Rawlins also evokes a kind of indeterminate change when he talks about the "dialectic of encapsulation", which represents relatively closed, regulated and narrowly circumscribed change. While Rawlins' (1989) conceptual discussion of encapsulation focuses most on patterns that reflect the selecting and sustaining of a dominant polarity over a secondary one, his descriptive data about actual behavioral practices emphasize indeterminate changes represented in cycles and spirals between fairly equally weighted polarities (Rawlins, 1983a, 1983b, 1992).

Conville's Relational Transitions Model

Conville (1983, 1988, 1991, 1998) integrates dialectical notions into a structural approach to understand the development of personal relationships. Specifically, Conville argues that during the process of resolving dialectical contradictions, partners are "out of kilter". This imbalance propels relationships through transitions, which link the times when partners are "in kilter", i.e., feel comfortable, occupy complementary roles and coordinate their actions. Moreover these periods of "in kilter" security are but one phase of a recursive process, driven by dialectical oppositions. Security is followed sequentially by the phases of disintegration, alienation and resynthesis to a new pattern of security.

These teleologically defined, relational transitions occur throughout the relationship course, which Conville likens to a spiral or helix. He stresses that the helix represents the recurrence of "second-order" or qualitative changes, which result in the restructuring of the social realities of a relationship, creating new grounds for relating. Conville contrasts this with first-order change, which is change within the context of the given grounds for interaction. For instance, partners deciding to spend more (or less) time together is a first-order change; partners redefining a relationship from "a romantic fling" to "a long-term romance" is a second-order change. According to Conville, partners can cycle through the second-order change process and security-disintegration–alienation–resynthesis many times over the course of their relationship's history, qualitatively transforming the definition of their relationship with the completion of each four-period cycle. In this way, Conville's model underscores the functionality of relationship crisis, which signifies the disintegration of an old relational state.

Conville's conception of contradiction stresses efficient causation. The structural constraint of sequenced episodes leading, always, from security to disintegration, to alienation, to resynthesis and to a new security, represents the assumption of standard, directional changes in relating. Additionally, Conville defines two "meta-dialectics" in this sequence, formed in the juxtapositions of security–alienation and of disintegration–resynthesis. These primary contradictions set the relational stage for the playing out of the secondary contradictions associated with the themes of time (i.e., past–future), intimacy (i.e., close–distant) and affect (i.e., positive–negative).

Conville has applied his structural model to understand a variety of relationship case studies, ranging from the friendship of Helen Keller and Anne Sullivan to the romantic and marital relationships of ordinary persons. His method is a form of interpretive structural analysis.

Baxter's and Montgomery's Dialectical Work

Until recently, each of us has contributed independently to the literature on dialectics in personal relationships. Baxter's work has involved both quantitative and qualitative studies of contradictions in friendships (Bridge & Baxter, 1992), romantic relationships (e.g., Baxter, 1988, 1990; Baxter et al., 1997; Baxter & Widenmann, 1993), marital couples (Baxter & Simon, 1993; Braithwaite & Baxter, 1995) and family relationships (Braithwaite, Baxter & Harper, 1998). Six internal and external contradictions have received attention in this work: the internal contradictions of autonomy–connection, predictability–novelty, and openness–closedness; and the external contradictions of separation–integration, conventionality–uniqueness, and revelation–non-revelation (Baxter, 1993, 1994). Montgomery's work (1984, 1992, 1993) has been characterized by its theoretical orientation, building up on the work of Bateson (1972, 1979) in articulating the ongoing flux of both internal and external contradictions experienced by relationship parties. We have both emphasized the praxis of contradiction; that is, how contradictions are created and sustained through communicative practices.

Most recently, however, we have collaborated in an articulation of ways to rethink the dialectical study of communication in personal relationships (Baxter & Montgomery, 1996). This recent articulation reflects a shift in our previous dialectical work and raises new possibilities for the dialectically-oriented work of others. In particular, we have been influenced by one specific variant of dialectical thinking, Bakhtin's dialogism. Despite variability in recent understandings of dialogism, scholarly opinion seems to be coalescing on the centrality of the "dialogue" to Bakhtin's lifelong intellectual work (Clark & Holquist, 1984; Holquist, 1990: Morson & Emerson, 1990; Todorov, 1984). Bakhtin was critical of the "monologization" of the human experience that he perceived in the dominant linguistic, literary, philosophical and political theories of his time. His intellectual project was a critique of theories that reduced the unfinalizable, open and heterogeneous nature of social life to determinate, closed, totalizing concepts (Bakhtin, 1965/1984, 1981, 1984, 1986; Voloshinov/Bakhtin, 1973[1]). To Bakhtin, social life was a "dialogue", not a "monologue". The essence of dialogue is a simultaneous differentiation from, yet fusion with, another. To enact dialogue, the parties need to fuse their perspectives while maintaining the uniqueness of their individual perspectives; the parties form a unity in conversation but only through two clearly differentiated voices. Dialogue, unlike monologue, is multivocal; that is, it is characterized by the presence of at least two distinct voices. Just as a dialogue is invoked by and also invokes unity and difference, Bakhtin (1981, p. 272) regarded all social processes as the product of "a contradiction-ridden, tension-filled unity of two embattled tendencies", the centripetal (i.e., forces of unity) and the centrifugal (i.e., forces of difference).

WHAT ARE YOUR CHOICES?

Now that you've read my "essential readings," how grounded do you feel in your knowledge of interpersonal communication? Do you see the range of paradigms, disciplines, and theoretical perspectives from which the study of communication process is derived? If you had to select your own five essential readings, what would they be, and why?

---

[1] Some scholars believe that Bakhtin, not Voloshinov, wrote *Marxism and the Philosophy of Language*. The most recent discussion of Bakhtin's authorship is Bocharov (1994). We will refer to "Voloshinov/Bakhtin" throughout.

7

Foundational Resources

In this chapter we will concentrate on technical aspects of locating and reading materials that support an entry-level course in interpersonal communication. You will find an introductory discussion on types of sources and how to read them efficiently, advice on building a personal library, and an annotated bibliography of 79 citations. This chapter will help increase your teaching effectiveness by showing you how to use foundational resources in an informed and systematic manner. Let's begin by looking at the types of resources available.

PRIMARY AND SECONDARY RESOURCES

Teachers need both primary and secondary sources to understand the scope of the field. Primary sources are the original findings reported by the authors and/or researchers themselves. This primary source material comprises our teaching foundation and is the initial word on the theory or concept in question. It is best to go to the original source whenever possible so that we can read for ourselves the researchers' principal ideas. In general, it is recommended that we read the research in the language of its time and in the source in which it was originally published because once a primary source is interpreted and printed somewhere else, ideas can change or become distorted. For example, Erving Goffman's *The Presentation of Self in Everyday Life* was published in 1959, yet we are still using many of his ideas about impression management and interpersonal persuasion. The phrase *impression management* wasn't used 45 years ago, so it is a good idea to read the original to get the holistic feel and understanding of his ideas. Also, the language and examples he uses are somewhat different from what an author might use today, so reading the original may help you recognize any distortions that could occur as contemporary authors invoke Goffman's book. Reading the original source makes you a more grounded reader intellectually and historically.

Secondary sources, such as textbooks, are valuable because they show us how our colleagues interpret knowledge. We need to see how others frame and interpret the scholarship of interpersonal communication because that is an indicator of how the material is valued and presented to students. Just looking at a textbook for its point of view, what is included and excluded, and how the material is organized tells a teacher a great deal about how the principles of interpersonal communication are taught. A secondary source is often a shortcut because someone else does the thinking for you. If you are short on time, this could be a quick answer to your need for knowledge. However, reading primary sources is the only way to fully ground yourself in original ideas. As a teacher, you need to make decisions about how central a role secondary sources will play in your teaching.

Consider the following instructive activity. Compare five interpersonal communication textbooks on the following points: overall organization, major themes, and main topic covered in each chapter. Where do these textbooks converge and diverge? What does this tell you about the general way instructors view the appropriate teaching of interpersonal communication? Do you agree or disagree with the general approach you see in these textbooks? How does an activity like this help you think about your teaching and resource selection?

Types of Primary and Secondary Sources

Primary and secondary sources come in various formats; following is a guide to help you identify the sources that may be found in the annotated bibliography at the end of this chapter. Note that different formats have unique structural features that determine how a reader should approach the material; I will point out those features. Types of sources you may read include:

Edited Anthology. This is a collection of essays or chapters by different authors that targets various aspects of the same general topic. Anthologies can be a collection of research reports, factual essays, historical pieces, critical articles, or a combination of these. One of the best ways to determine the structure of an anthology is to read the editor's preface or introduction. Then study the table of contents to see how the articles relate to the central theme of the anthology.

Both Sage and Lawrence Erlbaum publishers are known for their excellent research anthologies on interpersonal communication topics. These anthologies typically comprise a combination of literature reviews, theoretical suggestions, and research reports. An anthology such as this would be considered primary because the research is original and the content theorizing. For example, in the annotated bibliography, the *Handbook of Communication and Social Interaction Skills* (2003), edited by John Greene and Brant Burleson, is a collection of literature reviews on a range of interpersonal contexts connected to competence. It is a research-based anthology that goes beyond what a textbook is designed to do and includes contributions from experts in the field.

Journal Articles. In the social sciences, journal articles are usually professional reports of scientific studies and are considered primary sources. These articles report research findings about human behavior, helping us to understand its patterns and the way research supports theories about human behavior. This type of text is best understood if you have a command of both scientific methods for conducting research and the typical vocabulary or jargon for that topic area. If you do not have knowledge of scientific research methods, do not be deterred. The article title reveals the main concept or theoretical area under investigation. If there is an abstract available, read it to get the summary and basic findings of the study. The body of most social science reports is divided into four parts: introduction, methods and procedures, results, and discussion and conclusions. The methods and procedures section will be the most technical, so if you don't have the background for it, you might want to concentrate more on the other three sections. There are valuable ideas to explore in all of the sections, but the discussion and conclusions will usually summarize the study for you.

Book. This type of source is a report of an entire theory, in most instances. A book is usually the culmination of many years of research wherein the author collects and presents his or her research findings into a coherent whole, rather than as a collection of piecemeal journal articles published over the testing of a theory. Books frequently include chapters on the theoretical framework, the instrumentation used to collect data, a review of the studies done over a period of time, the propositions and models that are the core of the theory, and some criticism of the theory. These books are valuable for the extended knowledge provided.

For example, Irwin Altman and Dalmas Taylor's book *Social Penetration: The Development of Interpersonal Relationships* (1973/1983), presents the theory of social penetration. Many interpersonal communication textbooks present the famous "onion model" from social penetration theory, but it's not until you read the primary source that you understand in depth what the model means. Reading the original source has helped me to clarify for students the model in the textbook, and it has directed me to teach the model beyond simply as a tool for understanding self-disclosure in relationship development.

Traditional Textbook. As was stated earlier, a traditional textbook is a secondary source. This type of source is often easy to read because the author uses many pedagogical tools (headings, boxes, discussion questions, a glossary, bold type, and exercises) to help you understand the content of the text. The annotated bibliography at the end of this chapter lists a few textbooks, which have been included either because they are considered classics in the field, such as Miller and Steinberg's *Between People* (1975), or because they are an extension of an author's original theorizing on an interpersonal communication topic, such as *Competent Communication* (1997) by O'Hair, Friedrich, Wiemann, and Wiemann. Such cases reveal some crossover between primary and secondary reporting of knowledge.

READING RESOURCES EFFICIENTLY

You have two immediate goals each time you sit down to read a source: (1) you want to be able to understand the main idea of the reading, and (2) you want to be able to teach intelligently the knowledge from the reading during your class discussion. To accomplish these goals, here are some tips:

- Examine the journal or book title and locate the description of the author(s). This information can give you clues about the author's point of view in writing the document. For example, a social psychologist may focus on slightly different issues than a communication theorist. To help you with this, I have identified the discipline with which each author is affiliated in the annotated bibliography.

- Review the headings and subheadings in the document before you start reading to get a feel for the main points and the progression of ideas.
- Start reading. Some readers are tempted to highlight or underline much of the material, but try not to overdo it. (Also, out of respect for the document and other readers, only highlight if the document is your personal property.) Look for key phrases in the beginning of the chapter to point you toward purposes, goals, themes, and topics. Highlight sparingly as you come upon key ideas. It can also be useful to make quick notes in the margins to help you locate ideas or concepts.
- On an index card or sheet of paper (that you will be able to slip into your textbook or teaching notebook) you might want to *briefly* record the following items:

  a. purpose or thesis statement
  b. main points
  c. type of evidence or support used to develop the ideas (research studies, interviews)
  d. key vocabulary terms and definitions (look for bold or italics)
  e. conclusions drawn by the author
  f. your reaction to the document:
     - Did you like the reading? Why or why not?
     - Is the reasoning sound?
     - Are the conclusions relevant to your life experience?
     - What did you learn?
  g. thoughts about how this document contributes to the course purpose and objectives (go back to the first page of your syllabus to think about this)
  h. anything you did not understand

- Use the references at the end of each document to find out who are the experts on this topic, locate sources for further reading, or locate materials for class exercises and activities.

BUILDING A PERSONAL LIBRARY

In order to maintain your theoretical knowledge, you should build a basic library of sources for yourself as you can afford to do so. Start with collecting items that you use frequently in the classroom; it can be disconcerting not to own materials that you need. There are three avenues you can take to build a personal collection of resources: first, photocopy or download journal articles (using tools such as Journal Finder from your campus library connection) and slip those into a file folder. Put in one item per file folder, label the folder, and file alphabetically by author last name. This will be your vertical, or hanging, file. If you subscribe to a number of journals, mark potential articles with Post-It notes so you can access them quickly.

Second, pay attention to the publishers' catalogues that come in the mail, and carefully scrutinize the interpersonal communication offerings to learn trends and determine what materials may be offered as courtesy items. Do not abuse this privilege! Order desk copies only for those items that you plan to consider for use. Also make a point of ordering library copies so that when you mention these sources in class, students can go and have a look for themselves. I advise against the habit of loaning your own materials. My experience is that personal materials often don't come back, or they are in worse shape than when you loaned them. I also find that I never know when I might need a resource from my own library. If it's loaned out, I don't have it to do my job. It may sound harsh not to loan to others, but the reality is that books and other materials are precious commodities that help you with your work. Protect them.

The third avenue for acquisition of materials is to buy books as you need to, or as you come across out-of-print items in used bookstores. (Amazon.com is not always the answer to your quest!) Keep in your wallet the titles of the top five out-of-print books on your wish list so that you can buy them when you find them. You may also want to spend more time at exhibitors' booths when attending conventions — that way you can actually look at books you are thinking of purchasing for your own library. There is usually a convention discount offered as well.

Why spend time reading and collecting a library? It is our professional obligation to stay current in the field. The one complaint we always had as students was when we took a class for which the professor had not updated the course readings in a decade! I vowed never to be one of those professors, and writing this chapter reinforces for me the need to be systematic in keeping a collection of materials up-to-date and, subsequently, the materials used in class up-to-date as well.

ANNOTATED BIBLIOGRAPHY

The following annotated bibliography lists 79 sources that will ground your knowledge in interpersonal communication and assist with teaching an introductory course in interpersonal communication. The bibliography is a compilation of both historic works and current resources and, although it consists primarily of books, lists some journal articles as well. Most of the publishers in the bibliography have specialties. For example, Sage Publications is known for up-to-date research anthologies. Knowing who publishes what may help you make decisions about which catalogs to keep up with and whose exhibition booth to attend when you are at a conference. Of course, you cannot teach without watching films, reading novels, and perusing Web sites, among the many sources of information available on personal relationships. However, the purpose here is to provide an academic grounding in the scholarship of interpersonal communication.

The bibliography has been constructed to provide you with more information than is normally found in a citation. First, I use the authors' full names so that you can become familiar with the most well-known researchers and writers in the field. Name recognition helps as you peruse sources and recommend scholars for your students to investigate. Second, I have identified the Library of Congress call number and the discipline within which the authors are trained. You will note that there are four primary fields from which we draw knowledge in interpersonal communication: communication, sociology, anthropology, and psychology. Within psychology we are informed by cognitive, social, and clinical approaches. Third, I include social science (empirical) and interpretive work to demonstrate the range of theory that underlies interpersonal communication. Even though many teachers find it easy to use a skills-based, or empirical, approach to teaching a basic undergraduate course, I cannot emphasize enough that philosophy, interpretation, and behavior all play important roles in our teaching and practice of interpersonal communication.

There are few journal articles in the bibliography for a reason. The sheer quantity of available journal articles makes it almost impossible to select something definitive. Instead, I have selected classic articles (e.g., Berger & Calabrese, 1975; Burgoon & Hale, 1988; Gibb, 1961; Knapp, Hart, & Dennis, 1974) to show you the beginnings of important concepts and theories and to remind you that it is pedagogically sound to cite research findings in class (e.g., Owen, 1984; Planalp & Honeycutt, 1985). Students do want to know "what the research says," and journal articles allow you to see the details of the communication process under study. As a professional, you should read regional (e.g., *Communication Quarterly*) and national (e.g., *Communication Monographs, Human Communication Research*) journals on a regular basis, but it is also helpful to read the interdisciplinary journals that pertain specifically to interpersonal communication, such as *Journal of Social and Personal Relationships* and *Personal Relationships*.

There are two ways you can use the annotated bibliography: as an alphabetical list by author, or as a guide to specific topic areas. In the table below you will find an alphabetical list of topic areas in the first column and a suggested set of sources by their number for those topics in the second column.

If you are interested in:	See items numbered:
Apprehension (Shyness, Reticence)	20, 39
Attraction	9, 19, 67
Attribution	15, 35, 60, 75
Communication Climate	28
Competence	6, 19, 32, 39, 51, 63, 68
Compliance Gaining	26, 47
Conflict Management	26, 27, 36, 38, 46, 48, 59, 76
Constructivism	21
Conversation	12, 50, 66
Culture	52, 55, 62, 78, 79
Dark Side	18, 19, 36, 77
Deception	12, 18, 42
Dialectics	6, 46, 54, 57

(Continued)

If you are interested in:	See items numbered:
Dialogue	6, 38, 66
Difficulty, Difficult People	25, 30, 39, 40, 64
Discourse (Conversation) Analysis	50, 71
Divorce	25
Empathy	11, 48, 58
Expectancies	13, 15, 67
Face, Facework, Face Negotiation	17, 24, 30
Family	25, 27, 32, 36, 38, 39, 53, 55, 64, 77
Friendship	14, 24, 32, 36, 53, 57, 60, 77
Gender, Sex Differences, Sexual Orientation	2, 22, 23, 24, 34, 36, 39, 55, 61, 77, 79
Humanistic Philosophy	11, 37, 58
Impression Formation and Management (See also Facework)	4, 29, 32, 60
Intercultural Communication	33, 46
Internet Relationships	2, 4, 79
Johari Window	45
Journal Articles	3, 7, 13, 28, 42, 47, 53, 55, 56, 61
Listening	10
Love and Romance	23, 36, 43, 60, 69, 77
Marriage	14, 26, 53, 79
Metacommunication	62, 74
Miscommunication	45, 49
Nonverbal Communication	12, 13, 33, 46
Paradox (Double Binds)	18, 74
Pedagogy	16, 72
Power	26, 27, 47, 52, 76
Prejudice and Racism	36, 71
Relational Culture	78
Relational Structure	6, 26, 74, 78
Relational Theories	1, 7, 21, 35, 52, 62, 65, 70, 73, 74
Relationship Development, Maintenance, Dissolution (Stage Theory)	1, 3, 14, 25, 40, 59, 60
Research Anthologies	18, 20, 23, 24, 25, 32, 34, 36, 39, 41, 54, 60, 79
Roles	4, 8, 27, 29, 55
Rules	14, 21, 55, 64, 78
Self-Awareness	11, 45, 58
Self-Disclosure	1, 22, 24, 37, 45, 48, 54, 59, 61
Social Cognition	7, 15, 41, 48, 56, 60, 75
Social Construction (Interpretive Approach)	8, 38, 44, 53, 63, 66

(Continued)

If you are interested in:	See items numbered:
Social Exchange and Equity	14, 59, 70, 73
Speech Accommodation	60
Stalking	19, 24
Stigma	31
Symbolic Interaction	8, 27, 63, 78
Systems Theory	5, 14, 27, 62, 74
Textbooks	2, 4, 10, 12, 21, 27, 38, 40, 46, 48, 51, 72, 75, 76, 77, 78
Uncertainty Reduction	7, 56

1 Altman, Irwin, & Taylor, Dalmas A. (1983). *Social penetration: The development of interpersonal relationships.* New York: Irvington Publishers. (Original work published 1973)
   HM132.A38 1983   Psychology
   One of the early conceptualizations of relational stages, social penetration theory examines dyads in light of growth and deterioration, breadth and depth of intimacy, personality, and costs and rewards. This is the source of the famous "onion model" that is often mistaken as a model of self-disclosure. Rather, what is described is a range of verbal and nonverbal communication behaviors that assist in social bonding.

2 Backlund, Philip M., & Williams, Mary Rose (Eds.). (2004). *Readings in gender communication.* Belmont, CA: Thomson/Wadsworth.
   P96.S48 R430 2004   Communication, Interdisciplinary
   This "edgy" anthology of 31 readings is written by both scholars and students, and the essays include research reports, stories, personal experiences, and interpretive analyses of a wide range of communication concepts. More practical than theoretical, the book will jump-start numerous class discussions on topics such as tattoos, cyberspace, urban music, clothes, and the many facets of gender manifestations in personal relationships.

3 Banks, Stephen P., Altendorf, Dayle M., Greene, John O., & Cody, Michael J. (1987). An examination of relationship disengagement: Perceptions, breakup strategies and outcomes. *The Western Journal of Speech Communication, 51,* 19–41.
   PN4071.W75   Communication
   Using a questionnaire to probe the relational disengagement behavior of 310 respondents, the researchers shed further light on earlier studies done by Baxter and Cody. The report is a practical look at the five strategies of disengagement: justification, avoidance, negative identity management, de-escalation, and positive tone. Results indicate that partners who wish to disengage do consider costs, intimacy, network influences, and quality of the dyad when selecting strategies.

4 Barnes, Susan B. (2003). Internet interpersonal relationships. In *Computer-mediated communication: Human-to-human communication across the Internet* (pp. 136–159). Boston: Allyn and Bacon.

HM851.B37 2002   Communication
This chapter demonstrates how interpersonal concepts are manifested on the Internet. Barnes examines motives for interacting online, types of Internet relationships, and relationship development. Relational structure, social exchange-reciprocity, language, social presence, roles, and impression management are all addressed. This informative essay takes the communication process into a medium that is fast becoming a preferred way for students to relate interpersonally.

5 Bateson, Gregory. (1972). *Steps to an ecology of mind.* New York: Ballantine.
GN6.B3 1972   Anthropology, Interdisciplinary
In this collection of three dozen essays and lectures written over 35 years, Bateson presents an accumulation of ideas he calls "minds." The broad range of ideas interacting in each essay requires the reader to know about anthropology, evolution, culture, psychiatry, theories of knowledge, and a systems-cybernetics perspective. His goal is to demonstrate an integrated set of ideas that create a literal mindset that he compares to how we understand eco-systems. Part III is most beneficial to communication instructors because it discusses relationships, double binds, and cybernetics.

6 Baxter, Leslie A., & Montgomery, Barbara M. (1996). *Relating: Dialogues and dialectics.* New York: Guilford.
P94.7 B39 1996   Communication
Relating provides both historical and theoretical background to the relational dialectics perspective. The authors compile a comprehensive review of their and others' research over ten chapters. Included are discussions on assumptions, history, rethinking aspects of interpersonal communication, dialogue, and competence. The 30-page reference list is a helpful resource for further study.

7 Berger, Charles R., & Calabrese, Richard J. (1975). Some explorations in initial interaction and beyond: Toward a theory of interpersonal communication. *Human Communication Research, 1,* 99–112.
P91.3H85   Communication
This original essay launched a 40-year research agenda to build and test uncertainty reduction theory. Initially proposing a developmental theory of interpersonal communication, Berger and Calabrese offer a theoretical model of 7 axioms and 21 theorems to explain what happens communicatively when people first meet and attempt to develop a relationship. The fundamental concept of uncertainty reduction remains a staple in the interpersonal communication course.

8 Berger, Peter L., & Luckmann, Thomas. (1966). *The social construction of reality: A treatise in the sociology of knowledge.* New York: Anchor Books.
BD175.B4 1989   Sociology
The original source for the interpretive perspective on interpersonal communication process, this book fully explains the claim that "reality is socially constructed." Part I establishes everyday life as a product of social

interaction and language, where communication maintains reality. Part II, on objective reality, examines how institutions help organize and control people through work and roles. Part III, on subjective reality, is a symbolic interaction look at how the self gets socialized through interaction with significant others and institutions.

9 Berscheid, Ellen, & Reis, Harry T. (1998). Attraction and close relationships. In Daniel T. Gilbert, Susan T. Fiske, & Gardner Lindzey (Eds.), *The handbook of social psychology, Vol. II* (4th ed., pp. 193–281). Boston: McGraw-Hill.
HM251.H224 1998 v. 2   Social Psychology
This chapter provides a comprehensive overview of attraction theory. Shifting from attraction in first encounters to acknowledging attraction in ongoing relationships, the review chronologically tracks the development of attraction as the concept functions throughout the life of a relationship. The authors situate the chapter empirically and then chronologically discuss the attraction literature in the field of social psychological theory. Looking at research as it has developed over time allows the reader to see that we have broadened our understanding of the concept from something that helps relationships to develop initially to the role attraction plays in partners' perceptions of ongoing satisfaction in a dyad. There is a wealth of information here that will assist in classroom discussion on this important topic.

10 Brownell, Judi. (2006). *Listening: Attitudes, principles, and skills* (3rd ed.). Boston: Pearson/Allyn and Bacon.
BF323.L5 B663 2006   Communication
Using a behavioral approach to improve listening skills, the book is framed around the HURIER model: hearing, understanding, remembering, interpreting, evaluating, and responding. This model is useful for a skills-based course, and the book provides many case studies and ideas for application. Even though the book is based on a relational perspective, the chapter on types of listening relationships demonstrates that the HURIER model needs appropriate application to work effectively.

11 Buber, Martin. (1970). *I and thou* (Walter Kaufmann, trans.). New York: Charles Scribner's Sons. (Original work published 1937)
B3213.B83 I213 1970   Theology, Philosophy
You do not need a background in religion or philosophy to understand the compassion for humanity or the concern for the loss of interpersonal connection that is the focus of Buber's classic treatise. Walter Kaufmann's translation, together with an extended prologue, is considered the definitive clarification on Buber's first (1923) and second (1957) editions of *I and Thou*. The book is divided into three parts: Part One looks at "I"; Part Two looks at the impersonal world of "it"; Part Three examines "you" as the spiritual connection of people through God. Buber argues that the I–You relationship accounts for the most valid understanding of a true interpersonal relationship because people are connected through each other and in the context of spirituality. He calls this "authentic interpersonalness."

12 Burgoon, Judee, Buller, David B., & Woodall, W. Gill. (1989). *Nonverbal communication: The unspoken dialogue.* New York: Harper & Row.
BF637.N66.B87 1989   Communication
This popular nonverbal communication textbook offers a more in-depth look at nonverbal codes and their function in relational communication. In addition to chapters on kinesics, proxemics, the environment, appearance, and so forth, the second half of the book puts these codes into play in relational processes such as conversation, deception, and the expression of emotion.

13 Burgoon, Judee K., & Hale, Jerold L. (1988). Nonverbal expectancy violations: Model elaboration and application to immediacy behaviors. *Communication Monographs,* 55, 58–79.
PN4077.S6   Communication
Although Expectancy Violations Theory (EVT) has been refined and extended for more than 25 years, this article outlines the fundamental concepts and propositions that are the foundation of the theory. The article also includes an empirical study that tests EVT for application to friendship and immediacy. The visual model presented is helpful, as are the explanations of its components: expectancies, violations and arousal, communicator reward valence, behavior interpretation and evaluation, and violation valence.

14 Cahn, Dudley D., Jr. (1987). *Letting go: A practical theory of relationship disengagement and reengagement.* Albany: SUNY Press.
HM132.C325 1986   Communication
Although this theoretical book is aimed at increasing advanced knowledge, the basic premise — that individuals' relationships deteriorate and then they reengage — is practical for anyone teaching relationship stages. Reengagment is simply overlooked much of the time, but is a focal point in this book. Other concepts of value include self-concept support, perceived understanding, and relationship satisfaction. This theory is explained in four chapters demonstrating a synthesis of systems, rules, communication, and social exchange. Part two takes a contextual look at these theoretical ideas in friendship, marriage, work, and student-teacher relationships.

15 Canary, Daniel J., Cody, Michael J., & Manusov, Valerie L. (2003). Four important cognitive processes. In Kathleen M. Galvin & Pamela J. Cooper (Eds.), *Making connections: readings in relational communication* (pp. 42–51). Los Angeles: Roxbury Publishing.
BF637.C45 M33 2003   Communication
This book is a collection of reprints on many basic interpersonal topics. The chapter by Canary and his colleagues summarizes crucial cognitive processes that most teachers address in interpersonal communication courses: interpersonal expectancies, attributions, person perception, and stereotypes. The resources at the end of the chapter provide suggestions for more in-depth reading in social cognition.

16 Cooper, Pamela J., & Simonds, Cheri J. (2003). *Communication for the classroom teacher* (7th ed.). Boston: Allyn and Bacon.

LB1033.C64 2003   Communication, Pedagogy

Although this book is aimed at students training to be communication teachers, there are a number of valuable charts and references to help any teacher improve his or her knowledge and practice of teaching. Because the authors are communication professors themselves, the perspective on teaching is one where the teacher-student relationship is seen as interpersonal. This book is a good motivator for practicing the kinds of skills we are teaching our students to master: listening, discussing, information sharing, and influencing.

17 Cupach, William R., & Metts, Sandra. (1994). *Facework*. Thousand Oaks, CA: Sage.

HM132.C86 1994   Communication

This book in the Sage Series on Close Relationships is an heuristic explication of face management theory that brings Goffman's (1967) original work into the field of communication. The authors argue that face is a salient issue in all interaction, but particularly in difficult interaction such as embarrassing situations and relationship dissolution. They examine gaining, maintaining, and losing face. Managing face constitutes a feature of competent interaction and is a skill for students to learn.

18 Cupach, William R., & Spitzberg, Brian H. (Eds.). (1994). *The dark side of interpersonal communication*. Hillsdale, NJ: Erlbaum.

BF637.C45.D335 1994   Communication

One of the first to focus on negative aspects of interpersonal interaction, this book has spawned much research since its publication. Thirteen chapters explore a range of understudied topics that balance our focus on positive aspects of relating. Such topics include incompetence, paradoxes, deception, relational transgression, privacy invasion, and abuse.

19 Cupach, William R., & Spitzberg, Brian H. (2004). *The dark side of relationship pursuit: From attraction to obsession and stalking*. Mahwah, NJ: Erlbaum.

HM1106.C86 2004   Communication

Continuing their interest in negative aspects of relating, Cupach and Spitzberg here focus on stalking, something many students have experienced. This book synthesizes the interdisciplinary research on obsessive relational intrusion (ORI) and stalking and theorizes an answer to "why?" using attachment theory and relational goal pursuit theory. As competence experts, the authors explore aspects of relationship management as a way to cope. Particularly useful to teaching is the information on motives, process, and the typology of stalking and ORI tactics.

20 Daly, John A., McCroskey, James C., Ayres, Joe, Hopf, Tim, & Ayres, Debbie M. (Eds.). (1997). *Avoiding communication: Shyness, reticence, and communication apprehension* (2nd ed.). Beverly Hills, CA: Sage.

BF575.B3 A96 1997   Communication

This book offers complete coverage of shyness and reticence in interpersonal communication. It defines terms and outlines research, measurement, treatment, and theoretical explanations of communication avoidance. Read selectively from the 17 chapters in this anthology as you may need to train yourself about how to appropriately teach these topics in an interpersonal communication course.

21 Delia, Jesse G., O'Keefe, Barbara J., & O'Keefe, Daniel J. (1982). The constructivist approach to communication. In Frank E. X. Dance (Ed.), *Human communication theory: Comparative essays* (pp. 147–191). New York: Harper & Row. BF637.C45H85 Communication
This chapter is the best general summary of Delia's constructivist approach and includes philosophical foundations, theory and research foci, methodology, research practices, and extensive references. Constructivism is outlined as an interpretive theory where communication is based on "schemes" that help people create social reality through interaction. Central to this approach is an understanding of how one's interpersonal construct system functions to guide interpretations, select communication strategies, and generally engage social interaction with others.

22 Derlega, Valerian, Metts, Sandra, Petronio, Sandra, & Margulis, Stephen T. (1993). *Self-disclosure.* Newbury Park, CA: Sage.
BF697.5 .S427 S43 1993 Social Psychology, Communication
Self-Disclosure can be viewed as a precursor to *Balancing the Secrets of Private Disclosures* (also cited in this bibliography). This short book synthesizes knowledge of self-disclosure and brings it to the center of close relationships. Four themes are set up to examine this centrality: the mutual transformation of relationships and self-disclosure, male-female differences, privacy regulation, and stress-reducing disclosure as a form of coping and social support.

23 Dindia, Kathryn, & Canary, Daniel (Eds.). (2006). *Sex differences and similarities in communication* (2nd ed.). Mahwah, NJ: Erlbaum.
P96.S48.S49 2006 Communication, Social Psychology
This anthology has done much to neutralize the common assumption that women and men are different and, therefore, cannot communicate effectively with each other. The second edition updates and adds new knowledge in four parts: framing chapters, theories, exploration of communication process, and a section devoted to romance. Because the research presented is based in social interaction, instructors of interpersonal communication can gain a balanced view on a topic that is often approached by students as "men versus women."

24 Dindia, Kathryn, & Duck, Steve. (Eds.). (2000). *Communication and personal relationships.* Chichester, England: Wiley.
HM1116.C65 2000 Communication
This book focuses on current topics that are part of teaching interpersonal communication. In nine chapters, the best names in interpersonal research (e.g., Bochner, Metts, Spitzberg, Baxter) contribute research-based essays

on topics such as stalking, disclosure, facework, stories, and cross-sex friendship. Many of the authors approach their topics by asking what they mean and where the research stands.

25 Fine, Mark A., & Harvey, John H. (Eds.). (2006). *Handbook of divorce and relationship dissolution.* Mahwah, NJ: Erlbaum.
    HQ814.H27 2006   Social Psychology, Interdisciplinary
    This timely, comprehensive anthology is an excellent resource for two reasons: first, there is not enough coverage of divorce in our teaching materials and second, students from divorced families seek to understand the impact of divorce on parent-child relationships. There are eight parts to this 700-page tome, but interpersonal communication instructors will benefit most from the sections on causes, consequences, coping, and variations in divorce (e.g., African American divorce).

26 Fitzpatrick, Mary Ann. (1988). *Between husbands and wives: Communication in marriage.* Thousand Oaks, CA: Sage.
    HQ728.F46 1988   Communication
    This well-known empirical study of marriage resulted in the marital types Fitzpatrick calls traditional, independents, and separates. The book outlines the research agenda and the three types. The heart of the book analyzes how the three marital types predict different outcomes regarding who wields power or has control in the marriage, how conflict is managed, how partners gain compliance from each other, and the communication of emotion. Fitzpatrick provides a realistic look at marital structure and communication processes.

27 Galvin, Kathleen M., Bylund, Carma L., & Brommel, Bernard J. (2004). *Family communication: Cohesion and change* (6th ed.). Boston: Pearson/Allyn and Bacon.
    HQ734.G19 2004   Communication
    The topic of family is prevalent in student discussion, and this well-known text provides depth of understanding of interpersonal process within a family context. Thirteen chapters cover a range of topics: theories, communication patterns, roles, conflict, power, and intimacy. Symbolic interaction and systems theories provide the basic framing for a descriptive discussion of the issues.

28 Gibb, Jack. (1961). Defensive communication. *Journal of Communication, 11,* 141–148.
    P87.J6   Communication
    This classic article is the starting point on reducing defensiveness in relationships. Although set up as descriptions of communication climates in group settings, the characteristics of defensiveness versus supportiveness are frequently prescribed as communication strategies in dyads. Gibb discusses the following pairs of communication and their effects on interaction: evaluation and description, control and problem orientation, strategy and spontaneity, neutrality and empathy, superiority and equality, certainty and provisionalism.

29 Goffman, Erving. (1959). *The presentation of self in everyday life*. New York: Anchor Books.
HM291.G6 1959   Sociology
Goffman's most famous book explores the interpersonal implications for impression management in social life. Using a dramatist's perspective — life is theatre — he demonstrates how people take on roles within work contexts to reach goals. The assumption that people have goals and, most often, interact interpersonally leads to managing an impression through role behavior. The ethical and moral dimensions of communication are an integral part of the study. After 45-plus years, this book still makes a strong practical impact.

30 Goffman, Erving. (1967). *Interaction ritual: Essays in face-to-face behavior*. Chicago: Aldine Publishing.
HM291.G59   Sociology
This ethnography of interaction is based on the premise that face-to-face behavior is ritualized communication that maintains the larger social order. The first essay, "On Face-Work," is the best known and sets the stage for theorizing the concept of facework (see Cupach and Metts in this bibliography). Interpersonal communication teachers will also learn about other concepts by reading the entire book. Particularly relevant are chapters on deference and demeanor, embarrassment, and alienation.

31 Goffman, Erving. (1986). *Stigma: Notes on the management of spoiled identity*. New York: Touchstone/Simon & Schuster. (Original work published 1963)
HM291.G624 1986   Sociology
Goffman's compact study of stigma, as related to identity and deviance, is a valuable tool for considering how a stigmatized individual manages social (interpersonal) interaction. Information control and group alignment are presented as two processes that have interpersonal implications when communicating from a stigmatized position. The book is relevant to a course on interpersonal communication when we consider how we interact with the many stigmatized individuals who are now mainstreamed into social life in the twenty-first century.

32 Greene, John O., & Burleson, Brant R. (Eds.). (2003). *Handbook of communication and social interaction skills*. Mahwah, NJ: Erlbaum.
HM1111.H36 2003   Communication
This handbook, ideal for a competence or skills-based course, includes literature reviews with extensive reference lists. Among the interaction skills reviewed, many are typical in interpersonal communication teaching: arguing, emotional support, friendship interaction, parenting, negotiating, and impression management. Although this is a research tool, the benefits for teaching include updated knowledge and a deeper understanding of what *competence* means.

33 Hall, Edward T. (1959). *The silent language*. New York: Anchor Books/ Doubleday.
HM258.H245 1990   Anthropology

It is difficult to teach (or read) about nonverbal communication in relation-ships without reference to Hall's influential book. Many basic concepts about cross-cultural communication, including perceptions of time and space, are part of what Hall calls "the cultural unconscious." These factors influence perceptions and subsequent behavior when people from different cultures attempt to communicate. Much like his contemporary, Erving Goffman, Hall uses examples from his fieldwork to illustrate principles of nonverbal communication.

34 Hecht, Michael L. (Ed.). (1998). *Communicating prejudice*. Thousand Oaks, CA: Sage.
    HM276.C625 1998   Communication
    Part II of this anthology focuses on spheres of prejudice and how prejudice is embedded in communication codes. Contributors include Molefi Asante, on racist language, Lana Rakow and Laura Wackwitz, on communicating sexism, Thomas Nakayama, on ways of communicating heterosexism, Dreama Moon and Garry Rolison, on classism, and Angie Williams and Howard Giles, on ageism. Each of these five chapters is useful as back-ground knowledge for teaching about "isms" and prejudice.

35 Heider, Fritz. (1958). *The psychology of interpersonal relations*. New York: Wiley.
    BF636.H383   Social Psychology
    Heider was one of the early relational theorists, and this book is the original source on attribution and balance theories, including the p, o, x logical state-ments that characterize much of the attribution literature. In this dense explication of what happens when two people engage one another psycho-logically in a relationship, Heider starts with the knowledge of naïve psy-chology in order to logically extend intuitive thought to a more explicit scientific approach to relationships. His claim is that common sense (intu-itive or naïve psychology) has much to offer science. He unfolds the idea that as people perceive and react to others in their environment, a kind of ordering process that he calls "attribution" occurs. The theoretical model that results is one that looks at the interaction of perception, action, moti-vation, sentiments, and norms.

36 Hendrick, Clyde, & Hendrick, Susan S. (Eds.). (2000). *Close relationships: A sourcebook*. Thousand Oaks, CA: Sage.
    HM1106.C55 2000   Social Psychology, Communication
    The best known theorists are represented in the 26 chapters of this anthol-ogy, which covers most topics taught in interpersonal communication. Chapters are structured as literature reviews and draw primarily on quanti-tative studies. A sampling of topics includes: friendship, multiracial dyads, family, gay/lesbian/bisexual dyads, emotion, conflict, gender, attachment, love, aging, social support, jealousy, depression, and aggression.

37 Jourard, Sidney M. (1971). *The transparent self* (Rev. ed.). New York: Van Nostrand Reinhold. (Original work published 1964)
    BF697.J65 1971   Clinical Psychology

Based on the premise that self-disclosure is related to positive health, Jourard's study of transparency is the exemplar of ideas that were swept up in the 1960s humanism movement in interpersonal communication. Historically, this book laid the groundwork for much of our teaching and changed our thinking about the nature and function of self-disclosure. Although it was intended as a tool for use in mental health settings, communication teachers can learn much about relational aspects of self-disclosure that can be applied to healthy dyads. The book also includes Jourard's Self-Disclosure Questionnaire.

38 Kellett, Peter M., & Dalton, Diana G. (2001). *Managing conflict in a negotiated world: A narrative approach to achieving dialogue and change.* Thousand Oaks, CA: Sage.
HM1126.K45 2001   Communication
Designed as a teaching tool, this book is about analyzing and responding to real-life stories of interpersonal conflict. The first half of the book uses personal narratives as the basis for learning how to dissect conflict and then engage dialogue to negotiate change in personal relationships. The second half of the book devotes chapters to conflicts in community, work, and family. The interpretive perspective framing this book is a significant alternative to most behavioral strategies models used in teaching about conflict.

39 Kirkpatrick, D. Charles, Duck, Steve, & Foley, Megan K. (Eds.). (2006). *Relating difficulty: The processes of constructing and managing difficult interaction.* Mahwah, NJ: Erlbaum.
BF637.I48.R45 2006   Communication, Sociology, Psychology
Part of Erlbaum's Series on Personal Relationships, this anthology includes 12 chapters that contribute to a more complex notion of what a "difficult" person is and how that impacts relationships. Scholars take on topics such as shyness, in-laws, long distance, money, hook-up experiences, gossip, and chronic illness to explore difficult experiences in relationships. We learn that difficulty is not as simple as dealing with personalities; rather, all the studies point toward a triangulation principle: two people in the dyad are influenced by an outside factor such as situation or other people. Thus, competent relating requires managing the interaction process rather than attributes of people.

40 Knapp, Mark L. (1978). Stages of coming together and coming apart. In *Social intercourse: From greeting to goodbye* (pp. 1–29). Boston: Allyn and Bacon.
HM132.K5   Communication
This is the first version of Knapp's often-used model of interaction stages, which describes growth and decay in interpersonal relationships. In this chapter the reader can see the influence of Altman and Taylor's social penetration theory. This historical essay is the precursor to Knapp's current version in his text with Anita Vangelisti entitled *Interpersonal Communication and Human Relationships*. (See Chapter 6 of this book for an excerpt.)

41 Knapp, Mark L., & Daly, John A. (Eds.). (2002). *Handbook of interpersonal communication* (3rd ed.). Thousand Oaks, CA: Sage.
BF637.C45 H287 2002   Communication
Like the two previous editions, the *Handbook* is considered a top-notch compilation of interpersonal communication research. Nineteen chapters are divided among five parts: basic issues and approaches, perspectives on inquiry, fundamental units, processes and functions, and contexts. The first chapter, on background and trends, provides historical information and themes to help frame thinking about the field in general. Looking at all three editions of the *Handbook* side by side will also show how the research on interpersonal communication has evolved in the last 20 years.

42 Knapp, Mark L., Hart, Roderick P., & Dennis, Harry S. (1974). An exploration of deception as a communication construct. *Human Communication Research, 1,* 15–29.
P91.3H85   Communication
This historical essay sets up some early baseline behaviors for the communication of deception. Empirical testing yielded support for both verbal and nonverbal behaviors used by deceivers in six categories of communication: uncertainty, vagueness, nervousness, reticence, dependence, and negative affect. At least 14 communication differences were found between deceivers and nondeceivers. After this article, Knapp continued to lead the field in research on deception.

43 Lee, John Alan. (1976). *The colors of love.* Englewood Cliffs, NJ: Prentice-Hall/Psychology Today.
BF575.L8 L33 1976   Sociology
Lee is the originator of the highly popular "lovestyles" theory derived from his study involving extensive interviews of 200-plus men and women about their love experiences. Using themes that emerged from the interviews, Lee developed the five styles of eros, ludus, storge, mania, and agape. He frames and interprets these styles using literature from Western civilization. The book is an in-depth explanation of the five styles of love, both separately and in some form of combination. It includes Lee's lovestyles instrument, allowing the reader to gauge his or her preferred style.

44 Leeds-Hurwitz, Wendy. (Ed.). (1995). *Social approaches to communication.* New York: Guilford.
HM258.S58 1995   Communication
This research anthology is one of the first to synthesize social — also known as interpretive — approaches to theorizing about interpersonal communication. The reader can understand the philosophy, methodology, and controversial politics surrounding interpretation as it came into vogue in our field during the 1990s. An application section includes chapters that can help an instructor make decisions about using case studies, ethnographies, and narratives as instructional strategies to study interpersonal relationships and communication process.

45 Luft, Joseph. (1969). *Of human interaction*. Palo Alto, CA: National Press Books.
HM133.L83   Social Psychology, Personality
Of all his writings, this is Luft's most clear source on the Johari Window, which he first developed in 1955 with Harry Ingham, as a tool for self-awareness. This book is organized around the four quadrants of the window: open, blind, hidden, and unknown. Implications for interpersonal learning are played out through such concepts as trust, miscommunication, leadership patterns, and self-disclosure.

46 Martin, Judith N., Nakayama, Thomas K., & Flores, Lisa A. (Eds.). (2002). *Readings in intercultural communication: Experiences and contexts* (2nd ed.). Boston: McGraw-Hill.
GN345.6 R43 2001   Communication
Intercultural communication is a specific kind of interpersonal communication process that involves much of the diversity that characterizes relationships in today's world. Many perspectives represent a range of cultural experience in these short chapters, but the editors use dialectical theory to broadly frame intercultural communication. This is a rich resource that can expand your approach to teaching about ethics, conflict, language, nonverbal communication, and identity; it also provides classroom activities.

47 Marwell, Gerald, & Schmitt, David R. (1967). Dimensions of compliance-gaining behavior: An empirical analysis. *Sociometry, 39,* 350–364.
HM1.S8 1   Sociology
This classic study was the first empirical attempt to distinguish clusters of strategies in interpersonal compliance-gaining situations. The authors found that 16 strategies clustered around five factors: rewarding activity, punishing activity, expertise, activation of impersonal commitments, and activation of personal commitments. These results correlated positively with French and Raven's power typology. Although much research has been conducted on how partners influence each other to comply and, concomitantly, to resist influence to comply, the 16 original strategies are still in use today.

48 Miller, Gerald R., & Steinberg, Mark. (1975). *Between people: A new analysis of interpersonal communication*. Chicago: Science Research Associates.
HM132.M52   Communication
Between People made a strong impact on the understanding and teaching of interpersonal communication when it was first published, and it is still referenced today. Because it was designed as a textbook, the content of the ten chapters is both descriptive and prescriptive. In framing relationships, the authors define interpersonal relationships as a mutual dyadic system in which thinking (cognitive) partners control their choices through communication skills to achieve outcomes in a given social environment. Historically, the book is an important look at many early concepts (trust, empathy, disclosure, conflict, transaction) that set the stage for how we teach undergraduates about relationships and communication.

49 Mortensen, C. David, with Ayres, Carter M. (1997). *Miscommunication*. Thousand Oaks, CA: Sage.
P90.M66 1997   Communication
The term *miscommunication* has been popularized by sociolinguist Deborah Tannen, and students commonly think of it as a cross-sex pattern. Mortensen's book is an in-depth and complex communication model of what happens when people miscommunicate. His analysis is based on personal accounts from 80 participants, and examples from the accounts are used throughout the book. What Mortensen accomplishes is an extended definition of miscommunication, including conditions that precipitate and aggravate negativity.

50 Nofsinger, Robert E. (1991). *Everyday conversation*. Newbury Park, CA: Sage.
BJ2121.N64 1991   Communication
Nofsinger presents a highly technical but very readable explication of conversation from a discourse analysis perspective. Through its use of real conversation, the book dispels the assumption that "everyone can communicate." In order to show how conversation works, chapters are organized to build off each other. An introduction on pragmatics leads to conversational action (speech acts) followed by chapters on action sequences, turn organization, and alignment. The last chapter deals with extended structures such as argument, storytelling, and relationships themselves.

51 O'Hair, Dan, Friedrich, Gustav W., Wiemann, John M., & Wiemann, Mary O. (1997). *Competent communication* (2nd ed.). New York: St. Martin's.
P90.C63467 1997   Communication
In this hybrid textbook, Parts One and Two constitute six chapters on basic communication processes and three chapters on interpersonal communication. Of note is the competence perspective that extends John Wiemann's work on the definition and components of relational competence. Rather than locating competence only in the individual communicators, Wiemann conceives of the dyad itself as competent. This was a major leap forward in conceptualizing the totality of interpersonal communication.

52 Orbe, Mark P. (1998). *Constructing co-cultural theory: An explication of culture, power, and communication*. Thousand Oaks, CA: Sage.
HM258.O63 1998   Communication
Co-cultural theory extends muted group and standpoint theories by looking at communication interaction initiated by co-cultural group members in the direction of dominant group members. Orbe documents 26 co-cultural strategies in Chapter 4 and then interprets co-cultural communication in Chapter 5 in terms of assimilation, accommodation, and separation. This useful typology of communication strategies helps students see how the choice of strategy changes the power dynamics in personal relationships involving dominant and socially marginalized partners.

53 Owen, William Foster. (1984). Interpretive themes in relational communication. *Quarterly Journal of Speech, 70*, 274–287.

PN4071.Q3   Communication
Owen's interpretive study is an example of how partners in relationships make sense of the episodes that characterize relational life in marriage, family dyads, relatives outside the nuclear family, and friendship. Analysis of self-reports from participants yielded seven themes that partners use to make sense of the relationships: commitment, involvement, work, unique/special, fragile, consideration/respect, and manipulation. This study is a way to see how partners characterize what is going in their relationships so they can *understand* the dyad and communicate accordingly. This is quite a different approach from the traditional empirical studies of skills and behaviors.

54 Petronio, Sandra. (Ed.). (2000). *Balancing the secrets of private disclosures.* Mahwah, NJ: Erlbaum.
BF697.5 .S427 B35 2000   Communication
This anthology of 20 chapters captures current knowledge on secrets and disclosures by framing the topic through the dialectical idea of private needs versus public exposure. The first three chapters provide an introduction and review of the literature by Lawrence Rosenfeld, Kathryn Dindia, and Sandra Petronio. More specialized chapters follow, including explorations of disclosure in health care contexts, in close relationships, and across cultures.

55 Philipsen, Gerry. (1975). Speaking "like a man" in Teamsterville: Culture patterns of role enactment in an urban neighborhood. *Quarterly Journal of Speech, 61,* 13–22.
PN4071.Q3   Communication
One of the earliest and most influential ethnographic studies of relationships, communication, and gender, Philipsen's study is still current. By discovering cultural rules of community, we can know how talk manifests social identity that is characterized by relationship status, SES, geographical boundaries, gender, and cultural values. Public and private places such as taverns, community centers, and the streets are bound by rules as well, and require competent knowledge by community members in order for relationships to function smoothly. Readers learn that competence is not just a matter of learning skills; rather, skills are implemented in social interaction to be effective.

56 Planalp, Sally, & Honeycutt, James M. (1985). Events that increase uncertainty in personal relationships. *Human Communication Research, 11,* 593–604.
P91.3H85   Communication
This study shows how uncertainty arises beyond initial interaction and what partners do to reduce uncertainty in friendship, marriage, and romance. Six types of events produced uncertainty in participants' experience: competing relationships, loss of closeness, sexual behavior, deception, change in personality, and betraying confidence. Results showed the emotional impact to be high and that communication strategies used included talking over and around the issue, arguing, and avoiding both the

issue and the partner. This study shows that coping with uncertainty is as important as reducing uncertainty.

57 Rawlins, William K. (1992). *Friendship matters: Communication, dialectics, and the life course.* Hawthorne, NY: Aldine de Gruyter.
HM132.5 R38 1992   Communication
Not only is this one of the earliest and best studies of friendship in the field of communication, but Rawlins also grounds his work in relational dialectics theory. Using 100 interviews as the basis of his data collection, Rawlins examines the tensions of friendships throughout life, including a look at children, adolescents, young adults, and older adults. Four dialectical tensions emerge to characterize communication processes in friendship: independent-dependent, affection-instrumentality, judgment-acceptance, and expressiveness-protectiveness.

58 Rogers, Carl R. (1995). *On becoming a person: A therapist's view of psychotherapy* (Peter D. Kramer, intro.). Boston: Houghton Mifflin. (Original work published 1961)
RC480.5 R62 1995   Clinical Psychology
Rogers's famous humanistic look at the client-therapist relationship is actually a collection of 30 years' worth of his writing. Lessons are given on self-awareness, empathy, relational understanding, and unconditional positive regard for others as conditions of self-actualization, or becoming a person. Of the seven parts of the book, Parts I, II, III, IV, and VI explicate Rogers's philosophy and method of approaching interpersonal relationships.

59 Roloff, Michael E. (1981). *Interpersonal communication: The social exchange approach.* Beverly Hills, CA: Sage.
HM132.R653   Communication
This book has a single focus on five theories under the umbrella of social exchange. The reader is able to clarify the contributions of the Operant Psychology Approach, the Economic Exchange Model, the Theory of Interdependence, Resource Theory, and Equity Theory as they relate to the theoretical concept that humans engage in social exchange as a fundamental process of relating. Roloff compares the assumptions of each theory, looks at how each theory views various interpersonal processes (relational development, self-disclosure, and conflict), and gauges strengths and weaknesses of each.

60 Roloff, Michael E., & Berger, Charles R. (Eds.). (1982). *Social cognition and communication.* Beverly Hills, CA: Sage.
HM132.S566 1982   Communication
In nine chapters, this anthology defines social cognition, explicates the relationship between social cognition and communication, and then applies the whole process to the following areas: impression formation and message production, attribution, relational trajectories in friendship and love, speech accommodation, legal trials, organizations, and mass commu-

nication. The first chapter by Roloff and Berger is known as one of the best statements in the field on what social cognition is ("organized thoughts people have about human interaction") and how it works.

61 Rosenfeld, Lawrence B. (1979). Self-disclosure avoidance: Why I am afraid to tell you who I am. *Communication Monographs, 46,* 63–74.
PN4077.S6   Communication
This study is a favorite in self-disclosure literature and among students. Instead of the usual "what" and "how much" approach, Rosenfeld empirically investigates why men and women avoid disclosing. Results from self-disclosure and avoidance measures showed similarity on avoiding disclosure so as not to project an undesired image, but there were also sex differences. Males primarily avoid disclosure so as not to lose control of the dyad, while females avoid disclosure so that information would not be used against them.

62 Ruesch, Jurgen, & Bateson, Gregory. (1951). *Communication: The social matrix of psychiatry.* New York: Norton.
RC602.R9   Psychiatry, Anthropology
This historic book is one of the first systematic (scientific) theories of interpersonal communication and the original source for the term *metacommunication.* Using a systems perspective, Ruesch (a psychiatrist) and Bateson (an anthropologist) locate interpersonal communication in dyads that function within a larger American social matrix. Communication is seen as an integrated system of information, cybernetics, cultural values, human interaction, and wholeness. The "levels of communication" model is also one of the first contextual conceptualizations of communication as intrapersonal, interpersonal, group, and cultural.

63 Sass, Carina P. (1994). On interpersonal competence. In Kathryn Carter & Mick Presnell (Eds.), *Interpretive approaches to interpersonal communication* (pp. 137–157). Albany: SUNY Press.
BF637.N66I68 1994   Communication
Using a symbolic interaction framework, Sass develops an interpretive model of interpersonal competence. She theoretically teases out "the social interaction of the individuals." Three assumptions (reflexivity, context, unification) ground her definition of *competence.* Competence is viewed as relational, mutually satisfactory, authentic, and having shared perception between partners. This interpretive model is an alternative to the more common behavioral approach to competence.

64 Satir, Virginia. (1972). *peoplemaking.* Palo Alto, CA: Science and Behavior Books.
HQ734.S266   Clinical Psychology
Satir is a family therapist whose work has been adopted by interpersonal communication teachers and trainers. In concentrating on healthy family process, she uses four key concepts: self-worth, communication, systems, and rules. Communicating in family relationships is overt or implied on

virtually every page of the book, but chapters 4, 5, and 6 concentrate on communication processes, including the famous patterns of placate, blame, compute, and distract.

65 Schutz, William C. (1966). *The interpersonal underworld.* Palo Alto, CA: Science and Behavior Books. (Originally published in 1958 as *FIRO: A three-dimensional theory of interpersonal behavior*)
HM132.S38 1966   Psychiatry
This highly empirical book presents Schutz's well-known theory of Fundamental Interpersonal Relations Orientation (FIRO). His simple contention that "people need people" is manifested in the three basic needs of inclusion, control, and affection (in that order). Further, he proposes that we both give ("expressed behavior") and receive ("wanted behavior") these basic needs. Compatibility is linked to these needs as a predictor of successful relationships. The FIRO-B questionnaire is included as chapter 4.

66 Shotter, John. (1993). *Conversational realities: Constructing life through language.* Thousand Oaks, CA: Sage.
P95.45.S56 1993   Communication, Psychology
A well-known social constructionist, Shotter offers a book that centers on the way language helps us construct interpersonal relationships. Shotter claims that communication interaction creates social life (reality) by revealing how we relate to each other and then make sense of our lives through that talk. His evidence for the claim is conversation analysis and a complicated synthesis of literature from psychology, European philosophy, rhetoric, and linguistics. He builds a framework to explain the process of "living dialogue" between people. The value of this book for interpersonal communication instructors is in being able to see how social construction works as perspective to teach concepts such as dialogue, conversation, and relationships.

67 Simpson, Jeffrey A., & Harris, Betty A. (1994). Interpersonal attraction. In Ann L. Weber & John H. Harvey (Eds.), *Perspectives on close relationships* (pp. 45–66). Boston: Allyn and Bacon.
BF511.P46 1994   Social Psychology
This chapter does an excellent job of summarizing the basic concepts of Ellen Berscheid's and Harold Kelley's original works on attraction. Using Kelley's model, the content of this chapter is divided into the P, E, O, and P X O variables that represent the four categories of variables that influence attraction. P variables are attributes a person brings to the situation; E variables are environmental influences; O variables are attributes of the other person; and P X O variables are the intersecting attributes of the two people. Familiar concepts within these categories include expectancies, proximity, attractiveness, and similarity.

68 Spitzberg, Brian H., & Cupach, William R. (1984). *Interpersonal communication competence.* Beverly Hills, CA: Sage.
BF637.C45 S67 1984   Communication

A compact overview of concepts and theories in interpersonal communication, this primer has served the field heuristically in teaching and research. A conceptual model based on five components in interaction is offered to organize the literature on competence: motivation, knowledge, skills, context, and outcomes. A short discussion in the last chapter considers pedagogical implications.

69 Sternberg, Robert J. (1988). *The triangle of love: Intimacy, passion, commitment.* New York: Basic Books.
BF575.L8 S78 1988 Social Psychology
Sternberg presents a social psychological theory of love based on the three factors of intimacy, passion, and commitment. Eight chapters include valuable discussions of attraction, liking versus loving, and the course of a relationship. Chapter 2, "The Ingredients of Love," offers a detailed explication of the theory. The Sternberg Triangular Love Scale, presented in chapter 3, could be a basis for class data collection and analysis.

70 Thibaut, John W., & Kelley, Harold H. (1986/2004). *The social psychology of groups.* New Brunswick, NJ: Transaction Publishers. (Original work published 1959)
HM131.T46 1986 Social Psychology
This is the original source of what most interpersonal texts call "social exchange theory." Thibaut and Kelley, however, call their explanation "interdependence theory" and maintain the idea that dyads are the basis of all social interaction where partners create patterns of interdependence in controlling outcomes. Chapters 1 through 10 lay out the theory, including explication of cost, rewards, CL, CLalt, power, and the outcome matrix. Their 1978 book, *Interpersonal Relations,* takes the theory out of a group context and more explicitly develops the dyadic implications.

71 Van Dijk, Teun A. (1987). *Communicating racism: Ethnic prejudice in thought and talk.* Newbury Park, CA: Sage.
HM291.D496 1987 Communication
Based on interview data from Amsterdam and San Diego, this study examines how Whites reproduce racism in everyday talk. Using discourse analysis, Van Dijk theorizes how prejudiced discourse is structured, how we cognitively organize prejudice, and, most important, how racism is communicated in interpersonal interaction. Although deeply detailed, this book provides a strong foundation for understanding racism as a social phenomenon manifested in communication among people.

72 Vangelisti, Anita, Daly, John A., & Friedrich, Gustav W. (Eds.). (1999). *Teaching communication: Theory, research, and methods* (2nd ed.). Mahwah, NJ: Erlbaum.
P91.3 T43 1999 Communication, Pedagogy
Written by experts in the field, this 38-chapter general resource offers various pieces of advice ranging from professionalism to course creation to instructional strategies to evaluation techniques. This advice is particularly valuable because it is contextualized within the communication field. The

chapter on teaching interpersonal communication offers a good starting point for thinking about course design.

73 Walster, Elaine, Walster, G. William, & Berscheid, Ellen. (1978). *Equity: Theory and research.* Boston: Allyn and Bacon.
HM251.W2658   Social Psychology
This is the definitive source on equity theory. Framed as a general theory, it examines notions of fairness in human relationships. Chapter 2 explicates the four basic propositions of equity theory: we maximize outcomes (1) as individuals and (2) in groups; (3) inequity equals distress; and (4) people in distress try to restore equity. Separate chapters apply the theory to four types of relationships: exploiter/victim, philanthropist/recipient, business, and intimate. The book concludes with its own theoretical critique. Despite the common tendency to treat equity theory as an extension or alternative to social exchange theory, it is conceptually distinct.

74 Watzlawick, Paul, Bavelas, Janet Beavin, & Jackson, Don D. (1967). *Pragmatics of human communication.* New York: Norton.
BF637.C45 W3   Clinical Psychology
No other book has had more influence on the teaching of interpersonal communication than *Pragmatics,* particularly the five axioms in chapter 2. The book broke new ground as the authors used their powers of behavioral observation to construct a "calculus," or model of interpersonal relationships, from a systems perspective. Although dense at times, the book contains now-familiar concepts: paradox or double bind, metacommunication, complementarity, symmetrical structure, and message punctuation. The book also includes an application to *Who's Afraid of Virginia Woolf?* (see Chapter 6 of this book for an excerpt).

75 West, Stephen G., & Wicklund, Robert A. (1980). *A primer of social psychological theories.* Monterey, CA: Brooks/Cole.
HM251.W573   Social Psychology
Part Three in this concept-oriented text has three chapters on attribution theory: Self-Perception Theory, the Theory of Correspondent Inferences, and Kelley's Attribution Theory. In about 50 pages, the book provides a solid discussion of the process of attribution, or how we assign causation to behavior — one of the top social cognition concepts taught in interpersonal communication courses.

76 Wilmot, William W., & Hocker, Joyce L. (2006). *Interpersonal conflict* (7th ed.). New York: McGraw-Hill.
HM1121.H62 2006   Communication, Clinical Psychology
Conflict is one of the most popular areas of interest to students, and this text provides in-depth coverage on the topic. In addition to the expected chapters on definition, power, styles, and negotiation, there is a chapter on forgiveness and reconciliation. The book is informative and practical from a skills-based perspective, and includes many applications for classroom use.

77 Wood, Julia T. (Ed.). (1996). *Gendered relationships*. Mountain View, CA: Mayfield Publishing.
HQ1075.G467 1995   Communication, Psychology
Wood's goal to "focus specifically on [the] reciprocal influence between gender and relationships" is met in this 15-chapter anthology divided into four parts: foundations, personal relationships, romance, and professional relationships. Particularly useful are the chapters on friendship, lesbian/gay romance, violence, sexual harassment, and workplace issues. This book can be used as both a primary text and a source of supplemental reading.

78 Wood, Julia T. (2000). Relational culture: The nucleus of intimacy. In *relational communication: Continuity and change in personal relationships* (2nd ed., pp. 76–100). Belmont, CA: Wadsworth.
BF637.C45 W66 1999   Communication
This chapter is a full realization of the ideas on relational culture that Wood first drafted in a 1982 *Communication Quarterly* essay. The chapter looks at relational dialectics; organizing structures; rules; and symbolic practices such as rituals, routines, placemaking, and scripts as the components of relational culture. Wood contends that each of these components of relational culture is enacted through communication. She claims that such communication processes, structures, and practices reveal the uniqueness of every relationship we participate in. This chapter provides a practical set of conceptual tools for students to use when analyzing a personal relationship.

79 Wood, Julia T., & Duck, Steve. (Eds.). (1995). *Under-studied relationships: Off the beaten track*. Thousand Oaks, CA: Sage.
HM132.U54 1993 v.6   Communication, Interdisciplinary
Volume Six in the Sage Understanding Relationship Processes Series examines notions of dyadic competence in relationships that had received little research attention at the time. The groundwork here opens the reader to what was known about long-distance communication, cyber relationships, gay-lesbian dyads, long-term marriages, and intracultural minority interaction. Model-building and theoretical framing are common approaches in the eight chapters that comprise the book.

References

Adler, R., Proctor, R. F., & Towne, N. (2005). *Looking out/looking in* (11th ed.). Belmont, CA: Wadsworth.

Albom, M. (1997). *Tuesdays with Morrie.* New York: Doubleday.

Altman, I., & Taylor, D. A. (1983). *Social penetration: The development of interpersonal relationships.* New York: Irvington. (Original work published 1973)

Anderson, L. W., & Krathwohl, D. R. (Eds.). (2001). *A taxonomy for learning, teaching, and assessing: A revision of Bloom's Taxonomy of Educational Objectives.* New York: Longman.

Applegate, J. L., & Morreale, S. P. (1999). Service-learning in communication: A natural partnership [Preface]. In D. Droge & B. O. Murphy (Eds.), *Voices of a strong democracy: Concepts and models for service-learning in communication studies* (pp. ix–xiv). Washington, DC: American Association for Higher Education.

Artz, L. (2001). Critical ethnography for communication studies: Dialogue and social justice in service-learning. *Southern Communication Journal, 66,* 239–250.

Bain, K. (2004). *What the best college teachers do.* Cambridge, MA: Harvard Univ. Press.

Banta, T. W. (2002). *Building a scholarship of assessment.* San Francisco: Jossey-Bass.

Barnes, S. B. (2003). *Computer-mediated communication: Human-to-human communication across the Internet.* Boston: Allyn & Bacon.

Bateson, M. C. (1989). *Composing a life.* New York: Grove Press.

Baxter, L. A. (1988). A dialectical perspective on communication strategies in relationship development. In S. W. Duck, D. F. Hay, S. E. Hobfoll, W. Iches, & B. Montgomery (Eds.), *Handbook of personal relationships* (pp. 257–273). Chichester, UK: Wiley & Sons.

Baxter, L. A. (1990). Dialectical contradictions in relationship development. *Journal of Social and Personal Relationships, 7,* 69–88.

Baxter, L. A., & Montgomery, B. M. (1996). *Relating: Dialogues & dialectics.* New York: Guilford.

Baxter, L. A., & Montgomery, B. M. (2000). Rethinking communication in personal relationships from a dialectical perspective. In K. Dindia & S. Duck (Eds.), *Communication and personal relationships* (pp. 31–53). Chichester, UK: John Wiley & Sons.

Bean, J. C. (1996). *Engaging ideas: The professor's guide to integrating writing, critical thinking, and active learning in the classroom.* San Francisco: Jossey-Bass.

Beebe, S., Beebe, S., & Redmond, M. (2005). *Interpersonal communication: Relating to others* (4th ed.). Boston: Allyn & Bacon.

Berger, P. L., & Luckmann, T. (1966). *The social construction of reality: A treatise in the sociology of knowledge.* New York: Anchor Books.

Bloom, B. S. (Ed.), Engelhart, M. D., Furst, E. J., Hill, W. H., & Krathwohl, D. R. (1956). *Taxonomy of educational objectives: The classification of educational goals, by a committee of college and university examiners.* New York: Longmans, Green.

Bochner, A. P. (1994). Perspectives on inquiry II: Theories and stories. In M. L. Knapp & G. R. Miller (Eds.), *Handbook of interpersonal communication* (2nd ed., pp. 21–41). Thousand Oaks, CA: Sage.

Bohm, D. (2004). *On dialogue*. New York: Routledge.

Buber, M. (1970). *I and thou* (W. Kaufmann, Trans.). New York: Charles Scribner's Sons. (Original work published 1937)

Burke, J. (2005). *A journey of change*. Unpublished manuscript, University of North Carolina at Greensboro.

Buscaglia, L. (1982). *Living, loving, and learning*. New York: Holt, Rinehart, & Winston.

Campbell, D. M. (Ed.). (2004). *How to develop a professional portfolio: A manual for teachers* (3rd ed.). Boston: Allyn and Bacon.

Canary, D. J., Cody, M. J., & Manusov, V. L. (2003). Four important cognitive processes. In K. M. Galvin & P. J. Cooper (Eds.), *Making connections: Readings in relational communication* (pp. 42–51). Los Angeles: Roxbury.

Cannon, L. W. (1989, May). *Meeting diversity in the college classroom*. Workshop presented at the Memphis State University Conference on Gender Balancing the Curriculum.

Carter, K., & Presnell, M. (1994). *Interpretive approaches to interpersonal communication*. Albany: SUNY Press.

Cayanus, J. L. (2004). Using teacher self-disclosure as an instructional tool. *Communication Teacher, 18*, 6–9.

Christ, W. G. (Ed.). (1994). *Assessing communication education: A handbook for media, speech and theatre educators*. Mahwah, NJ: Erlbaum.

Civikly-Powell, J. (1999). Creating a new course. In A. L. Vangelisti, J. A. Daly, & G. W. Friedrich (Eds.), *Teaching communication: Theory, research, and methods* (2nd ed., pp. 61–72). Mahwah, NJ: Erlbaum.

Comstock, J., Rowell, E., & Bowers, J. W. (1995). Food for thought: Teacher nonverbal immediacy, student learning and curvilinearity. *Communication Education, 44*, 251–266.

Confucius. (1979). *The analects*. (D.C. Lau, Trans.). London: Penguin.

Cooper, P. J., & Simonds, C. J. (2003). *Communication for the classroom teacher*. (7th ed.). Boston: Allyn and Bacon.

Craig, R. T. (1999). Communication theory as a field. *Communication Theory, 9*, 119–161.

Curzon, L. B. (2004). *Teaching in further education: An outline of principles and practice* (6th ed.). London: Continuum.

Cushman, D. P., & Kovacic, B. (Eds.). (1995). *Watershed research traditions in human communication theory*. Albany: SUNY Press.

DeVito, J. A. (2004). Interpersonal relationships: Growth and deterioration. In *The interpersonal communication book* (10th ed., pp. 252–279). Boston: Pearson/Allyn & Bacon.

DeVito, J. A. (2004). *The interpersonal communication book* (10th ed.). Boston: Pearson Education.

DeVito, J. A. (2006). *The interpersonal communication book* (11th ed.). Boston: Pearson Education.

Droge, D., & Murphy, B. O. (Eds.). (1999). *Voices of a strong democracy: Concepts and models for service-learning in communication studies*. Washington, DC: American Association for Higher Education.

Duck, S. (1982). A topography of relationship disengagement and dissolution. In S. Duck (Ed.), *Personal relationships 4: Dissolving personal relationships* (pp. 1–29). London: Academic Press.

Etzioni, A. (1996). *The new golden rule: Community and morality in a democratic society*. New York: Basic Books.

Farrell, T. B. (1987). Beyond science: Humanities contributions to communication theory. In C. R. Berger & S. H. Chaffee (Eds.), *Handbook of communication science* (pp. 123–139). Newbury Park, CA: Sage.

Feeley, T. H. (2002). Evidence of halo effects in student evaluations of communication instruction. *Communication Education, 51,* 225–236.

Filene, P. (2005). *The joy of teaching.* Chapel Hill: University of North Carolina Press.

Friedrich, G. W., & Cooper, P. (1999). The first day. In A. L. Vangelisti, J. A. Daly, & G. W. Friedrich (Eds.), *Teaching communication: Theory, research, and methods* (2nd ed., pp. 287–296). Mahwah, NJ: Erlbaum.

Frymier, A. B., & Houser, M. L. (2000). The teacher-student relationship as an interpersonal relationship. *Communication Education, 49,* 207–219.

Fulghum, R. (1989). *All I really need to know I learned in kindergarten: Uncommon thoughts on common things.* New York: Villard Books.

Gerbner, G. (1990). Epilogue: Advancing on the path of righteousness (maybe). In N. Signorielli & M. Morgan (Eds.), *Cultivation analysis: New directions in media effects research* (pp. 249–262). Newbury Park, CA: Sage.

Gibb, J. (1961). Defensive communication. *Journal of Communication, 11,* 141–148.

Glater, J. D. (2006, February 21). To: Professor @university.edu subject: Why it's all about me. *New York Times.* Retrieved February 21, 2006, from http://www.nytimes.com

Goffman, E. (1959). *The presentation of self in everyday life.* New York: Anchor Books.

Goldstein, G. S., & Benassi, V. A. (1994). The relation between teacher self-disclosure and student classroom participation. *Teaching of Psychology, 21,* 212–216.

Graham, E. E., & Shue, C. K. (2001). Reflections on the past, directions for the future: A template for the study and instruction of interpersonal communication. *Communication Research Reports, 18.* (Reprinted from *CRR, 17,* pp. 337–348. Volume 18 is the complete version with the same page numbers as Volume 17.)

Gronlund, N. E., & Linn, R. L. (1990). *Measurement and evaluation in teaching* (6th ed.). New York: Macmillan.

Grunert, J. (1997). *The course syllabus: A learning centered approach.* Bolton, MA: Anker.

Gulley, H. E. (1968). *Discussion, conference, and group process* (2nd ed.). New York: Holt, Rinehart and Winston.

Hayakawa, S. I., & Hayakawa, A. R. (1992). *Language in thought and action* (5th ed.). Ft. Worth: Harcourt Brace.

Hendrix, K. G. (2000). *The teaching assistant's guide to the basic course.* Belmont, CA: Wadsworth.

Higgins, R. (1994). Classroom management and organization. In K. W. Prichard & R. M. Sawyer (Eds.), *Handbook of college teaching: Theory and applications* (pp. 403–414). Westport, CT: Greenwood Press.

Houser, M. L. (2004). Understanding instructional communication needs of nontraditional students. *Communication Teacher, 18,* 78–81.

Howard, R. (Producer/Director). (2001). *A beautiful mind* [Motion picture]. United States: Universal Studios.

Intrator, S. (Ed.). (2002). *Stories of the courage to teach: Honoring the teacher's heart.* San Francisco: Jossey-Bass.

Jones, E. A. (1994). *Essential skills in writing, speech and listening, and critical thinking for college graduates: Perspectives of faculty, employers, and policymakers.* University Park, PA: National Center for Postsecondary Teaching, Learning, and Assessment.

Jourard, S. M. (1971). *The transparent self* (Rev. ed.). New York: Van Nostrand Reinhold. (Original work published 1964)

Kennedy, G. A. (Ed. & Trans.). (1991). *Aristotle on rhetoric: A theory of civic discourse.* New York: Oxford University Press.

Kibler, R. J., Barker, L. L., & Miles, D. T. (1970). *Behavioral objectives and instruction.* Boston: Allyn & Bacon.

Knapp, M. L., & Daly, J. A. (Eds.). (2002). *Handbook of interpersonal communication* (3rd ed.). Thousand Oaks, CA: Sage.

Knapp, M. L., & Vangelisti, A. L. (1992). Stages of coming together and coming apart. In *Interpersonal communication and human relationships* (2nd ed., pp. 29-63). Boston: Allyn & Bacon.

Knapp, M. L., & Vangelisti, A. L. (2005). Stages of coming together and coming apart. In *Interpersonal communication and human relationships* (5th ed., pp. 31-67). Boston: Allyn & Bacon.

Krathwohl, D. R. (2002). A revision of Bloom's taxonomy: An overview. *Theory into Practice, 41,* 212-218.

Laing, R. D. (1969). *Self and others.* London: Tavistock.

Leeds-Hurwitz, W. (Ed.). (1995). *Social approaches to communication.* New York: Guilford.

Lucas, R. W. (2005). *People strategies for trainers: 176 tips and techniques for dealing with difficult classroom situations.* New York: Amacom.

Luft, J. (1969). *Of human interaction.* Palo Alto: National Press Books.

McCarthy, C. (1998). *Cities of the plain.* New York: Alfred A. Knopf.

McKeachie, W. J. (1969). *Teaching tips: A guidebook for the beginning college teacher* (6th ed.). Lexington, MA: D.C. Heath.

Mead, G. H. (1934). *Mind, self and society.* Chicago: University of Chicago Press.

Mehrabian, A. (1971). *Silent messages.* Belmont, CA: Wadsworth.

Miller, K. (2002). *Communication theories: Perspectives, processes, and contexts.* Boston: McGraw-Hill.

Moore, A., Masterson, J. T., Christophel, D. M., & Shea, K. A. (1996). College teacher immediacy and student ratings of instruction. *Communication Education, 45,* 29-39.

Morreale, S., & Backlund, P. M. (1999). Assessment: Coming of age. *Popular Measurement. Journal of the Institute for Objective Measurement, 2* (1), 22-23.

Natalle, E. J. (2003, September). *Teaching excellence and the Confucian ideal.* College of Arts and Sciences Teaching Excellence Award Lecture, University of North Carolina at Greensboro.

Natalle, E. J., & Bodenheimer, F. R. (2004). *The woman's public speaking handbook.* Belmont, CA: Wadsworth.

Nicholson, J., & Duck, S. (1999). Teaching interpersonal communication. In A. L. Vangelisti, J. A. Daly, & G. W. Friedrich (Eds.), *Teaching communication: Theory, research, and methods* (2nd ed., pp. 85-98). Mahwah, NJ: Erlbaum.

Nussbaum, J. F. (1992). Effective teacher behaviors. *Communication Education, 41,* 167-180.

O'Hair, D., Friedrich, G. W., Wiemann, J. M., & Wiemann, M. O. (1995). *Competent communication.* New York: Bedford/St. Martin's.

Orbe, M. P. (1998). *Constructing co-cultural theory: An explication of culture, power, and communication.* Thousand Oaks, CA: Sage.

Orbe, M. P. (2004). Negotiating multiple identities within multiple frames: An analysis of first-generation college students. *Communication Education, 53,* 131-149.

Orbe, M. P., & Bruess, C. J. (2005). *Contemporary issues in interpersonal communication.* Los Angeles: Roxbury Publishing.

Partridge, J. (n.d.). *Plato's cave and The Matrix.* Retrieved May 31, 2005, from http://whatis thematrix.warnerbros.com/rl_cmp/new_phil_partridge.html

Phillips, G. M., & Wood, J. T. (1983). *Communication and human relationships: The study of interpersonal communication.* New York: Macmillan.

Pickering, J. W. (2006, January). Assessment measures: The right tools for the job. Presentation at the University of North Carolina at Greensboro Office of Academic Assessment Workshop, *Assessment, skills, and knowledge: Tools you can use,* Greensboro, NC.

Plato. (1985). *The Republic/Plato* (R. W. Sterling & W. C. Scott, Trans.). New York: W. W. Norton.

Prichard, K. W., & Sawyer, R. M. (Eds.). (1994). Methods of college instruction. In *Handbook of college teaching: Theory and applications* (pp. 83–84). Westport, CT: Greenwood Press.

Putnam, R. D. (2000). *Bowling alone: The collapse and revival of American community.* New York: Simon and Schuster.

Quinlan, K. M. (2002). Inside the peer review process: How academics review a colleague's teaching portfolio. *Teaching and Teacher Education, 18,* 1035–1049.

Quintilian. (1965). *On the early education of the citizen-orator* (Rev. J. S. Watson, Trans.). Indianapolis: Bobbs-Merrill.

Rawlins, W. K. (1992). *Friendship matters: Communication, dialectics, and the life course.* Hawthorne, NY: Aldine de Gruyter.

Rawlins, W. K. (2000). Teaching as a mode of friendship. *Communication Theory, 10,* 5–26.

Reid, T. R. (1999). *Confucius lives next door.* New York: Vintage Books.

Rogers, C. R. (1961). *On becoming a person: A therapist's view of psychotherapy.* Boston: Houghton Mifflin.

Roloff, M. E., & Berger, C. R. (Eds.). (1982). *Social cognition and communication.* Beverly Hills, CA: Sage.

Rosen, J. (2003, September 7). How to reignite the culture wars. *New York Times Magazine,* pp. 48ff.

Rubin, R. B. (1995, November). *The undergraduate student canon: Standards and assessment.* Paper presented at the annual meeting of the National Communication Association, San Antonio, TX.

Rubin, R. B. (1999). Evaluating the product. In A. L. Vangelisti, J. A. Daly, & G. W. Friedrich (Eds.), *Teaching communication: Theory, research, and methods* (2nd ed., pp. 425–444). Mahwah, NJ: Erlbaum.

Rubin, R. B., & Morreale, S. P. (1996). Setting expectations for speech communication and listening. In M. Kramer (Series Ed.) & E. A. Jones (Vol. Ed.), *New directions for higher education: Vol. 96. Preparing competent college graduates: Setting new and higher expectations for student learning* (pp. 19–29). San Francisco: Jossey-Bass.

Ruesch, J., & Bateson, G. (1951). *Communication: The social matrix of psychiatry.* New York: W. W. Norton.

Salkind, N. J. (2006). *Tests & measurement for people who (think they) hate tests & measurement.* Thousand Oaks, CA: Sage Publications.

Satir, V. (1972). *peoplemaking.* Palo Alto, CA: Science and Behavior Books.

Schrodt, P. (2003). Students' appraisals of instructors as a function of students' perceptions of instructors' aggressive communication. *Communication Education, 52,* 106–121.

Shepherd, G. J., St. John, J., & Striphas, T. (Eds.). (2006). *Communication as . . . Perspectives on theory.* Thousand Oaks, CA: Sage.

Smith, A. L. (1973). *Transracial communication.* Englewood Cliffs, NJ: Prentice-Hall.

Souza, T. (1999). Service-learning and interpersonal communication: Connecting students with the community. In D. Droge & B. O. Murphy (Eds.), *Voices of a strong democracy: Concepts and models for service-learning in communication studies* (pp. 77–86). Washington, DC: American Association for Higher Education.

Spitzberg, B. H. (1995). The conversational skills rating scale: An instructional assessment of interpersonal competence. Annandale, VA: Speech [National] Communication Association.

Spitzberg, B. H., & Cupach, W. R. (1984). *Interpersonal communication competence.* Beverly Hills, CA: Sage.

Stevens, D., & Levi, A. (2005). *Introduction to rubrics.* Sterling, VA: Stylus.

Stewart, J. (Ed.). (2002). *Bridges not walls: A book about interpersonal communication* (8th ed.). New York: McGraw-Hill.

Suskie, L. (2004). *Assessing student learning: A common sense guide.* Bolton, MA: Anker.

Syre, T. R., & Pesa, J. A. (2001). Teaching portfolios: Suggested contents. *College Student Journal, 35,* 260–261.

Tannen, D. (1998). *The argument culture.* New York: Random House.

Taylor, J. (2000). On being an exemplary lesbian: My life as a role model. *Text & Performance Quarterly, 20,* 58–73.

Teven, J. J. (2001). The relationships among teacher characteristics and perceived caring. *Communication Education, 50,* 159–169.

Teven, J. J., & McCroskey, J. C. (1997). The relationship of perceived teacher caring with student learning and teacher evaluation. *Communication Education, 46,* 1–9.

Thweatt, K. S., & McCroskey, J. C. (1998). The impact of teacher immediacy and misbehaviors on teacher credibility. *Communication Education, 47,* 348–358.

Trenholm, S., & Jensen, A. (2004). *Interpersonal communication* (5th ed.). New York: Oxford University Press.

Turner, P. K. (2001). Central States outstanding teaching award winners: Wisdom, eloquence, and a little bit of yourself: A philosophy for teaching. *Communication Studies, 52,* 272–277.

Vangelisti, A. L. (1999). Evaluating the process. In A. L. Vangelisti, J. A. Daly, & G. W. Friedrich (Eds.), *Teaching communication: Theory, research, and methods* (2nd ed., pp. 409–423). Mahwah, NJ: Erlbaum.

Verderber, K. S., & Verderber, R. F. (2004). *Inter-act: Interpersonal communication concepts, skills, and contexts* (10th ed.). New York: Oxford University Press.

Verderber, K. S., Verderber, F. V., & Berryman-Fink, C. (2006). *Inter-Act: Using interpersonal communication skills* (11th ed.). New York: Oxford University Press.

Wachowski, A., & Wachowski, L. (Producers/Directors). (1999). *The matrix* [Motion picture]. United States: Warner Brothers.

Wambach, C., & Brothen, T. (1997). Teacher self-disclosure and student classroom participation revisited. *Teaching of Psychology, 24,* 262–263.

Wanzer, M. B., & Frymier, A. B. (1999). The relationship between student perceptions of instructor humor and students' reports of learning. *Communication Education, 48,* 48–62.

Wardrope, W. J. (1999). A curricular profile of U.S. communication departments. *Communication Education, 48,* 256–258.

Watzlawick, P., Bavelas, J. B., & Jackson, D. D. (1967). *Pragmatics of human communication: A study of interactional patterns, pathologies, and paradoxes.* New York: W. W. Norton.

Wiemann, J. M. (1977). Explication and test of a model of communicative competence. *Human Communication Research, 3,* 195–213.

Wood, J. T. (2007). *Interpersonal communication for everyday encounters* (5th ed.). Belmont, CA: Wadsworth.

Wood, J. T., & Lenze, L. F. (1991). Gender and the development of self: Inclusive pedagogy in interpersonal communication. *Women's Studies in Communication, 14,* 1–23.

Worley, D. W. (2001). Central States outstanding teaching award winner: A teaching philosophy. *Communication Studies, 52,* 278–283.

Acknowledgments

Leslie A. Baxter, Barbara M. Montgomery. "Rethinking Communication in Personal Relationships from a Dialectical Perspective." From *Communication and Personal Relationships*. Edited by Kathryn Dindia and Steve Duck. Copyright © 2000 by John Wiley & Sons, Ltd. Reprinted by permission of the publisher.

Martin Buber. "I and Thou." From *I and Thou*, by Martin Buber, translated by Walter Kaufman. Copyright © 1970 by Charles Scribner Sons. Introduction copyright © 1970 by Walter Kaufman. Reprinted with permission of Scribner, an imprint of Simon & Schuster Adult Publishing Group. All rights reserved.

M. L. Knapp, A. L. Vangelisti. "Stages of Coming Together and Coming Apart." From Mark L. Knapp and Anita L. Vangelisti, *Interpersonal Communication and Human Relationships*, 2e © 1992. Published by Allyn and Bacon, Boston, MA. Copyright © 1993 by Pearson Education. Reprinted by permission of the publisher.

Paul Watzlawick, Janet Beavin Bavelas, Don D. Jackson, "Some Tentative Axioms of Communication." From *Pragmatics of Human Communication: A Study of Interactional Patterns, Pathologies and Paradoxes* by Paul Watzlawick, Janet Beavin Bavelas, and Don D. Jackson. Copyright © 1967 by W. W. Norton & Company, Inc. Used by permission of W. W. Norton & Company, Inc.

John M. Wiemann. "Explication and Test of a Model of Communicative Competence." From *Human Communication Research*, 3:3 (1977: Spring). Copyright © 1977 by Blackwell Publishers. Reprinted by permission of the publisher.